T0254874

Lecture Notes in Computer Science 11862

More information about this series at http://www.springer.com/series/7409

José Pagán · Mounir Mokhtari ·
Hamdi Aloulou · Bessam Abdulrazak ·
María Fernanda Cabrera (Eds.)

How AI Impacts Urban Living and Public Health

17th International Conference, ICOST 2019
New York City, NY, USA, October 14–16, 2019
Proceedings

Editors
José Pagán
New York University
New York, NY, USA

Hamdi Aloulou
Digital Research Centre of Sfax
Sfax, Tunisia

María Fernanda Cabrera
Technical University of Madrid
Madrid, Spain

Mounir Mokhtari
Institut Mines-Télécom
Paris, France

Bessam Abdulrazak
Université de Sherbrooke
Sherbrooke, QC, Canada

ISSN 0302-9743 ISSN 1611-3349 (electronic)
Lecture Notes in Computer Science
ISBN 978-3-030-32784-2 ISBN 978-3-030-32785-9 (eBook)
https://doi.org/10.1007/978-3-030-32785-9

LNCS Sublibrary: SL3 – Information Systems and Applications, incl. Internet/Web, and HCI

This Springer imprint is published by the registered company Springer Nature Switzerland AG
The registered company address is: Gewerbestrasse 11, 6330 Cham, Switzerland

Preface

This year we organized the 17th ICOST conference, an event which has succeeded in bringing together a community from different continents for over a decade and half and raised awareness about frail and dependent people's quality of life in our societies.

After 16 very successful conferences held in France (2003, 2009, 2017), Singapore (2004, 2013, 2018), Canada (2005, 2011), Northern Ireland (2006), Japan (2007), USA (2008, 2014), Korea (2010), Italy (2012), Switzerland (2015), and China (2016), we decided to open the conference to public health experts and tackle emerging challenges related to AI technologies for health and well-being. This 17th edition of the International Conference on Smart Living and Public Health (ICOST 2019), was hosted by the College of Global Public Health at New York University (NYU) and the New York Academy of Medicine (NYAM) in New York City, USA, during October 14–16, 2019. The theme of the conference this year was "How Does AI Impact Urban Living and Public Health?"

ICOST 2019 provided a premier venue for the presentation and discussion of research in the design, development, deployment, and evaluation of AI for health, smart urban environments, assistive technologies, chronic disease management, and coaching and health telematics systems. ICOST 2019 aimed to understand and assess how research impacts public health policies when facing emerging social and economic challenges. ICOST 2019 brought together stakeholders from health care, public health, academia and industry along with end users and family caregivers to explore how to utilize technologies to foster health prevention, independent living, and offer an enhanced quality of life. The ICOST 2019 conference featured a dynamic program incorporating a range of technical, clinical, and industrial related keynote speakers, oral and poster presentations, along with demonstrations and technical exhibits. Specific use cases were presented, such as the PULSE European funded project aiming at accelerating the use and vision of Big Data by designing a system to exploit Big Data Value (BDV) in the public health sector. PULSE (Participatory Urban Living for Sustainable Environments) is incorporating several major cities as test beds: Barcelona (Spain), New York City (USA), Paris (France), Birmingham (United Kingdom), Singapore, Keelung (Taiwan) and Pavia (Italy).

ICOST 2019 was proud to extend its hospitality to an international community consisting of researchers from major universities and research centers, representatives from industry and users from 13 different countries. We would like to thank the authors for submitting their current research work and the Program Committee members for their commitment to reviewing submitted papers. The ICOST proceedings have now reached over 150,000 downloads, and are in the top 25% of downloads of Springer LNCS.

We were very pleased to host world-renowned keynote speakers from multiple backgrounds coming from all over the world. We are extremely thankful to our sponsors for their commitment and support to the vision and mission of ICOST.

October 2019

José Pagán
Mounir Mokhtari
Hamdi Aloulou
Bessam Abdulrazak
María Fernanda Cabrera

Organization

General Chair

José Pagán	New York University and the New York Academy of Medicine, USA

Conference Co-chairs

Mounir Mokhtari	Institut Mines-Télécom, France, and Image and Pervasive Access Lab., Singapore
Maria Fernanda Cabrera	University Politecnica de Madrid, Spain

Steering Committee

Mounir Mokhtari	Institut Mines Télécom, France, and Image and Pervasive Access Lab., Singapore
Sumi Helal	Lancaster University (2017–present), UK, and University of Florida (1998–2017), USA
Bessam Abdulrazak	University of Sherbrooke, Canada
Hamdi Aloulou	University of Monastir, Tunisia, and Institut Mines-Télécom, France
Jose Pagan	New York University and the New York Academy of Medicine, USA
Maria Fernanda Cabrera	University Politecnica de Madrid, Spain

Scientific Advisory Board

Daqing Zhang	Institut Mines Télécom, Télécom SudParis, France
Hisato Kobayashi	Hosei University, Japan
Jongbae Kim	Science and Technology Research Center, Yonsei University, South Korea
Christian Roux	Institut Mines Télécom, France
Dong Jin Song	National University of Singapore, Singapore, and Griffith University, Australia
Sungyoung Lee	College of Electronics and Information, Kyung Hee University, South Korea
Timo Jämsä	EAMBES, University of Oulu, Finland
Daby Sow	IBM Research AI, USA

Program Committee

Chairs

Bessam Abdulrazak	University of Sherbrooke, AmI-Lab., Canada
Hamdi Aloulou	University of Monastir, Tunisia, and Institut Mines-Télécom, France

Members

Abdallah M'Hamed	Télécom SudParis - Evry, France
Belkacem Chikhaoui	University of Sherbrooke, Canada
Benoît Encelle	Université de Lyon, CNRS Université Lyon 1, LIRIS, France
Boussada Rihab	National School for Computer Science (ENSI), Tunisia
Charles Gouin-Vallerand	Télé-Université du Québec, Canada
David Menga	EDF R&D, France
Diane Cook	Washington State University, USA
Farah Arab	Université Paris 8, France
Hisato Kobayashi	Hosei University, Japan
Hongbo Ni	Northwestern Polytechnical University, China
Houssem Aloulou	Faculté des Sciences Économiques et de Gestion de Sfax, Tunisia
Ibrahim Sadek	Singapore University of Technology and Design (SUTD), Singapore
Jeffrey Soar	University of Southern Queensland, Australia
Laurent Billonnet	University of Limoges, France
Manfred Wojciechowski	University of Applied Sciences Duesseldorf, Germany
Salim Hima	ESME-SUDRIA, France
Sofia Ben Jebara	Ecole supérieure des communications de Tunis (SUPCOM), Tunisia
Timo Jämsä	University of Oulu, Finland
Victor Manuel Ponce Diaz	Université de Sherbrooke, Canada
Vigouroux Nadine	Institut de Recherche en Informatique de Toulouse (IRIT), France
Yves Demazeau	Laboratoire d'Informatique de Grenoble (LIG), France

Industry Liaison Committee

Peter Wu	ASUS Cloud, Taiwan
Daby M. Sow	IBM Research AI, USA
Vladimir Urosevic	Belit, Serbia
Suzanne Ballard	FCL, UK

Organizing Committee

Chair

Nina Raffio	NYU College of Global Public Health, USA

Members

Elisa Fisher	The New York Academy of Medicine, USA
Hamdi Aloulou	University of Monastir, Tunisia, and Institut Mines-Télécom, France
Antoine de Marassé Enouf	CNRS, Singapore
Valentina Tageo	European Connected Health Alliance, Spain

Sponsors

Institut Mines Télécom, Paris, France
National Center for Scientific Research, France
PULSE H2020 Project, Europe
New York University College of Global Public Health, USA
The New York Academy of Medicine, USA

Contents

E-health Technology Design

Well-being Technology

Biomedical and Health Informatics

E-health Technology Design

Privacy and Security of IoT Based Healthcare Systems: Concerns, Solutions, and Recommendations

Ibrahim Sadek[1(✉)], Shafiq Ul Rehman[2], Josué Codjo[3], and Bessam Abdulrazak[3]

[1] Faculty of Engineering, Biomedical Engineering Department, Helwan University, Cairo, Egypt
ibrahim_ibrahim@h-eng.helwan.edu.eg

[2] ST Electronics-SUTD Cyber Security Laboratory, Singapore University of Technology and Design, Singapore, Singapore

[3] Département d'Informatique, Faculté des sciences, Université de Sherbrooke (UdeS), Sherbrooke, Canada

Abstract. Although emerging IoT paradigms in sleep tracking have a substantial contribution to enhancing current healthcare systems, there are several privacy and security considerations that end-users need to consider. End-users can be susceptible to malicious threats when they allow permission to potentially vulnerable or leaky third-party apps. Since the data is migrated to the cloud, it goes over insecure communication channels, all of which have their security concerns. Moreover, there are alternative data violation concerns when the data projects into the proprietor's cloud storage facility. In this study, we present some of the existing IoT sleep trackers, also we discuss the most common features associated with these sleep trackers. As the majority of end-users are not aware of the privacy and security concerns affiliated with emerging IoT sleep trackers. We review existing solutions that can apply to IoT sleep tracker architecture. Also, we describe a deployed IoT platform that can address these concerns. Finally, we provide some of the recommendations to end-users and service providers to ensure a safer approach while leveraging the IoT sleep tracker in caregiving. This incorporates recommendations for software updates, awareness programs, software installation, and social engineering.

1 Introduction

The 2019 "World Economic Forum" global risk report[1] has nominated cyber attacks and data breaches as the fourth and fifth deliberate risks facing the world today. It is the second year in a row that these threats feature in the top five list of risks. Healthcare, among others, was offended with more cybersecurity breaches, in which several situations can lead to these breaches, for example,

[1] World Economic Forum. The Global Risks Report 2019. Retrieved May 29, 2019, from https://www.weforum.org/reports/the-global-risks-report-2019.

J. Pagán et al. (Eds.): ICOST 2019, LNCS 11862, pp. 3–17, 2019.
https://doi.org/10.1007/978-3-030-32785-9_1

credential-stealing malware, an insider who either systematically or accidentally unveils patient data, or lost laptops or other mobile devices. On the illegal market, "Protected Health Information" (PHI) is more important than credit card credentials or even personally identifiable information. Hence, there is a higher motivation for cybercriminals to target medical databases, and so they can sell the PHI or adapt it for their benefits.

Throughout the world, healthcare challenges can exist in different shapes and forms. Subsequently, this presents tremendous pressure on the current system. Even though every society faces various demands and encounters several effects, it is still practicable to determine the overall global risk to current healthcare systems. These demands are a fundamental starting point for the work ahead. Population aging, the prevalence of chronic diseases, shortage of healthcare specialists, and the unpredictable rise of healthcare costs, among other reasons, are the considerable challenges facing today's healthcare systems. For dealing with these issues, public and private sector players should collaborate to find more innovative and affordable methods that can be deployed in out-of-hospital environments [14]. Healthcare IoT based systems are multiples and vary from wearable to mobile sensors going through actuators, that acquire patient biosignals, motion, or contextual information. Amongst those systems, we have Zio Patch depicted in [24] which measures heart rate and electrocardiogram (ECG) and Myo [9] which is a motion controller used in orthopedics for patients who need to exercise after a fracture. None of the above performs in multiple information gathering. Therefore, we have systems, which can combine biosignals, motion, and contextual information such as sleep trackers.

In this paper, we focus on sleep tracking as a significant vector of quality of life. Sleep is crucial to our health and sleep disorders can often be a symptom of a disease; or likewise may be a signal of a subsequent illness such as depression. As a result, assessment of sleep is a fundamental component of any health check. Understanding cardiovascular and respiratory systems are essential for analyzing sleep and sleep cycles. This is because the active processes in the human body are different in sleep and wakefulness.

Nowadays, we can render the Internet of Things (IoT) and Cloud services to improve access to caregiving by remotely strengthen the quality of caregiving and above all cut down the cost of caregiving. As different sleep trackers, i.e., IoT devices are used to collect the user data and transfer it to the cloud. The collected data is later being analyzed by sleep experts to enhance these devices for better results. According to the "ABI Research" report[2] currently, there are over 10 billion wirelessly connected IoT devices, and by 2020, the number will exceed 30 billion devices. Some of these devices will fall within the category of sleep-tracking devices. Nevertheless, these emerging technologies are vulnerable to adversarial attacks because of their design. The data breach can have severe consequences both on individual users and the company's reputation. Moreover,

[2] ABI Research. Over 30 Billion Devices Will Wirelessly Connect to the Internet of Everything in 2020. Retrieved May 29, 2019, from https://www.abiresearch.com/press/more-than-30-billion-devices-will-wirelessly-conne/.

compromised IoT sleep tracking devices can allow intruders to monitor the user's private lives actively.

The main contribution of this study is to highlight the privacy and security concerns of IoT sleep trackers and provide an insight into how precise mechanisms or approaches can be applied to prevent or mitigate such adversarial attempts. We anticipate this research to guide future researchers to use and apply specific solutions for IoT in healthcare problems based on the proposed approaches and mechanisms by security experts.

The rest of the paper is organized as follows: IoT sleep trackers and their types are described in Sect. 2. We state the security and privacy issues that are associated with IoT sleep trackers in Sect. 3. We present some existing solutions in Sect. 4, then we depict an IoT based case study in Sect. 5, while we mention the recommendations in Sect. 6. We outline the conclusion in Sect. 7.

2 IoT Sleep Trackers

The healthcare system desperately needs reform to rein in costs, improve quality, and expand access. Medical diagnosis consumes a large part of hospital bills. Technology can move medical check routines from a hospital (hospital-centered) to the home (home-centered) of the patient. A new paradigm, known as the IoT, widely applies in many areas, including healthcare. The full application of this paradigm in healthcare is a mutual hope, as it enables medical centers to function more efficiently and patients to receive better treatment. There are unique benefits with the use of this technology that could improve the quality and efficiency of treatments and thus improve patient health.

IoT technology permits and facilitates remote monitoring of patients who do not have ready access to adequate health monitoring. Likewise, it helps to thoroughly reduce costs and promote health by increasing the availability and quality of care [12]. The IoT is a network of smart devices and other objects integrated with electronics, software, sensors, and network connectivity that permit these objects to get and exchange data. The concept of IoT provides healthcare professionals and caregivers to access a patient's medical history, vitals, lab results, medical and prescription histories either on-site or remotely via tablets or smartphones. Patients can be observed and notified from anywhere [9]. We can use IoT based solutions to record patient health data securely from several sensors, apply complicated algorithms to analyze the data and then distribute it through wireless connectivity with medical specialists who can make suitable health recommendations [21].

Typically, examining a person's sleep requires an overnight sleep test (Fig. 1) or polysomnography (PSG) that allows the monitoring of several physiological functions besides sleep cycles [4,22]. Although the PSG, or as known as the gold standard for sleep monitoring, provides real-time and accurate information about sleep, it is cumbersome, expensive, and time-consuming. Thus, the healthcare community is inquiring novel nonintrusive solutions that can improve the quality of healthcare for the patient while sustaining the cost of the service provided [19].

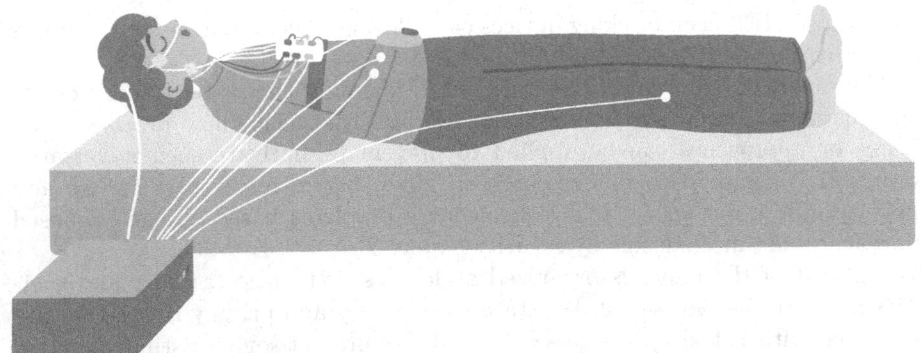

Fig. 1. An illustration of the location of the various electrodes and sensors used during the overnight sleep. Adapted from: mattressclarity.com

Actigraph is a very famous example that can be used for sleep analysis. The device is not as accurate as of the PSG. However, its information, which is based on the users' activity, is critical for healthcare professionals to interpret and analyze the sleep behavior of the users. As hardware and software technology is advancing quickly, several devices and mobile apps have been developed for general healthcare monitoring, including sleep. These devices could be wearables such as bracelets, smart-watches, smart-shirts, or smart-rings (Fig. 2) or non-wearable like bed-sensors that can be installed underneath the user's bed mattress (Fig. 3).

Sleep monitoring is described as getting qualitative sleep metrics by monitoring a person's sleep during the night. These serve two functions. One is to formulate an objective view of the quality of a person's sleep, while the other role is to determine the trends in sleep. Respiratory rate and body movements are considered the most detailed measurements for sleep monitoring during the sleeping session. The respiratory rate and respiratory rate variability are used for rapid eye movement (REM) sleep identification, while the movement metrics are utilized to discriminate between deep sleep, light sleep, and then waking stages of sleep. We can also extract several sleep parameters, for example, the duration of a sleep period, the number of awakenings, duration of disturbed sleep periods, and the time required to fall asleep. In recent years, various sensor technologies have been exploited, especially to monitor sleep-wake patterns simultaneously with the gold standard PSG and actigraphy; these sensor technologies are commonly denoted as consumer sleep tracking devices. Consumer sleep tracking devices are just like actigraphs because they allow users to be mobile and sleep as usual while being monitored closely.

Most of the consumer sleep monitors pretend to help provide information about sleep duration and quality of sleep, enabling subjects to awaken only from the light sleep. Typically, the data gained from consumer sleep tracking devices are not intended for routine diagnosis of sleep disorders. However, scientific improvements in hardware and software, accessibility, and ready availability

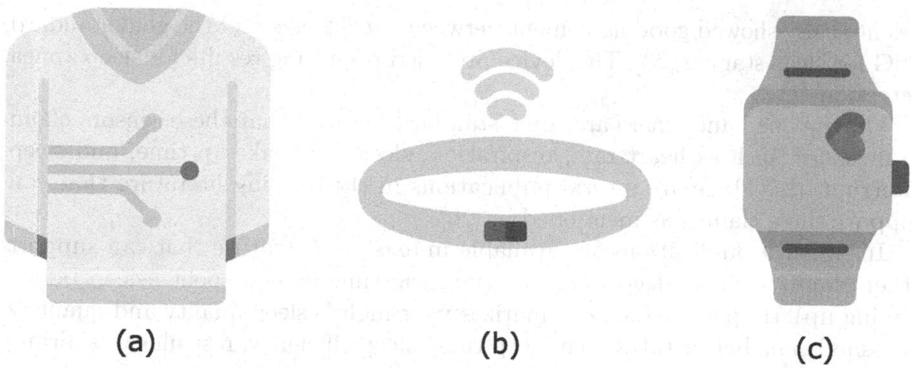

Fig. 2. Illustrations for wearable sleep trackers; (a) smart-shirt, (b) smart-bracelet, and (c) smart-watch. Icons made by Freepik from: flaticon.com

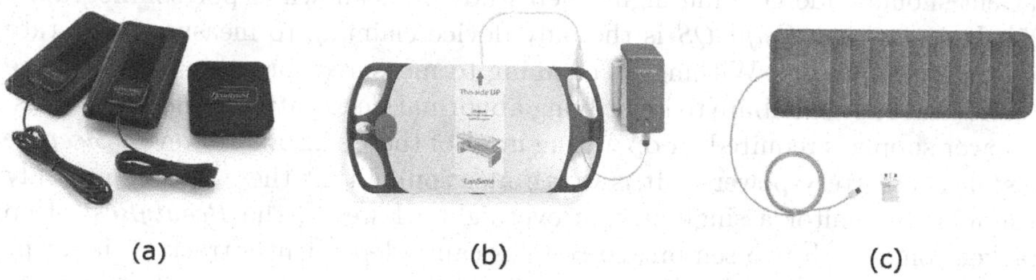

Fig. 3. Some examples of non-wearables sleep trackers; (a) Beautyrest © 2019 Simmons Bedding Company LLC, (b) EarlySense © 2019 Early Sense, and (c) Withings © 2019 Withings.

allow the public to adopt them for clinical purposes. These devices include *Emfit QS*, *Beddit*, *Withings*, *Sleepace Reston*, *Beautyrest*, and *Juvo*. Figure 3 shows three examples of existing bed-based sleep trackers.

These sensors are designed and packaged in a way that makes them invisible to the subjects. For instance, we can easily integrate them into home furniture such as beds, pillows, chairs, or even weighing scales [26]. These sensors technologies are preferred than those popular sensors (e.g., ECG) when we are considering long-term (trend over time, early detection and intervention by sending alarms to family members or caregivers through well-designed user interfaces), mobile, convenient and practical (aging-in-place, senior activity centers). However, in critical situations, gold-standard methods should be considered [20].

Most of the existing products implement the piezoelectric technology for nonintrusive monitoring of vital signs (for example, *Beddit*, *Withings*, *Sleepace Reston*, and *Beautyrest*) which shows the popularity and suitability of the piezoelectric material for measuring the slight vibrations caused by the heart movements that is transmitted through the bed mattress. Another famous sleep tracker sensor using a piezoelectric sensor is *EarlySense*. The system can report information about heart rate, respiration, snoring, coughing, and movement. A recent study showed good agreement between *EarlySense* and the gold standard PSG for sleep staging [23]. The device provided promising results for sleep apnea detection [7].

On the one hand, there are some standard features that these sensors claim to measure, such as heart rate, respiration, sleep and wake-up time, and sleep interruptions. There are several publications in the existing literature that can support these claims, as mentioned in [20].

Insufficient publications are available in existing literature that can support other claims such as sleep efficiency (i.e., the time in bed spent asleep before waking up), sleep score (i.e., summarizes your night's sleep quality and quantity in a single number, it takes your sleep time, sleep efficiency, restfulness, snoring, and heart rate into account), smart alarm (i.e., to awaken the wearer at an optimal time within a time-window that ends in the final alarm setting) and sleep stages. For example, to get accurate results about the different stages of sleep, the patient should undergo a full-night sleep study or as known as polysomnography [25]. It seems that *Emfit QS* is the only device claiming to measure heart rate variability. Similarity, Withings is claiming to measure a breathing disturbance metric that can contribute to identifying abnormal sleep patterns such as apneas. A power supply is required for operating most of these sensors. However, *Sleepace Reston* is a battery-powered. It is worth mentioning that these sensors are only designed to monitor a single person overnight. However, the *BeautyRest* sleep tracker comes with two sensors, so couples can independently track their sleep.

Having said that, although the security and privacy feature of these sensors are essential, most of the end-users might not fully know of weaknesses and potential risks in their existing devices. Therefore, we present in the ensuing sections, the security and privacy features associated with existing IoT sleep trackers.

3 Privacy and Security Concerns

According to Deborah Lupton's report[3], during her Research she found there are risks associated with data collection (a) from IoT tracking devices such as devices' storage, (b) while transmitting it over the network and (c) finally, in the cloud where data is stored for analyses. The same risk applies to the IoT Sleep Tracker Architecture, where these devices are being used for collecting data while users are asleep, later transmitted to cloud via wireless communication.

Sleep tracking devices aid us in practical applications in gaining quality sleep, thus improving our lives by measuring our heart rates and movements as described in Sect. 2. However, they can possess severe security and privacy risks. Since the sleep tracker users can become a victim to malware by downloading the insecure third-party apps and thus gives permission to the potential adversary to access the device remotely, Later, the users operate these sleep

[3] The Irish Times. Fitness trackers run into resistance over data security concerns. Retrieved May 29, 2019, from https://www.irishtimes.com/business/technology/fitness-trackers-run-into-resistance-over-data-security-concerns-1.3119483.

trackers knowingly or unknowingly in their private places, i.e., home, considering their devices are secure enough to be compromised. Mostly IoT sleep-tracking devices communicate over the public networks. As the data is being transferred to the cloud, the adversary can intercept over the communication channel by carrying out various attacks such as Botnet, Denial of Service (DoS) and Man in the Middle (MITM) attacks. Moreover, there are data breach concerns, as the adversary can remotely access the data stored in the cloud by compromising it via malicious software. Once the device/storage is hacked, a hacker can gain the user's confidential data about sleeping habits such as sleep talking, snoring sounds, and sensual activities. Such a data breach can have a severe impact on the user's reputation. Besides, a hacker can induce the noise by speaking or producing some sounds to disturb the user while asleep, which can consequently result in inadequate sleep.

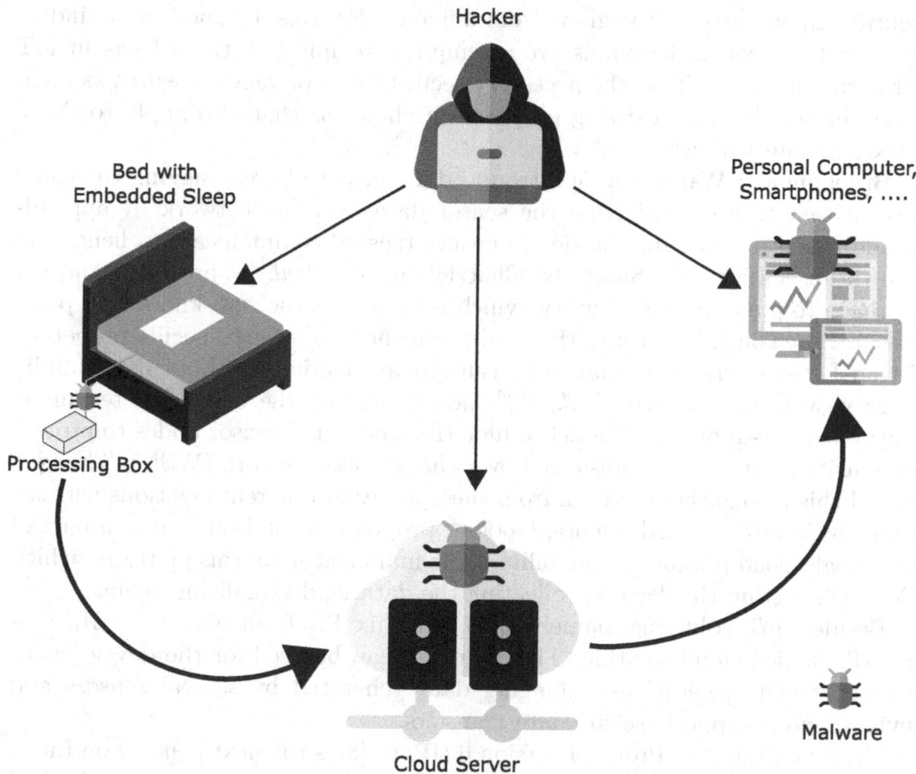

Fig. 4. An illustration of a sleep-tracking mat as an example of an IoT device in a medical setting and how an attacker can exploit the several stages of data processing, i.e., from data acquisition to end-users.

Similarly, there is a risk of data profiling which is defined as "collecting a person's behavior and analyzing psychological characteristics to predict or assess their ability in a certain sphere or to identify a particular group of people." This means the data generated by the sleep tracker devices can be exploited to create profiles of such device users, which can be afterward used for target advertisements. The reason being that an individual's data is collected through wirelessly connected devices means there is a need for advanced measures to ensure the security and privacy of end-users. Research has shown [1], that because of the heterogeneous nature of IoT, it has raised various privacy and security concerns. For instance, data confidentiality, integrity, availability, user authentication, authorization, and anonymity. Figure 4 depicts the different attack scenarios that can affect the remote monitoring of sleep.

4 Existing Security and Privacy Solutions

While considering these IoT privacy and security concerns, the researchers and security experts around the globe from different domains, i.e., academia, industry, and technical backgrounds are attempting to mitigate these flaws in IoT infrastructure by fulfilling the necessary security and privacy measures as mentioned in Sect. 3. Some existing proposed mechanisms that also apply to sleep-tracker architecture are as follows:

Bruening and Waterman [5] introduced a concept of data tagging to ensure data privacy while transferring the sensor data over the network. It appends an additional tag to data transfer to ensure trusted communication, hence can hide the user's identity. Similarly, Chatzigiannakis *et al.* [6] proposed another approach to preserve user identity, which is known as the zero-knowledge proof (ZKP). Based on this concept, the sender can show to receive specific properties of transferred information that can ensure its authenticity without revealing its identity. Moreover, Henze *et al.*, [11] have examined the clustering technique known as the k-anonymity model to hide the location of sensor nodes to protect the sensitive data being transferred over the wireless network (WSN). The idea behind this is to gather the data from these nodes at different positions without being easily traced. Furthermore, Google[4] proposed a solution that is a part of the Google cloud platform. Scalability is the main feature of this platform, which allows connecting the devices, collecting the data, and visualizing them.

Besides, IoT solutions, namely IBM Bluemix Platform offered by IBM, is an IoT-enabled cloud solution. This platform can be used for the development of cloud-based applications managing data generated by several sensors and devices, and it supports secure data transfers.

Moreover, Internet Protocol version 6 (IPv6) [8] is the next-generation Internet protocol, which is being deployed as a communication protocol in the IoT environment. However, because of its nature, it is vulnerable to DoS attacks [17]. Such vulnerability can interrupt the communication between the nodes in a network. To resolve this problem, the Rule-based mechanism [16] and a lightweight, encrypted scheme known as Secure-DAD [18] have been proposed by Rehman

[4] Google Cloud IoT - Fully managed IoT services — Google Cloud. Retrieved May 29, 2019, from https://cloud.google.com/solutions/iot/.

and Manickam. The former technique can detect any attempt of the DoS attack, while a later system can prevent it from occurring. Thus, by deploying such mechanisms, we can ensure a trusted communication between the IoT nodes in a heterogeneous environment.

Recently, Dwivedi *et al.* [10] proposed an IoT framework based on a modified blockchain model. The authors claim that the proposed framework provides a solution that is based on advanced cryptographic primitives for IoT data applications and secure transactions. Also, it can provide anonymity of users over the blockchain-based network.

To complement, in Sect. 5, we present an IoT-based case study (i.e., AMI-IoT platform) to show how these security concerns as aforementioned can be addressed in a real-life scenario.

5 AMI-IoT Deployed Platform

The Ami-lab has been developing several IoT architectures for the past decade and following; we described how we addressed the previously discussed security issues. We have mainly focused on privacy, data profiling, the man-in-the-middle-attack, data corruption, which can undermine the end-to-end communication from the environmental nodes to the database. The AMI-IoT platform as depicted in Fig. 5 is composed of three main components, which are, end-users environment, network, and cloud architecture. Based on the work of Mendonça *et al.* [2], we assume that the three elements, Sensing Approach (SA), Awareness & Security (AS) and Responsibility & Actions (RA), are essentials to address the IoT security concerns.

5.1 Sensing Approach (SA)

The SA element is the entry point of the architecture. It ensures data detection and its migration from environmental nodes to the database. It also represents the listening state of other components as well as the architecture. At this point, making sure of the working state of environmental nodes is crucial. Data gathered by nodes will be sent through a network path built by the node and its peer. This element is the foundation of IoT architecture, enabling endpoint sleep trackers and allowing them to submit information through the entire network, giving the opportunity to experts to process the data. Sleep tracker such as a smart mat has been used, transmitting data to a node that will serve as a broker and publish the information. On the other hand, a unique peer will be subscribing to that broker getting the data in time through a canal. A gateway will be used to monitor and redirect the traffic from the peer to the smart mat. Nevertheless, during the SAP, neglecting the user's privacy, the authenticity of the information sent, and the security of the database on which information is stored does not respect the security standards Raza *et al.* [15]. It's from this perspective that we build the same element.

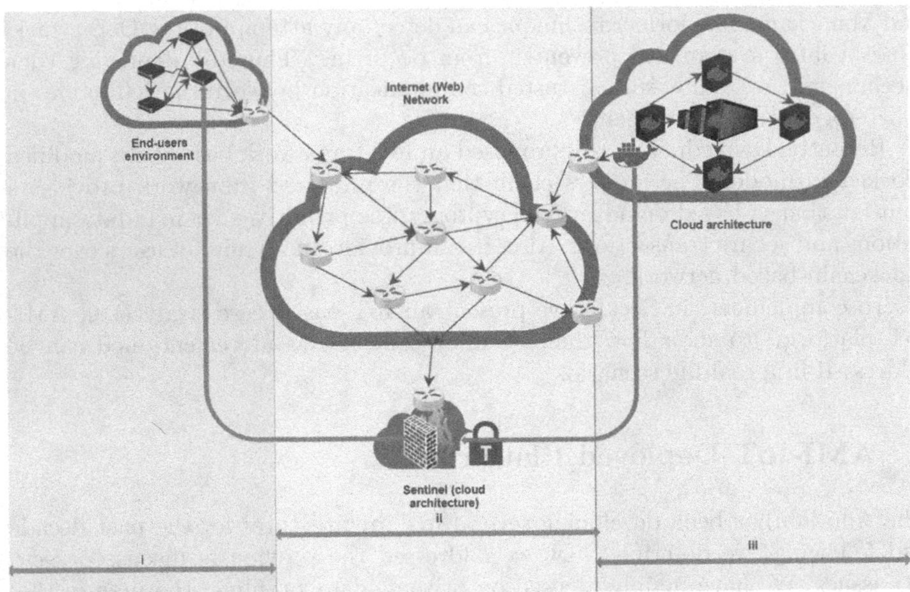

Fig. 5. Ami-IoT Architecture issues addressed (i. Jamming, Flooding, Phishing, Connection Timed out, Battery, Not responsible, Privacy, Data profiling; ii. The sinkhole, Man-in-the-middle, Hello Flood, Connection persistence, Packet loss, Botnet; iii. Flooding, Dos, Data stealing, Data loss, Data modification, privacy)

5.2 Awareness and Security (AS)

This element intends to make the system aware of abnormalities and breaches, which can occur and put the needed security to prevent a possible attack. On this note, a system cannot be protected if we are not aware of the situations and the risks surrounding it. Based on that, the Ami-lab will be relying on the three components of the architecture.

End-User Environment. It regroups all the environmental nodes gathering the data. This component is the favorite spot of attackers due to the negligence of users and their compliance with the attacks mentioned previously. This component is subject to external attacks and faces issues such as privacy, access, data profiling. To face those challenges, Ami-lab implemented firewalls Raza *et al.* [15] in every node deployed on thc cnd-user side. Those firewalls have been added, preventing external attacks and allowing just one communication at a time. Regarding privacy, we concluded that even the node should be identified by their ID and not the users. Thus, yet if the attacker has the identifier, he won't be able to know whose information he has access to. Moreover, rules have also been applied so that the user will have limited access to the node. It will restrict phishing attacks, which can compromise the system. Also, all incoming connections are blocked, accepting just the one responsible for collecting data. These techniques lead to securing the End-users environment component.

Cloud Architecture. It represents the core of the Ami-lab system. It's all the technologies and methods put together to enable a peer for each environmental node and the storing in the database. Data corruption, data stealing, data loss, privacy, data modification are various problems undermining this component. Ami-lab took some countermeasures such as defining a firewall on each server composing this part, to restrict intrusion. Every rule is set carefully, to block every incoming traffics and allowing single traffic from the listener to its peer (environmental node). Every outgoing traffic is controlled. Self-configuration and optimization being part of our architecture, everything adapts itself to the new configuration in our cloud. Thus, we are avoiding "data corruption" and any other kind of intrusion. We are keeping the use of the environmental node identifier and data compression to address the privacy issue. It comes to another concern, the bridge.

Internet (Network). Named in IoT architecture, the weak link, due to its public nature, it can be subject to many attacks mentioned in the previous sections. It relates the end-users environment to the cloud environment serving as a bridge. While an attack cannot reach the first component of the architecture, there is still a chance to intercept the data while it's been sent. Then, botnet attacks, man-in-the-middle attacks, which will block the transaction or worst prevent data from storing in the database. To avoid this weak point, we created a secure tunnel known just by our peers. The Internet will serve to, will be retrieving the certificates and then establishing a secured channel between the environmental node and the cloud node. Every communication has been made to guarantee that each environmental node has its peer and can communicate just with that peer. In case something happened, it won't affect the whole system since we made them independent. To reinforce the security, a high level of encryption has been used as well as data compression.

5.3 Responsibility and Actions (RA)

This element is the last piece conferring "responsibility" feature to a system and is based on Angarita and Kelaidonis *et al.* work [3,13]. Making a system able to take action, depending on the outcome of a situation is the key role of this part. Being part of our future work, Ami-lab strives to achieve a self-healing architecture. The concept of "responsibility" should be transmitted to the architecture enabling its self-management. A responsible environment based on awareness feature should be able to react in time when a situation occurs. A system should be able to define the right action to take and complete it in an optimal way. Indeed, an IoT system, when facing an intrusion issue, should be able to take action and keeps working. For instance, if there is an attack on the environmental node, the node should be able to detect and close all the connections, then re-enable the peer connection. We achieved "the responsibility" feature on the environmental nodes. It allows them to take action against intrusion, connectivity issues, and data transmission issues. Processing information, and creating an adapted virtual object dynamically to decipher the correct information, is also part of our future work. This feature grants autonomy to the applications letting the system creating an environment suited to the end-user. It gives the required access to the user, based on its knowledge and background. Regarding the listening peers for data retrieval, our system can take action upon peers' failure by replacing them in time. A monitoring system such as Prometheus or Zabbix will be listening to applications, environmental nodes, cloud nodes, and servers and networks to transmit the right information, while the nodes themselves will decide the communication state.

6 Recommendations

Apart from the given possible solutions as described in Sects. 4, and 5 certain things need to be considered by both parties, i.e., sleep tracker end-users as well as the healthcare service providers, to ensure a safer approach while leveraging the IoT sleep tracker in caregiving. This section outlines some of these recommendations.

- **Application/Firmware Updates:** Hackers are always in search of finding the weak links to attack victims, which could be via mobile apps, IoT sleep trackers. For instance, outdated mobile apps are the most vulnerable to security threats. Similarly, healthcare system providers rarely provide the latest firmware updates on existing IoT sleep trackers, which open the doors for possible side-channel attacks on end-user devices. Therefore, healthcare service providers should offer the regular updates on mobile apps and ensure availability of sleep tracker device's latest firmware to mitigate the zero-day attacks i.e., latest security threats which are unknown to security systems, while end-users should update their device apps and keep IoT sleep tracker's firmware updated to prevent possible security breaches.
- **Software Installation:** After ensuring the mobile app and IoT sleep tracker are updated. End-users should also refrain from downloading any untrusted third-party software, applications or click on any adware link by doing so, and they are inviting the malware into their mobile devices. For example, end-users receive any health promotion ads by clicking on the link or by downloading a malicious app, IoT sleep tracker users allow the attacker to gain access, thus can monitor their privacy remotely. After compromising the mobile user device, an attacker can secretly get the private information that most of the time, IoT sleep tracker users are unaware of. Therefore, before downloading any app or clicking such links, IoT sleep tracker users should confirm their source or authenticity to prevent malware installation into their mobile devices.

- **Social Engineering:** With the massive impact of social media, end-users share their personal information publicly on social media sites such as Facebook, Instagram, etc. With such a large user-base, these platforms are seen by cybercriminals as a new and lucrative platform to spread malware. Therefore, IoT sleep tracker users should not reveal their personal details with an unknown person over these sites or the phone's calls.
- **Awareness Program:** Moreover, healthcare service providers should conduct awareness programs such as online surveys and workshops to keep educating their IoT sleep tracker customers regularly so that end-users can gain awareness about the latest hacking tactics, cybercrimes, and their possible countermeasures.

By applying these suggestions into practice, the possibilities of privacy and security threats targeted against the IoT sleep tracker environment can be prevented. Thus, to enable a safe and secure remote caregiving.

7 Conclusion

With the rapid advancement and deployment of the IoT in the healthcare domain, these technologies are closely related to people; therefore, privacy and security are major concerns. To highlight these two critical aspects of IoT, we reviewed in this paper the progress of the research works related to IoT sleep trackers and found that these concerns need to be addressed. Moreover, to mitigate such threats, some proposed solutions from researchers and security experts are described. Furthermore, there are certain things that we recommend for both end-users and service providers to deploy a resilient IoT infrastructure to ensure a secured sleep tracker.

References

1. Aldowah, H., Ul Rehman, S., Umar, I.: Security in internet of things: issues, challenges and solutions. In: Saeed, F., Gazem, N., Mohammed, F., Busalim, A. (eds.) IRICT 2018. AISC, vol. 843, pp. 396–405. Springer, Cham (2019). https://doi.org/10.1007/978-3-319-99007-1_38
2. de Almeida, F.M., de Ribamar Lima Ribeiro, A., Moreno, E.D.: An architecture for self-healing in internet of things. In: UBICOMM 2015, p. 89 (2015)
3. Angarita, R.: Responsible objects: towards self-healing internet of things applications. In: 2015 IEEE International Conference on Autonomic Computing, pp. 307–312, July 2015. https://doi.org/10.1109/ICAC.2015.60
4. Boulos, M.I., Jairam, T., Kendzerska, T., Im, J., Mekhael, A., Murray, B.J.: Normal polysomnography parameters in healthy adults: a systematic review and meta-analysis. Lancet Respir. Med. **7**(6), 533–543 (2019). https://doi.org/10.1016/S2213-2600(19)30057-8. http://www.sciencedirect.com/science/article/pii/S2213260019300578
5. Bruening, P.J., Waterman, K.K.: Data tagging for new information governance models. IEEE Secur. Priv. **8**(5), 64–68 (2010). https://doi.org/10.1109/MSP.2010.147

6. Chatzigiannakis, I., Pyrgelis, A., Spirakis, P.G., Stamatiou, Y.C.: Elliptic curve based zero knowledge proofs and their applicability on resource constrained devices. In: 2011 IEEE Eighth International Conference on Mobile Ad-Hoc and Sensor Systems, pp. 715–720, October 2011. https://doi.org/10.1109/MASS.2011.77
7. Davidovich, M.L.Y., Karasik, R., Tal, A., Shinar, Z.: Sleep apnea screening with a contact-free under-the-mattress sensor. In: 2016 Computing in Cardiology Conference (CinC), pp. 849–852, September 2016. https://doi.org/10.23919/CIC.2016.7868876
8. Deering, S., Hinden, R.: Internet protocol, version 6 (IPv6) specification. RFC 8200, RFC Editor, July 2017. https://tools.ietf.org/pdf/rfc8200.pdf
9. Dimitrov, D.V.: Medical internet of things and big data in healthcare. Healthcare Inform. Res. **22**(3), 156–163 (2016). https://doi.org/10.4258/hir.2016.22.3.156
10. Dwivedi, A.D., Srivastava, G., Dhar, S., Singh, R.: A decentralized privacy-preserving healthcare blockchain for IoT. Sensors **19**(2) (2019). https://doi.org/10.3390/s19020326. http://www.mdpi.com/1424-8220/19/2/326
11. Henze, M., Hermerschmidt, L., Kerpen, D., Häußling, R., Rumpe, B., Wehrle, K.: A comprehensive approach to privacy in the cloud-based internet of things. Future Gener. Comput. Syst. **56**, 701–718 (2016). https://doi.org/10.1016/j.future.2015.09.016. http://www.sciencedirect.com/science/article/pii/S0167739X15002964
12. Islam, S.M.R., Kwak, D., Kabir, M.H., Hossain, M., Kwak, K.S.: The internet of things for health care: a comprehensive survey. IEEE Access **3**, 678–708 (2015). https://doi.org/10.1109/ACCESS.2015.2437951
13. Kelaidonis, D., et al.: A cognitive management framework for smart objects and applications in the internet of things. In: Timm-Giel, A., Strassner, J., Agüero, R., Sargento, S., Pentikousis, K. (eds.) MONAMI 2012. LNICST, vol. 58, pp. 196–206. Springer, Heidelberg (2013). https://doi.org/10.1007/978-3-642-37935-2_15
14. Niewolny, D.: How the internet of things is revolutionizing healthcare. Healthcare Segment Manager, Freescale Semiconductor, October 2013. freescale.com/healthcare
15. Raza, S., Wallgren, L., Voigt, T.: SVELTE: real-time intrusion detection in the internet of things. Ad Hoc Netw. **11**(8), 2661–2674 (2013). https://doi.org/10.1016/j.adhoc.2013.04.014. http://www.sciencedirect.com/science/article/pii/S1570870513001005
16. Rehman, S.U., Manickam, S.: Rule-based mechanism to detect denial of service (DOS) attacks on duplicate address detection process in IPv6 link local communication. In: 2015 4th International Conference on Reliability, Infocom Technologies and Optimization (ICRITO)(Trends and Future Directions), pp. 1–6. IEEE (2015)
17. Rehman, S.U., Manickam, S.: Denial of service attack in IPv6 duplicate address detection process. Int. J. Adv. Comput. Sci. Appl. **7**, 232–238 (2016)
18. Rehman, S.U., Manickam, S.: Improved mechanism to prevent denial of service attack in IPv6 duplicate address detection process. Int. J. Adv. Comput. Sci. Appl. **8**(2), 63–70 (2017)
19. Sadek, I., Seet, E., Biswas, J., Abdulrazak, B., Mokhtari, M.: Nonintrusive vital signs monitoring for sleep apnea patients: a preliminary study. IEEE Access **6**, 2506–2514 (2018). https://doi.org/10.1109/ACCESS.2017.2783939
20. Sadek, I., Biswas, J., Abdulrazak, B.: Ballistocardiogram signal processing: a review. Health Inf. Sci. Syst. **7**(1), 10 (2019). https://doi.org/10.1007/s13755-019-0071-7
21. Sadek, I., Demarasse, A., Mokhtari, M.: Internet of things for sleep tracking: wearables vs. nonwearables. Health Technol. (2019). https://doi.org/10.1007/s12553-019-00318-3

22. Shustak, S., et al.: Home monitoring of sleep with a temporary-tattoo EEG, EOG and EMG electrode array: a feasibility study. J. Neural Eng. **16**(2), 026024 (2019). https://doi.org/10.1088/1741-2552/aafa05
23. Tal, A., Shinar, Z., Shaki, D., Codish, S., Goldbart, A.: Validation of contact-free sleep monitoring device with comparison to polysomnography. J. Clin. Sleep Med. **13**(3), 517–522 (2017). https://doi.org/10.5664/jcsm.6514
24. Tung, C.E., Su, D., Turakhia, M.P., Lansberg, M.G.: Diagnostic yield of extended cardiac patch monitoring in patients with stroke or TIA. Front. Neurol. **5**, 266 (2015). https://doi.org/10.3389/fneur.2014.00266. https://www.frontiersin.org/article/10.3389/fneur.2014.00266
25. Tuominen, J., Peltola, K., Saaresranta, T., Valli, K.: Sleep parameter assessment accuracy of a consumer home sleep monitoring ballistocardiograph beddit sleep tracker: a validation study. J. Clin. Sleep Med. **15**(03), 483–487 (2019). https://doi.org/10.5664/jcsm.7682
26. Zaunseder, S., Henning, A., Wedekind, D., Trumpp, A., Malberg, H.: Unobtrusive acquisition of cardiorespiratory signals. Somnologie **21**(2), 93–100 (2017). https://doi.org/10.1007/s11818-017-0112-x

Designing an ICT Solution for the Empowerment of Functional Independence of People with Mild Cognitive Impairment: Findings from Co-design Sessions with Older People

Silvia de los Ríos[1(✉)], Rebeca I. García-Betances[1(✉)], Miguel Páramo[1], María Fernanda Cabrera-Umpiérrez[1], Marta Vancells[2], Maite Garolera[2], Jakub Kaźmierski[3], and María Teresa Arredondo Waldmeyer[1]

[1] Universidad Politécnica de Madrid, ETSI Ingenieros de Telecomunicación, 28002 Madrid, Spain
{srios,rgarcia,mparamo,chiqui,mta}@lst.tfo.upm.es

[2] Grupo de investigación clínica del cerebro, cognición y conducta, Consorci Sanitari de Terrassa, Barcelona, Spain
{mvancells,mgarolera}@cst.cat

[3] Department of Old Age Psychiatry and Psychotic Disorders, Medical University of Lodz, Łódź, Poland
jakub.kazmierski@umed.lodz.pl

Abstract. Mild Cognitive Impairment (MICI) symptoms are one of the main issues that contribute, in older people, to the difficulty to live independently, social isolation and loss of autonomy. INFINITy solution provides a set of services aimed to reinforce and support the daily routines of people with MCI for both indoor and outdoor scenarios. A co-design session with end-users were performed in order to better adapt the INFINITy solution to the needs and characteristics of the target beneficiaries. Results show the feedback received form end-users regarding different aspects of the solution such as: functionalities, use cases, and interfaces. The results were useful to improve the INFINITy solution to better address user's needs and preferences.

Keywords: Co-design · Participatory design · Older users · Functional independence · Mild cognitive impairment · Dementia

1 Introduction

It is estimated that 75 million of people will live with Dementia in 2030 worldwide and this number is expected to double every 20 years, to 132 million in 2050. Due to its widespread high incidence the World Health Organization recommended that Dementia should be treated and handled as a major public health issue [1] and its prevention and treatment currently represent one of the major challenges for researches, health and social services worldwide. Impairments in memory and spatial navigation

J. Pagán et al. (Eds.): ICOST 2019, LNCS 11862, pp. 18–26, 2019.
https://doi.org/10.1007/978-3-030-32785-9_2

associated with aging and, in some cases, to a cognitive condition such as Mild Cognitive Impairment (MCI) or Dementia, are one of the main issues that contribute to the difficulty to live independently, social isolation and a progressive loss of autonomy [1]. Behavioral changes and spatial disorientation that leads to develop a wandering behavior and reduce social activities and interactions, are important early indicators of a potential evolution from normal aging to other more severe cognitive conditions [2]. Different ICT solutions could help to prevent the evolution to these conditions or maintain as long and possible a condition in which people could live independently and continue to perform their daily routines, but most of them do not provide the necessary support and tools while performing outdoor activities [3].

Based on this, the INFINITy project offers a technological solution to cover some of the needs of people with MCI, with the ambition of safeguarding their independence and autonomy while performing their daily routines for as long as possible. The main objective is to have a positive impact on the Quality of Life (QoL) of these people and their main caregiver, while preserving their functionality and extending their autonomy in indoor and outdoor activities by using a technological solution.

Currently there are two main directions collecting data from users with cognitive impairments. Either within the framework of clinical trials which often entails large cohorts of users but rarely focuses on ICT solutions but rather on the medicinal effects, or studies involving the effect of ICT solutions to people with cognitive impairments focused on cognitive impairment as co-morbidity or results because of the primary health condition. The important of QoL metrics and techniques are of vital importance for testing quality of living assessment in older people. The primary INFINITy innovation is to estimate the real-life depiction of the potentially positive effect of ICT solution on cognitive decline in both indoors and outdoors activities of daily living.

The manuscript presents the process followed to design an ICT solution together with potential end users. Section 2 presents the materials used, the sample, and methods followed to conduct the co-design sessions with end-users. Section 3 describe the design of the INFINITy solution showing the use cases defined and the first designs of the solution (i.e. interfaces and NFC tags formats) used as an initial visual material. Section 4 presents the key findings from co-design sessions regarding system designs and defined use cases. Finally, Sect. 5 presents the conclusions.

2 Materials and Methods

The following sub-sections present the materials used and the methods followed to carry out the co-design sessions with end-users. The findings obtained following this approach provide useful information that will be used to define and develop the final INFINITy solution.

2.1 Materials

The main materials used for the co-design sessions were: (1) the questionnaires used to collect user's feedbacks, both standardized and designed for the occasion questionnaires, including questions regarding social and leisure activities, technology use, interfaces look and feel, functionalities and use cases; (2) the interface mock-ups of the INFINITy solution; and (3) the NFC tags presented in different formats.

Technologies used for the INFINITy solution (e.g. NFC, BLE) were selected based on their low costs, easiness to use, availability and compatibility with current smartphones, and communication capabilities that fulfill the main purpose of the features provided by INFINITy.

Specifically, the standardized questionnaires used were: Socioeconomic Subjective Status (SES) [4], Montreal Cognitive Assessment (MoCa) [5], Lawton & Brody test [6], and Memory Failures of Everyday (MFE) [7].

Consent must be obtained from all participants including the individuals who act as their informal caregiver. Participants were provided with the information they need to make an informed decision. In the occurrence of a change in the informal carer during the testbed duration, consent must be obtained from the new carer before they can become involved in the evaluation. A series of Consent Form Sheets were provided in English to all clinical partners, detailing the list of items to be consented. All participants completed the consent before the start of the co-design session.

2.2 Sample

The study involved 20 participants from Spain and Poland (10 participants by site) including people with MCI and their caregivers. Caregivers participated during the co-design sessions as supporters of the MCI participants as well as providing their opinions specifically in the definition of features and use cases. Demographic data collected from MCI participants is the following: age mean of 72.7 (sdv 5.96), 50% of the sample is in the age range from 71 to 80 years old; 8 females and 2 males; schooling level with a mean of 8.4 (sdv 4.06) years of schooling; MoCa mean score of 23.9 (sdv 2.13); a functionality level of 6.8 (sdv 1.03); and SES mean score of 4.7 (sdv 1.159).

2.3 Co-design Sessions Protocol

The co-design sessions aim to design and improve different technical aspects of the application in terms of interface design and workflow of functionalities. The session consists of an interview conducted by a project member of testbed site, where the participant and the caregiver will go through different questions related to interface design and functions of the proposed solution. The questions were defined in an easy and understandable way in order to collect the opinions and suggestions from MCI participants and their caregivers.

Specifically, the objectives of the co-design sessions were:

- Define the format and icons design of NFC tags (using questionnaires and set of NFC cards and media material)
- Assess first set of use cases and get ideas for new use cases (using questionnaires and videos of the Smart Cards)
- Get feedback regarding the mock-ups of the interface (using the mock-ups and the questionnaires)

Each session had an approximate duration of 90 min. A written informed consent was provided to the participant and caregiver in order to be part of the co-design session and to approve video recording of the session to later visualize and analyze the answers. These recordings will only be viewed by members of the project, and subsequently deleted from the system.

Three main phases of the study were defined: (1) socio-demographic assessment; (2) psychometric assessment; and (3) qualitative assessment.

Socio-demographic Assessment: In this phase information regarding age, sex, years schooling, profession, marital status and socioeconomic status (SES questionnaire) were collected from participants.

Psychometric Assessment: The MoCa questionnaire and the Lawton & Brody test were used to collect information about cognitive and functional state. Additionally, the Subjective Cognitive Complaints were measured using the most important items from the MFE questionnaire. The items used are the following: forgetting where you have put something; having to go back to check whether you have done something; forgetting that you were told something yesterday; and getting lost on a place where you have only been once or twice before.

Qualitative Assessment: A questionnaire designed for the occasion questions related to social and leisure activities, technology use, interfaces, functionalities and use cases was provided to participants. The project member guiding the session went through all the specific questions complementing the information provided in the questionnaire with additional materials such as screen shots of the interfaces and NFC tags in different formats.

3 INFINITy Solution Design

The INFINITy solution is aimed to support daily life activities of older people with MCI in indoor and outdoor environments in order to reinforce their functional abilities and safeguard their independence and autonomy while performing daily routines. It is constituted by a smartphone App (on Android) and a set of cards with the contact less technology Near-Field-Communication (NFC). In addition, a set of Bluetooth Low Energy (BLE) beacons located around the city are used to activate automatic messages while walking around.

3.1 Use Cases

3.1.1 Support to Indoor and Outdoor Activities with NFC Cards

Different use cases (UC) with NFC cards were designed in order to support daily life activities in both, indoors and outdoors scenarios. Table 1 shows the description of each defined UC. These use cases were pre-defined in order to assess and refine them during the co-designed session with MCI participants and with their caregivers.

Table 1. Use cases with NFC cards.

Environment	UC name	Description
Indoors	Voice mail	It allows a bidirectional communication between the user and their caregiver by sending (recording) and receiving (listening) voice messages through two paired of NFC cards
	Battery	It provides the battery status of the smartphone
	Pre-fixed message	It sends a predefined message to the caregiver
	Date and time	It provides the current date and time
	Agenda	It allows to create an event on the agenda or consult the existing ones
Outdoors	Go home	It guides the user to go home from wherever he is
	Go to a POI	It guides the user to go to a specific Point of Interest from wherever he is
	Call a contact	It makes a phone call to a contact
	Share a GPS	It sends the GPS location of the user to their caregiver

3.1.2 Automatic Messages to Reinforce Abilities

In addition to the use cases described in the previous section, there is an additional use case related to the reinforcement of the abilities through the stimulation of the declarative memory using associative principles to link two pieces of information by content and context relationships. While the user with MCI is walking around the city, the city sends them messages to their smartphone with the aim to support their daily life activities. Messages are in the form of quick games (or quizzes) and healthy or well-being tips and are launched every time that a user passes nearby a Point of Interest mapped with GPS or with a BLE beacon.

3.2 Interface First Designs

Based on the previous use cases, the INFINITy App was designed as a launcher application that enables the different functionalities of the system. It provides a simple and user-friendly interface, where the caregiver can access to set up the initial configuration of the system and where the user with MCI can access normally their standard applications installed on the phone.

3.2.1 Main Menu (Launcher) Interface

Different mockups of the main interface were designed to offer a variety of options for the co-design sessions: two options in portrait mode (A and B), two options in landscape mode (C and D), two options with soft colors (A and C), and two options with vivid colors (B and D). Figure 1 shows the four design options of the main menu interface.

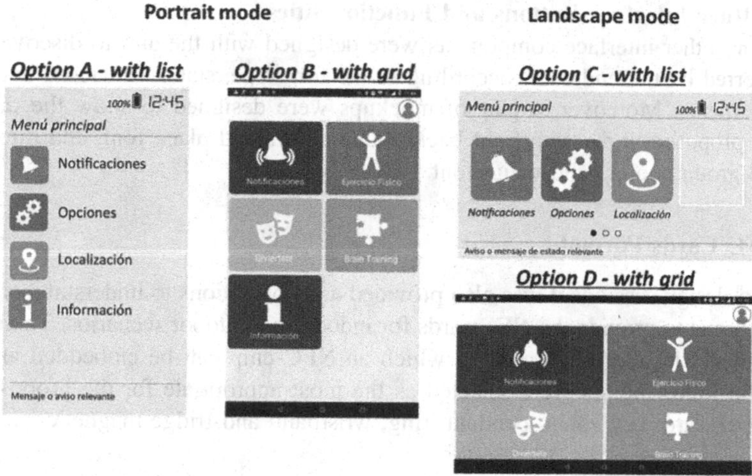

Fig. 1. Four design options for the user interface of the main menu.

In addition, two themes were designed: one with light background (A) and one with dark background (B), as presented in Fig. 2.

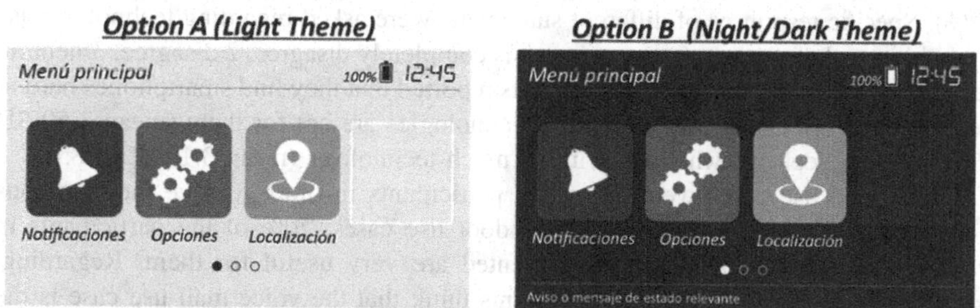

Fig. 2. Two design option with different themes.

3.2.2 Automatic Messages Interface

Three mockups defined to provide the messages to reinforce abilities while the user is walking around the city. The first presents message launched when a user passes nearby a region (POI) mapped with GPS or BLE in the INFINITy system. This screen informs the user that he is walking nearby a concrete type of POI and asks whether a quick quiz can be launched. The second one presents the quiz and provides the user with two options to answer the question proposed. The third provides the tip/recommendation related to the POI.

3.2.3 Other Interface Buttons and Functionalities

In addition, other interface components were designed with the aim to discover what was preferred by the end users according to the font type, status bar, icons and navigation elements. Moreover, a pair of mockups were designed to show the different contrasts proposed, three with light background colors and black font, and three with dark background colors and white font.

3.3 NFC Cards Format

During co-design sessions it was also provided a set of options to understand which is the best format to provide the NFC cards for indoor and outdoor scenarios. Taking into account the wide offer of formats in which an NFC chip can be embedded and presented, the following six were selected as the most appropriate for the proposed use cases: credit card, key chain, pendant, ring, wristband and fridge magnetic.

4 Key Findings from Co-design Sessions

Before analyzing the results obtained regarding the functionalities and interface design of the solution, it is important to analyze the overall general opinion about technologies, perceived level of difficulty of smartphones and technology usage.

Regarding technological level of participants, the majority do not use smartphones (70%). Specific responses of different statements were asked regarding technology use with a liker scale from 1 to 5 where 1 means completely disagree, 2 disagree, 3 neutral, 4 agree and 5 completely agree. Participants reported that they find smartphones hard to use (mean 3.30 SD 1.34), feel that new technologies are not for them (mean 3.50 SD 1.65) and they feel overwhelmed with so much technology (mean 3.10 SD 1.85).

Pre-defined use cases were assess by participants in order to give their opinons about their usefulness. In the case of outdoor use cases, 70% of the participants in general perceive that all use cases presented are very useful for them. Regarding, indoor use cases the 90% of the participants think that the voice mail use case is the most useful for them, followed by send pre-fixed messages, with 70%, and know the battery level with a 60%. The use cases that MCI participants liked the most were: phonebook management, use of calendar, know date and time, outdoors guidance, make calls and send messages.

Specifically, where asked about their opinions regarding the additional use case related to the reinforcement of the abilities through the stimulation of the declarative memory. In this respect, 50% of participants find it useful, the other half thinks that in some cases could represent an additional workload (30%) and could be annoying (40%).

Results regarding the interface designs participants likes more option B (portrait mode with grid) and think it is clean, pretty and that the size of the elements are correct. In terms of screen look and feel (e.g. colors) they think that option A (portrait mode with list) colors will not tire their eyesight (70%). Overall, 80% of participants prefer the list format although they liked more option B with a grid format, they think that having a list would be most simple to them. In the case of other interface buttons and functionalities, users prefered the options that make it more intuitive and readable, for example: icons text in plain instead of italic; navigation bars with buttons and with text; and a good contrast between background colors and font.

Futhermore, participants were asked to choose their prefered format of NFC tags for both types of use cases, indoors and outdoors. In general the most voted was the card format (40%).

5 Conclusions

Co-design sessions were a fruitful experience to start involving end users from the early stages of the prototype definition, in order to better adapt the product to the target beneficiaries of the solution.

After the co-design sessions were carried out, we could conclude that a positive feedback was collected that helped us to understand the user needs and choose their preferred elements when developing the system. Feedback from end-users will be used to improve the first designs of the solutions and to identify potential new use cases and functionalities.

Acknowledgments. This work was financially supported by the EIT Health, a body of the European Union, under the activity code: 19342.

References

1. World Health Organization (WHO): Global action plan on the public health response to dementia 2017–2025 (2017). ISBN 978-92-4-151348-7
2. Alzheimer's Association: 2018 Alzheimer's disease facts and figures. Alzheimer's & Dementia 14, no. 3, pp. 367–429 (2018). https://doi.org/10.1016/j.jalz.2018.02.001
3. Teipel, S., Babiloni, C., Hoey, J., Kaye, J., Kirste, T., Burmeister, O.K.: Information and communication technology solutions for outdoor navigation in dementia. Alzheimer's Dementia **12**(6), 695–707 (2016). https://doi.org/10.1016/j.jalz.2015.11.003
4. Adler, N.E., Epel, E.S., Castellazzo, G., Ickovics, J.R.: Relationship of subjective and objective social status with psychological and physiological functioning: preliminary data in healthy, White women. Health Psychol. **19**(6), 586 (2000). https://doi.org/10.1037/0278-6133.19.6.586
5. Montreal Cognitive Assessment (MoCa). Spanish version. https://www.mocatest.org/pdf_files/test/MoCA-Test-Spanish.pdf. Polish version https://www.mocatest.org/pdf_files/test/MoCA-Test-Polish.pdf

6. Lawton, M.P., Brody, E.M.: Assessment of older people: self-maintaining and instrumental activities of daily living. Gerontologist **9**(3), 179–186 (1969)
7. Montejo, P., Peña, M., Sueiro, M.: The memory failures of everyday questionnaire (MFE): internal consistency and reliability. Spanish J. Psychol. **15**, 768–776 (2012). https://doi.org/10.5209/rev_SJOP.2012.v15.n2.38888

Deployment of an IoT Solution for Early Behavior Change Detection

Hamdi Aloulou[1,2(✉)], Mounir Mokhtari[3], and Bessam Abdulrazak[4]

[1] Centre de Recherche en Numérique de Sfax, Sfax, Tunisia
hamdi.aloulou@isima.u-monastir.tn
[2] Université de Monastir, Institut Supérieur d'Informatique de Mahdia, Mahdia, Tunisia
[3] Institut Mines Télécom, Paris, France
[4] Université de Sherbrooke, Sherbrooke, Canada

Abstract. Today, numerous factors are causing a demographic change in many countries in the world. This change is producing a nearly balanced society share between the young and aging population. The noticeable increasing aging population is causing different economical, logistical and societal problems. In fact, aging is associated with chronic diseases in addition to physical, psychological, cognitive and societal changes. These changes are considered as indicators of aging peoples' frailty. It is therefore important to early detected these changes to prevent isolation, sedentary lifestyle, and even diseases in order to delay the frailty period. This paper presents an experiment deployment of an Internet of Thing solution for the continuous monitoring and detection of elderly people's behavior changes. The objective is to help geriatricians detect sedentary lifestyle and health-related problems at an early stage.

Keywords: Behavior change · Internet of Things · Frailty

1 Introduction

Aging is often related to significant changes in physical activities, mobility, nutrition, social life and cognitive status. These changes considerably affect elderly people quality of life. According to the World Health Organization (WHO) [1], the biggest health risk for seniors is the adoption of a sedentary lifestyle that causes isolation, depression and many other diseases such as cardiovascular disease, obesity, high blood pressure, etc.

In this paper, we present our experience in deploying an Internet of Things (IoT) solution for the continuous monitoring and detection of elderly people's behavior changes. The objective is to help geriatricians detect sedentary lifestyle and health related problems at early stage, without the need to perform classical psycho-geriatric tests that have many limitations like assessment inaccuracies

Supported by H2020 European Project City4Age.

J. Pagán et al. (Eds.): ICOST 2019, LNCS 11862, pp. 27–35, 2019.
https://doi.org/10.1007/978-3-030-32785-9_3

and the difficulty for elderly people to recall past events. The work was performed as part of the European project City4Age based on 6 pilot sites: Athens, Birmingham, Lecce, Madrid, Montpellier and Singapore. In this paper, we will focus and detail the deployment performed in the pilot site of Montpellier.

2 Literature Review and Related Work

Early detection of ageing people behavior change can improve medical assessments and enable proactive intervention. In fact, aging-related health problems generate long-term behavior changes, such as possible instabilities, variations, impairments, declines, increases or improvements [2]. Nowadays, geriatricians use psycho-geriatric scales and questionnaires to analyze behavior and investigate possible changes [3,4]. These psycho-geriatric approaches are insufficient to monitor patients on a daily basis [5]. Thus, geriatricians need technological services to acquire new objective observations that complete their medical observations. Monitoring technologies can help follow-up elderly people at home and in city, in order to early detect possible health changes [6].

Contrary to existing technological solutions that target Short-term Health Change Detection [7], retrospectively investigate possible changes after change occurrence [8] and use intrusive technologies to capture video sequences, collect daily questionnaire-based information and record physical data using body sensors [9], our proposed approach analyzes overall behavior over long periods, in order to detect long-term changes in health status. These long-term changes require weeks and months to emerge, and are difficult to detect due to normal continuous variation in human behavior [10]. In addition, it continuously analyzes monitoring data on a daily basis, in order to early detect possible changes. This proactive change detection provides opportunity for daily assessment and subsequent intervention. Finally, it uses unobtrusive monitoring technologies that are embedded in our real environment or in objects of daily living, do not interfere with natural behavior of elderly people and do not change their daily habits.

3 Montpellier Pilot Setup

Montpellier pilot site goal is to quickly and unobtrusively detect possible aging people's behavior changes. Detected behavior changes are afterwards analyzed and confirmed by collaborating geriatricians to provide adequate intervention.

The pilot site is Coordinated by the French National Center for Scientific Research (CRNS) and is collaborating with local authorities such as Montpellier Metropolis, the ETAPE (health autonomy pole) association and healthcare professionals from Beausoleil Clinic and Saint Vincent De Paul nursing home.

The proposed solution deployed in the pilot site of Montpellier consists of a set of sensors deployed in the participants' homes and in the city as shown in Fig. 1. For indoor monitoring, the pilot uses motion sensors, contact sensors and bed sensors. Outdoor monitoring is based on Smartphones carried by participants and beacons deployed in places of interest of participants in the city. These sensors allow to collect raw data and objective information in real time, which are processed to detect behavior changes.

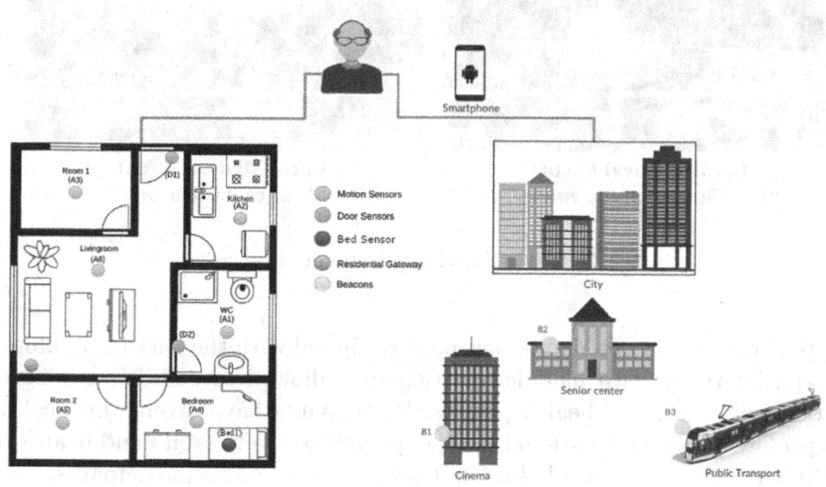

Fig. 1. Montpelier pilot site global setup

4 Recruitment and Engagement

Each of the six pilot sites followed a specific ethical approval process, related to specific countries' regulation, in order to recruit participants. For Montpellier pilot site, the ethical process consists in sending the specifications of the deployment to CNRS's Data Protection Correspondent (Correspondants Informatique et Libertés: CIL). In parallel, an application was also submitted to the Institutional review board (Comités de Protection des Personnes: CPP).

After obtaining the ethical approval, we started the recruitment process. We have approached around 40 potential participants with the help of ETAPE association and Saint Vincent De Paul nursing home. In fact, we have presented the solution in several local events to promote the project and identify interested people to be included in the study. As shown in Fig. 2, briefing and presentation sessions were organized in the Montpellier pilot site to better promote experimentation objectives, quickly launch recruitment process and keep recruited participants involved in the experimentation. These events allowed to have in depth discussions with interested aging people who accepted to visit a demonstration house, see a live demonstration of the system and have their feedback. The demonstration house highlights the unobtrusiveness of the technological solution proposed for the potential participants. Interested people also observe sensor events in real-time and examples of real data over weeks and months indicating significant changes in health status. Potential participants asked for information about employed technological solutions, real benefits of adopting them at home and possible risks.

Local Medical Event "Pass'Sport Santé Séniors"

Local Medical Event "France Parkinson"

Fig. 2. Briefing and involvement sessions

19 participants accepted and have been equipped with the City4Age solution. An initial interview with included participants allowed to collect some indications on their social and health profiles. Participants have diverse medical and social profiles such as educational level, dependence level, habits and health status. Table 1 presents regular habits and health info of some participants.

Table 1. Examples of Montpelier pilot site participants habits and health status

Patient	Regular habits	Health info
98	Wakes up at 8 h. Home aid 4 times per day. Stays most often at home. Sometimes goes out with daughter or caregiver	Alzheimer Diabetes Vision and audition problems
101	Wakes up at 7 h30–8 h. Home aid visits 3 times per day (morning, midday and evening). Niece and neighbor visits during the day. Sleeps earlier than before (at 20 h, and before at 22 h)	Alzheimer Some falls and hospitalizations
102	Wakes up at 6 h–7 h. Home aid visits each day in the morning. Lives alone. Daughter house is nearby. Monthly visits to and from daughter	Heart problems Urinary infection

5 Technologies and Data Collection

The system proposed in Montpellier pilot site uses indoor and outdoor technologies to monitor daily living activities of participants. For indoor monitoring, the pilot is proposing a set of sensors (motion sensors, contact sensors and bed sensors). These sensors operate discreetly and allow to collect raw data and objective information in real time. The objective is to be able to accurately determine the "habitual behaviours" of people by collecting data over time. Outdoor monitoring is based on beacons deployed in the participants' places of interest in the city (e.g. bus and metro stations, cinemas, restaurants, etc.) and smartphones with dedicated mobile application carried by the participants. Thus, it is possible to collect data on the activities of our participants' even when they are in outdoor in the city. Figure 3 showcases some deployed sensors in Montpellier pilot site.

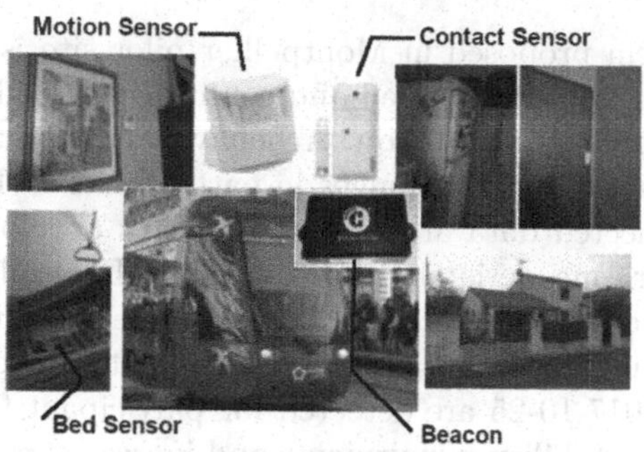

Fig. 3. Indoor and outdoor sensors deployment

All indoor and outdoor data are collected in Montpellier pilot site local server where local treatment for Low Elementary Actions (LEAs) and measures identification is performed. Low Elementary Actions are basic participants' actions which are inferred from received sensors' events (e.g. Start Moving, Stop Moving, Change Room, Visit Restaurant, etc.). Measures are quantified data extracted from LEAs (e.g time in the bedroom/day, number of toilet visits /day, number of shops visits/week, etc.). Later, these information are transferred to the City4Age repository and analytic algorithm where further treatments are performed in order to produce visualisations for the geriatrician. The complete architecture of the City4Age solution and the performed deployment and data analysis in Montpellier pilot site is presented in Fig. 4.

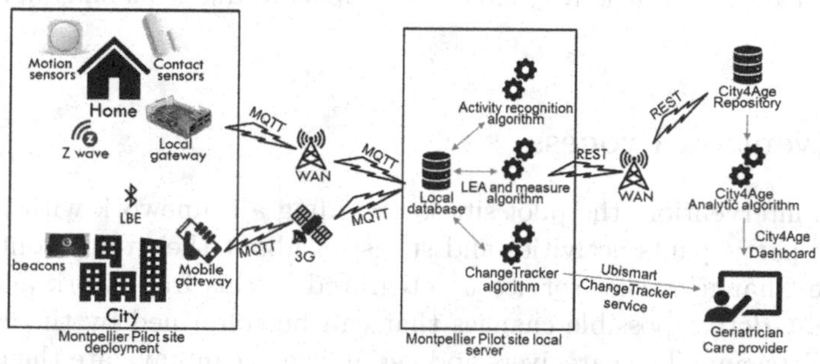

Fig. 4. Complete architecture of Montpellier pilot site's deployment

The deployment of this system in France allowed to collect around two years of real data. We have collected 310.590 of Low Elementary Actions (LEA) and 49.659 of Measures for 19 participants.

6 Data Interpretation

The goal of the system proposed in Montpellier pilot site is to detect possible behavior changes that will be analysed and confirmed by collaborating geriatricians to provide adequate intervention. A behavior change tracker service [11] was developed allowing to detect changes in participants' behavior using statistical algorithms. Collected data are analyzed by this developed algorithm and presented to collaborating geriatricians from clinic Beausoleil. Figure 5 showcases some behavior changes detected by the ChangeTracker service for one of the participants in the pilot site. In Fig. 5, 3 consecutive decreases on 2017-02-15, 2017-06-20 and 2017-10-25 are detected for participant 91. Participant and family doctor confirm mobility impairments and increased risk of dependence in managing activities of daily living. Professional caregiver helps with medication taking and household from 2017-05-04.

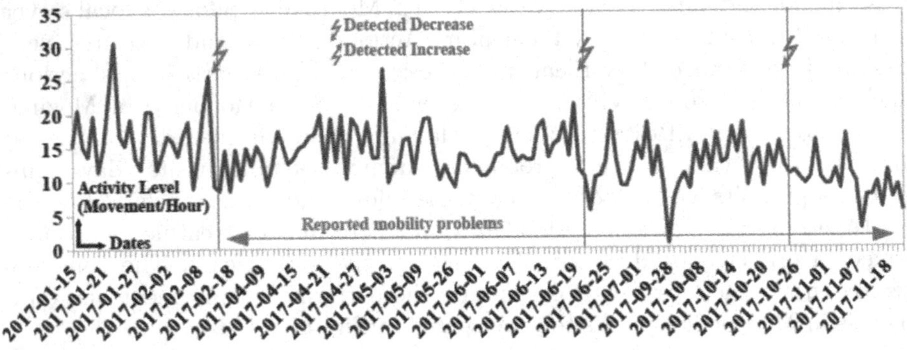

Fig. 5. Detected changes in activity level of participant 91 due to mobility impairments

7 Intervention Process

To perform intervention, the pilot site is providing a framework with visualizations about participants activities and statistics about their daily routines and habits. The ChangeTracker service is integrated in this framework allowing to automatically detect possible changes that can be confirmed by the caregivers and the geriatrician. The caregivers and geriatricians can navigate the data provided by these visualizations and decide on the type and form of intervention when needed. As an example, after detecting a decrease in outdoor and indoor activities for participant 96, nursing home stuff decided to initiate home assistance.

8 Validation

8.1 Detection Process Validation

The ChangeTracker service has being validated with the help of our stakeholders. Detected changes are being correlated with medical observation and health records to validate the used algorithms and their performances.

The ChangeTracker service sends change notifications. Change notifications provide opportunity to confirm that detected changes are really permanent and investigate possible correlations with geriatric observations. Regular review meetings with elderly people, family members and family doctors allow to accurately investigate possible causes of detected changes. Review meetings investigate mutli-dimensional correlations of detected changes, such as identifying parallel decreases in activity level and time out home related to mobility impairments, and consecutive increases in sleep interruptions and toilet entries after treatment change. Figure 6 shows some results of changes detected by ChangeTracker service and their correlation with medical observations and participant feedback.

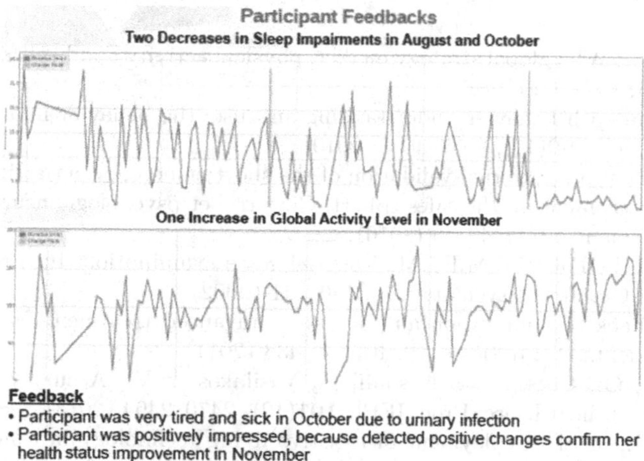

Participant Feedbacks
Two Decreases in Sleep Impairments in August and October
One Increase in Global Activity Level in November
Feedback
• Participant was very tired and sick in October due to urinary infection
• Participant was positively impressed, because detected positive changes confirm her health status improvement in November

Fig. 6. Detected behavior changes by ChangeTracker and corresponding participant feedback

8.2 Results and Performance

In total, we have detected 340 changes for all participants with an average of 0.97 change per month. Participants show diverse changes in monitoring period that are associate with diverse medical reasons, such as physical problems (45.59% of detected changes), health improvements (36.76%), nutritional problems (8.82%), personal changes (7.35%) and social problems (1.47%).

9 Conclusion

Montpellier pilot site was a proof of concept of our IoT proposed solution for the early identification of behavior changes. In total, 340 changes have been detected for all participants. These changes have been validated and classified with the help of local geriatrician and by correlation with Medical Observations. This solution could be of great value for the geriatricians. In fact, the technological observations provided by the proposed solution enrich their medical observation for better assessments of frailty and MCI. The solution is also valuable for nursing homes. In fact, nursing homes need to maintain independent living at home and identify elderly people at risk who really require entry to nursing home.

Acknowledgment. This work was supported by the European project City4Age that received funding from the Horizon 2020 research and innovation program under grant agreement number 689731. We would like to thank all the participants who accepted to be part of this experimentation and all our collaborating geriatricians and professional and informal caregivers.

References

1. Waxman, A.: Who global strategy on diet, physical activity and health. Food Nutr. Bull. **25**(3), 292–302 (2004)
2. Cao, L.: In-depth behavior understanding and use: the behavior informatics approach. Inf. Sci. **180**(17), 3067–3085 (2010)
3. Tardieu, E., et al.: External validation of the short emergency geriatric assessment (SEGA) instrument on the safes cohort. Geriatrie et psychologie neuropsychiatrie du vieillissement **14**(1), 49–55 (2016)
4. Cockrell, J.R., Folstein, M.F.: Mini-mental state examination. In: Principles and Practice of Geriatric Psychiatry, pp. 140–141 (2002)
5. Lökk, J.: Lack of information and access to advanced treatment for Parkinson's disease patients. J. Multidisc. Healthc. **4**, 433 (2011)
6. Acampora, G., Cook, D.J., Rashidi, P., Vasilakos, A.V.: A survey on ambient intelligence in healthcare. Proc. IEEE **101**(12), 2470–2494 (2013)
7. Aloulou, H., et al.: Deployment of assistive living technology in a nursing home environment: methods and lessons learned. BMC Med. Inform. Decis. Making **13**(1), 42 (2013)
8. Sprint, G., Cook, D.J., Schmitter-Edgecombe, M.: Unsupervised detection and analysis of changes in everyday physical activity data. J. Biomed. Inform. **63**, 54–65 (2016)
9. Avvenuti, M., Baker, C., Light, J., Tulpan, D., Vecchio, A.: Non-intrusive patient monitoring of Alzheimer's disease subjects using wireless sensor networks. In: 2009 World Congress on Privacy, Security, Trust and the Management of e-Business, pp. 161–165. IEEE (2009)
10. Lally, P., Van Jaarsveld, C.H., Potts, H.W., Wardle, J.: How are habits formed: modelling habit formation in the real world. Eur. J. Soc. Psychol. **40**(6), 998–1009 (2010)

11. Kaddachi, F., Aloulou, H., Abdulrazak, B., Fraisse, P., Mokhtari, M.: Long-term behavior change detection approach through objective technological observations toward better adaptation of services for elderly people. Health Technol. **8**(5), 329–340 (2018)

Long Short Term Memory Based Model for Abnormal Behavior Prediction in Elderly Persons

Meriem Zerkouk[1(✉)] and Belkacem Chikhaoui[2(✉)]

[1] Department of Computer Science, USTO-MB University, Oran, Algeria
zerkouk.meriem@gmail.com

[2] LICEF Research Center, Department of Science and Technology, TELUQ University, Montreal, Canada
belkacem.chikhaoui@teluq.ca

Abstract. Smart home refers to the independency and comfort that are ensured by remote monitoring and assistive services. Assisting an elderly person requires identifying and accurately predicting his/her normal and abnormal behaviors. Abnormal behaviors observed during the completion of activities of daily living are a good indicator that the person is more likely to have health and behavioral problems that need intervention and assistance. In this paper, we propose a method, based on long short-term memory recurrent neural networks (LSTM), to automatically predicting an elderly person's abnormal behaviors. Our method allows to model the temporal information expressed in the long sequences collected over time. Our study aims to evaluate the performance of LSTM on identifying and predicting elderly persons abnormal behaviors in smart homes. We experimentally demonstrated, through extensive experiments using a dataset, the suitability and performance of the proposed method in predicting abnormal behaviors with high accuracy. We also demonstrated the superiority of the proposed method compared to the existing state-of-the-art methods.

Keywords: Smart home · ADL · LSTM · Anomaly detection

1 Introduction

Internet of Things (IoT), which is an emerging domain, promises to create a world where all the objects around us are connected to the Internet and communicate with each other with minimum human intervention. The crucial goal is to create a better world for human beings, where objects around us are context awareness, that can respond to questions: what we want, what we need and where we are. Smart homes represent one of the main application domains of IoT that received particular attention from researchers [1].

The smart homes become a safe and secure environment for dependent people. They offer the ability (1) to track residents' activities without interfering in their daily life, and (2) to track residents' behaviors and to monitor their health by using sensors embedded in their living spaces [2]. The data collected from smart homes needs to be

J. Pagán et al. (Eds.): ICOST 2019, LNCS 11862, pp. 36–45, 2019.
https://doi.org/10.1007/978-3-030-32785-9_4

deeply analyzed and investigated, in order to extract useful information about residents' daily routines, and more specifically (specific) activities of daily living.

Activity recognition [3], as a core feature of smart home, consists of classifying data recorded by the different integrated environmental and/or wearable sensors, into well-defined and known movements. However, dependent persons are usually exposed to different types of problems causing them mostly to perform activities of daily living in a wrong way. Therefore, detecting abnormal behaviors is of great importance for dependent people in order to ensure that activities are performed correctly without errors [4]. This will also ensure their safety and well-being.

Detecting an anomaly in the activities of daily living (ADL) of a person is usually performed by detecting nonconformities from their usual ADL patterns. This has been conducted in various works using classical machine learning algorithms [5, 6]. Telehealth care requires systems with high accuracy, less computational time and less user intervention because data are becoming larger and more complex [7]. However, deep learning architectures provide a way to automatically extract useful and meaningful spatial and temporal features of a raw data without the need for data labeling which is time consuming, complex and error prone. This makes deep learning models easily generalizable to different contexts. LSTM is a powerful deep learning model for sequence prediction and anomaly detection in sequential data [8]. LSTM models are able to extract temporal features with long time relationships. This property is of great importance in smart homes in order to understand person's behaviors, they change over time, and particularly any deviations from normal execution of activities of daily living.

In this paper, we propose an LSTM model to identify and predict elderly people's abnormal behaviors. The rationale of using LSTM model in our work is threefold: (1) it is capable of handling multivariate sequential time-series data, (2) it can identify and accurately predict abnormal behavior in time-series data [9, 10], and (3) it can automatically extract features from massive time-series data, which makes it possible to be easily generalizable to other types of data. Therefore, the contributions of our paper can be summarized as follows:

1. Proposing an LSTM model for automatic prediction of abnormal behaviors in smart homes.
2. Managing the problem of imbalanced data by oversampling minority classes.
3. Conducting extensive experiments to validate the proposed LSTM model.

The paper is organized as follows: Sect. 2 presents an overview of anomaly detection models and related work in machine learning algorithms. Section 3 presents Materials and methods to conduct our work and the obtained results. Section 4 gives a comparison of different machine learning algorithms. Finally, Sect. 5 discusses the outcomes of the experiments and perspectives for future work.

2 Related Work

Tracking user behavior for abnormality detection has gain a large attention and becomes one of the main goals for certain researchers [11]. Abnormal behavior detection approaches are based mainly on machine learning algorithms, and more specifically supervised learning techniques [12]. Supervised classification techniques need labelled data points (samples) for the models to learn. This kind of classification requires to train a classifier on the labelled data points and then evaluate the model on new data points. Therefore, in case of normal and abnormal classes, the model learns the characteristics of these data points and classify them as normal or abnormal. Any data point that does not conform to this normal class, will be classified as an anomaly by the model. Various classification techniques have been applied for abnormal behavior detection.

Pirzada et al. [13] explored KNN as a classifier which works well to classify data in categories. They performed a binary classification where they classify activity as good or bad to distinguish the anomaly in the user behavior. Eventually, the proposed KNN applied to predicts whether the class belongs to regular (good) or irregular (bad) class. The performed work monitor health conditions of elderly person living alone using sensors in unobtrusive manner.

Aran et al. [4] proposed a method to automatically observe and model the daily behavior of the elderly and detect anomalies that could occur in the sensor data. In their proposed method, the anomaly relies on signal health related problems. For this purpose, they have created a probabilistic spatio-temporal model to summarize daily behavior. They define anomalies as significant changes from the learned behavioral model and detected, the performance is evaluated by cross-entropy measure. Once the anomaly is detected, the caregivers are informed accordingly.

Ordonez et al. [14] presented an anomaly detection method based on Bayesian statistics that identify anomalous human behavioral patterns. Their proposed method assists automatically the elderly person's with disabilities who live alone, by learning and predicting standard behaviors to improve the efficiency of their healthcare system. The Bayesian statistics are choosen to analyze the collected data, the estimation of the static behavior is based on three probabilistic features that introduce, namely sensor activation likelihood, sensor sequence likelihood and sensor event duration likelihood.

Yahaya et al. [11] proposed novelty detection algorithm known as One-Class Support Vector Machine (SVM) which is applied for detection of anomaly in activities of daily living. The anomaly is situated in sleeping patterns, which could be a sign of Mild Cognitive Impairment (MCI) in older adults or other health-related issues.

Palaniappan et al. [15] interested in detecting abnormal activities of the individuals by ruling out all possible normal activities. Authors define abnormal activities as unexpected events that occur in random manner. Multi-class SVM method is used as classifier to identify the activities in form of a state transition table. The transition table helps the classifier in avoiding the states which are unreachable from the current state.

Hung et al. [16] proposed a novel approach that mix SVM and HMM to a homecare sensory system. RFID sensor networks are used to collect elder's daily activities, Hidden Markov Model (HMM) used to learn the data, and SVMs used to estimate whether the elder's behavior is abnormal or not.

Bouchachia et al. [17] proposed an RNN model to deal the problem of activity recognition and abnormal behavior detection for elderly people with dementia. The proposed method suffered from the lack of data in the context of dementia.

The aforementioned methods suffer from one or more of the following limitations:

1. The presented methods focus on the spatial and the temporal anomalies in user assistance. However, we noted that the abnormal behavior does not treated in the case of the smart home.
2. These methods require feature engineering, which is difficult specifically when data becomes larger.
3. The abnormality identification and prediction lack of good accuracy.

These points motivate us to propose a method, which tries to overcome these limitations and to be useful in smart homes for assistance.

3 Proposed Method

In this section, we present a description of our problem related to the identification and prediction of elderly person's abnormal behaviors.

3.1 Problem Description

Abnormality detection is an important task in health care monitoring, particularly for monitoring elderly in smart homes. Abnormality consists in finding unexpected activities, variations in normal patterns of activities, finding the patterns in data that do not conform to the expected behavior [18] because humans usually perform their ADLs in a sequential manner. According to [19], the abnormality can be categorized into temporal, spatial, and behavioral abnormality. Our work focuses on the behavioral anomaly because this kind of abnormality depends on the same on time (when performing the activity) and location (where performing the activity). Each activity is defined by a sequence of sub-activities and if the person violates the expected sequence then it is an abnormality.

3.2 LSTM for Anomaly Description

LSTMs [20] are a recurrent neural network architecture, the principal characteristic is the memory extension that can be seen as a gated cell, where gated means that the cell decides whether or not to store or delete information, based on the importance it assigns to the information. The assignment of importance happens through weights, which are also learned by the algorithm. This simply means that it learns over time, which information is important.

LSTM architecture consists of three layers: Input layer, hidden layer and output layer. The hidden layers are fully connected to the input and output layers. A layer in LSTM is composed from blocs, and each block has three gates: input, output and forget gates. Each gate is connected to each other. These gates decide whether or not to let new input in (input gate), delete the information because it isn't important (forget gate) or to let it impact the output at the current time step (output gate).

As we mentioned previously, our motivations in using LSTM rely on the fact that it enables to remember their inputs over a long period of time which allows to remember the data sequences. Abnormality detection aims to identify a small group of samples, which deviate remarkably from the existing data. That why, we choose LSTM to identify and accurately predict the abnormality behavior from a long sequential data given that persons perform their ADL in a sequential manner, less human intervention in the identification and prediction process.

The LSTM input layer development requires reshaping the data. It needs the input data to be 3-dimensions as training sample, time step, and features. We add for this layer an activation function (ReLu). To avoid overfitting problem in LSTM architectures, we used the dropout method [24] and improve model performance. In our proposed model, the dropout is applied between the two hidden layers and between the last hidden layer and the output layer. We setup the dropout at 20% as recommended in literature [24].

The last layer (dense layer) defines the number of outputs which represents the different activities and anomaly (classes). The output is considered as vector of integer which is converted into binary matrix. The anomaly prediction is formulated as multi classification problem which requires to create 7 output values, one for each class, Softmax as activation function and categorical_crossentropy is used as the loss function. The Fig. 1 indicate the LSTM architecture development.

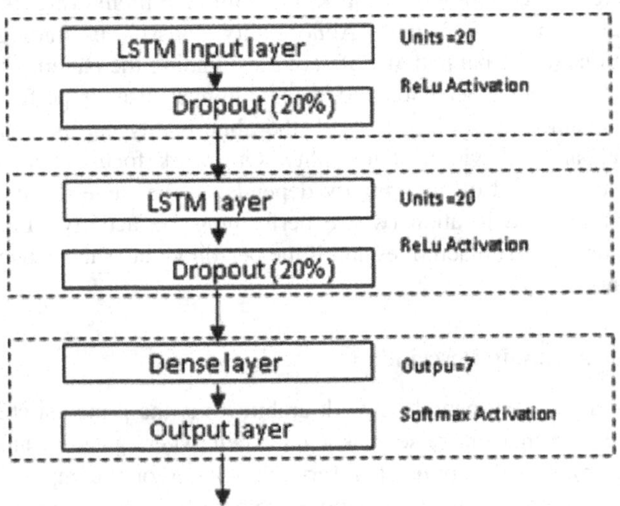

Fig. 1. LSTM development.

4 Experiment Study

In this section, we present our dataset that we want to analyze, overcome to the problem of imbalanced data by oversampling our data with SMOTE. After that, we identify and predict the abnormal behavior based on LSTM model.

4.1 Dataset

This research uses SIMADL [21] dataset generated by OpenSHS [22] which is an open source simulation tool that offered the flexibility needed to generate the inhabitant's data for classification of ADLs. OpenSHS was used to generate several synthetic datasets that includes 29 columns of binary data representing the sensor values, each binary sensor has two states, on (1) and off (0). The sensors can be divided into two groups, passive and active. The passive sensors react without explicitly the participants interact with them. Instead, they react to the participant movements and positions.

The sampling was done every second. Seven participants were asked to perform their simulations using OpenSHS. Each participant generated six datasets resulting in forty-two datasets in total. The participants self-labelled their activities during the simulation. The labels used by the participants were: Personal, Sleep, Eat, Leisure, Work, Other and Anomaly. The simulated anomalies are behavioral and are described in Table 1. Note that each user has his/her own behavioral abnormality to simulate.

Table 1. Anomalies description

Participants	Description
Participant 1	Leaving the fridge door open
Participant 2	Leaving the oven on for long time
Participant 3	Leaving the main door open
Participant 4	Leaving the fridge door open
Participant 5	Leaving the bathroom light on
Participant 6	Leaving tv on
Participant 7	Leaving light bedroom and wardrobe open

4.2 Imbalanced Data

The distribution of the classes (that represent the different ADL) is not uniform, leads to imbalanced classes. This situation appears because of rare abnormal behavior which is clear in the Fig. 2. As shown in Fig. 2, the class anomaly represent a minority. We tackle this problem in order to improve our classification performance. Dealing with imbalanced datasets requires strategies such as oversampling techniques before providing the data as input to the LSTM model. Oversampling strategy consists in augmenting the minority class samples to reach a balanced level with the majority class.

4.2.1 Oversampling

We deal with abnormality, called also anomaly, detection problem as a supervised learning that refers to correctly classifying rare class samples as compared to majority samples.

Therefore, anomalies are a minority in the whole behavior, which create an imbalanced data problem. Therefore, we have to oversample our data and after that, we can classify correctly.

A subset of data is taken from the minority samples as an example and then new synthetic similar data points are created. These synthetic data points are then added to the original dataset. The new dataset is used to train the classification models. The main objective of balancing classes is to either increasing the samples of the minority class or decreasing the samples of the majority class. In oversampling, we increase the minority class samples. This is done in order to obtain approximately the same number of instances for both the classes as demonstrated in Fig. 2. Our motivation in the use of this strategy is to avoid overfitting. We use SMOTE statistical method [23] to over-sample our classes as indicated in Fig. 2. We note that the x-axes indicate the number of classes and y-axes indicate the number of input data.

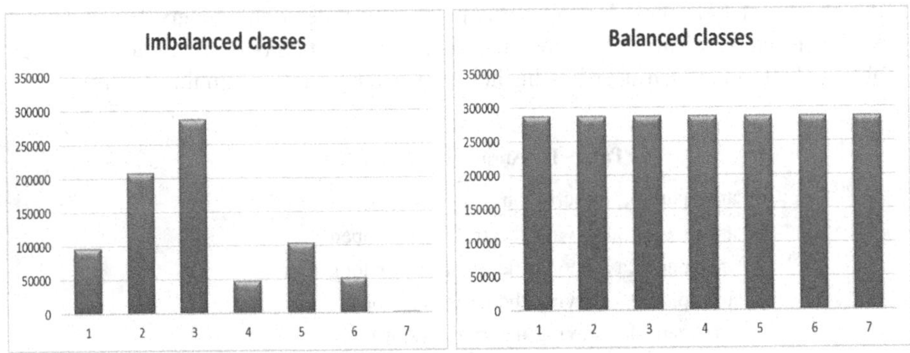

Fig. 2. Imbalanced classes vs Balanced classes

4.3 Network Architecture and Hyper-parameters Tuning

The crucial task is to find a suitable network structure for training the data, specifically to choose the right amount of nodes and layers. Many experiments were run by varying LSTM networks architecture as shown in Table 2 to find the suitable units number. We varied this number from 20, 30, 50, 60, 100 to 200. The number of layers was experimentally fixed to four layers.

To compile and fit the model, we experimentally fixed mini-batch size to 128 samples, with ADAM [25] as optimizer, which is an algorithm that can used instead of the classical stochastic gradient descent procedure to update the network weights iterative based on training data.

Our experiment with LSTM were implemented in Python language using Keras library [26] with Tensorflow [27]. The Fig. 1 shows the development of our LSTM network and the adjusted parameters to obtain the appropriate results.

4.4 Performance Metrics Analysis

High performance system should have less false positive and false negative rates. The performance of our proposed method is evaluated in terms of precision, recall and f-score [28]. Table 2 presents the obtained results.

Table 2. LSTM experiment.

Units	Precision	Recall	F-score
20	0.91	0.91	0.91
30	0.87	0.85	0.86
50	0.90	0.90	0.90
60	0.86	0.86	0.86
100	0.90	0.90	0.90
200	0.90	0.90	0.90

Table 2 refers to the results obtained on SIMADL dataset for abnormal behavior detection and shows that LSTM with 20 units gives the best precision of 0.91%, recall of 0.91% and f-score of 0.91%. The rest of the results is expressed in the Table 2 for which we have varied the unit number to 30, 50, 60, 100 and 200.

To demonstrate the superiority of the proposed method, we conducted comparison with existing state-of-the-art methods. The results are summarized in Table 3.

Table 3. LSTM comparison with the state of the art.

Models	Precision	Recall	F-score
LSTM	0.91	0.91	0.91
SVM	0.90	0.90	0.90
NB	0.79	0.79	0.79
KNN	0.89	0.89	0.89
NN	0.77	0.77	0.77

According to Table 3, we note that LSTM gives a good result by comparing to machine learning methods such as: SVM, NB, KNN and NN.

5 Conclusion

We proposed an LSTM based abnormal behavior prediction method. Our method identifies and predicts abnormal behaviors with a high degree of accuracy and with less user intervention in order to automate the identification and prediction process. We note that before to classify the activities, we have checked the distribution of classes, we detected an imbalanced classes, to deal with this problem we have applied SMOTE for oversampling classes.

The future work can focus on using real dataset from environmental and physiological sensors to understand the health condition of the elderly person's for better wellbeing.

References

1. Perera, C., Zaslavsky, A., Christen, P., Georgakopoulos, D.: Context aware computing for the internet of things: a survey. IEEE Commun. Surv. Tutor. **16**, 414–454 (2014)
2. Lê, Q., Nguyen, H.B., Barnett, T.: Smart homes for older people: positive aging in a digital world, pp. 607–617 (2012). https://doi.org/10.3390/fi4020607
3. Mehr, H.D., Polat, H., Cetin, A.: Resident activity recognition in smart homes by using artificial neural networks (2016)
4. Aran, O., Sanchez-Cortes, D., Do, M.-T., Gatica-Perez, D.: Anomaly detection in elderly daily behavior in ambient sensing environments. In: Chetouani, M., Cohn, J., Salah, A.A. (eds.) HBU 2016. LNCS, vol. 9997, pp. 51–67. Springer, Cham (2016). https://doi.org/10.1007/978-3-319-46843-3_4
5. Omar, S., Ngadi, A., Jebur, H.H.: Machine learning techniques for anomaly detection: an overview. Int. J. Comput. Appl. **79**, 33–41 (2013)
6. Grover, A.: Anomaly detection for application log data (2018)
7. Ismail Fawaz, H., Forestier, G., Weber, J., Idoumghar, L., Muller, P.A.: Deep learning for time series classification: a review. Data Min. Knowl. Discov. **33**, 917–963 (2019)
8. Wang, J., Chen, Y., Hao, S., Peng, X., Hu, L.: Deep learning for sensor-based activity recognition: a survey. Pattern Recognit. Lett. **119**, 3–11 (2019)
9. Chandola, V.: Anomaly detection : a survey, pp. 1–72 (2009)
10. Paudel, R., Eberle, W., Holder, L.B.: Anomaly detection of elderly patient activities in smart homes using a graph-based approach, pp. 163–169 (2016)
11. Yahaya, S.W., Langensiepen, C., Lotfi, A.: Anomaly detection in activities of daily living using one-class support vector machine. In: Lotfi, A., Bouchachia, H., Gegov, A., Langensiepen, C., McGinnity, M. (eds.) UKCI 2018. AISC, vol. 840, pp. 362–371. Springer, Cham (2019). https://doi.org/10.1007/978-3-319-97982-3_30
12. Mukhopadhyay, S.C.: Next generation sensors and systems. Next Gener. Sens. Syst. **16**, 1–330 (2015)
13. Pirzada, P., White, N., Wilde, A.: Sensors in smart homes for independent living of the elderly. In: Proceedings of 5th International Multi-Topic ICT Conference Technology Future Generation, IMTIC 2018 (2018)
14. Ordóñez, F.J., de Toledo, P., Sanchis, A.: Sensor-based Bayesian detection of anomalous living patterns in a home setting. Pers. Ubiquit. Comput. **19**, 259–270 (2015)
15. Palaniappan, A., Bhargavi, R., Vaidehi, V.: Abnormal human activity recognition using SVM based approach. In: International Conference on Recent Trends Information Technology, ICRTIT 2012, pp. 97–102 (2012)
16. Hung, Y.-X., Chiang, C.-Y., Hsu, Steen J., Chan, C.-T.: Abnormality detection for improving elder's daily life independent. In: Lee, Y., et al. (eds.) ICOST 2010. LNCS, vol. 6159, pp. 186–194. Springer, Heidelberg (2010). https://doi.org/10.1007/978-3-642-13778-5_23
17. Arifoglu, D., Bouchachia, A.: Activity recognition and abnormal behaviour detection with recurrent neural networks. Proc. Comput. Sci. **110**, 86–93 (2017)
18. Novák, M., Jakab, F., Lain, L.: Anomaly detection-2013, vol. 3 (2013)
19. Zhu, C., Sheng, W., Liu, M.: Wearable sensor-based behavioral anomaly detection in smart assisted living systems. IEEE Trans. Autom. Sci. Eng. **12**, 1–10 (2015)
20. Hochreiter, S., Schmidhuber, J.: LSTM. Neural Comput. **9**, 1–32 (1997)
21. Alshammari, T., Alshammari, N., Sedky, M., Howard, C.: SIMADL: simulated activities of daily living dataset. Data **3**, 11 (2018)
22. OpenSHS by openshs. https://github.com/openshs/

23. Chawla, N.V., Bowyer, K.W., Hall, L.O., Kegelmeyer, W.P.: SMOTE: synthetic minority over-sampling technique. J. Artif. Intell. Res. **16**, 321–357 (2002)
24. Hinton, G.: Dropout: a simple way to prevent neural networks from overfitting. J. Mach. Learn. Res. **15**, 1929–1958 (2014)
25. Kingma, D.P., Ba, J.L: Adam: a method for stochastic optimization, pp. 1–15 (2014)
26. FAQ - Keras Documentation. https://keras.io/
27. TensorFlow. https://www.tensorflow.org/
28. Hossin, M., Sulaiman, M.N.: A review on evaluation metrics for data classification evaluations. Int. J. Data Min. Knowl. Manag. Process **5**, 1–11 (2015)

Well-being Technology

A Deep Learning Method for Automatic Visual Attention Detection in Older Drivers

Belkacem Chikhaoui[1(✉)], Perrine Ruer[2], and Évelyne F. Vallières[1]

[1] LICEF Research Center, TELUQ University, Montreal, QC, Canada
belkacem.chikhaoui@teluq.ca, Evelyne.Vallieres@teluq.ca
[2] HEC Montreal, Montréal, QC, Canada
pruer.pro@gmail.com

Abstract. This paper addresses a new problem of automatic detection of visual attention in older adults based on their driving speed. All state-of-the-art methods try to understand the on-road performance of older adults by means of the Useful Field of View (UFOV) measure. Our method takes advantage of deep learning models such as Long-short Term Memory (LSTM) to automatically extract features from driving speed data for predicting drivers' visual attention. We demonstrate, through extensive experiments on real dataset, that our method is able to predict the driver's visual attention based on driving speed with high accuracy.

Keywords: UFOV · Deep learning · LSTM · Classification · Divided attention · Older drivers

1 Introduction

Visual and cognitive abilities are important parameters for safe driving. These abilities tend to decrease naturally with aging, and many older adults become unable to drive because of a serious decline in their visual and cognitive abilities. The decline in visual and cognitive abilities may lead to unsafe driving [1].

One of these abilities concerned divided attention, which is defined as the ability to construct information from multiple sources that are critical to the execution of a specific task (e.g., driving) [1], has received particular interest from researchers as a good indicator of driving performance in older drivers [1,2]. In fact, in the context of driving, drivers face multiple stimuli coming from the environment including the car, the road, other drivers, the weather, and driving time of day. These stimuli create a complex context, particularly for older drivers, that requires from them to shift attention between all these stimuli in order to ensure safe driving.

The Useful Field of View (UFOV) [3] is a well known and widely used test to measure visual attention [4]. It consists of three subtests of visual attention: processing speed, divided attention, and selective attention. The first one

J. Pagán et al. (Eds.): ICOST 2019, LNCS 11862, pp. 49–60, 2019.
https://doi.org/10.1007/978-3-030-32785-9_5

is to identify peripheral targets, the second and third subtests are to identify peripheral target presented either in the presence or absence of distractors while completing a central discrimination task [5–7].

The UFOV test has been shown to be highly effective in predicting driving outcomes such as (1) predicting crash risk among older adults [8–10], (2) predicting on-road performance [1,11], (3) predicting driving in the presence of distracters [12].

The overall studies using UFOV focus on driving outcomes and performance based on obtained UFOV test results. In this regard, our work is original and tries to predict the UFOV divided attention results based on older adults performances during driving, more specifically driving speed. To the best of our knowledge, no prior studies have examined the relationship between driving speed and divided attention. Therefore, the present research was initiated as it may have a great potential in developing assistance systems to help older adults drivers improve their safety while driving. In the research presented in this paper, we resort to deep learning models, particularly Long-Short Term Memory model (LSTM), to automatically detect older adult's divided attention based on his/her driving speed. The rationale of using LSTM models is threefold: (1) it allows to analyze raw speed data in order to automatically extract important features to perform predictions, (2) it allows to learn features across time by using their internal memory, and (3) it allows to process arbitrary sequences of inputs (speed data) unlike other existing feedforward neural network models. The major contributions of this paper can be summarized as follows:

- Proposing a LSTM based method to automatically detect older adults drivers' visual attention based on driving speed data.
- Conducting extensive experiments through real data to validate the proposed method.
- Demonstrating the performance and superiority of our proposed method compared to the state-of-the-art methods.

The rest of the paper is organized as follows. First, we give an overview of related work in Sect. 2. Section 3 describes the proposed model in terms of LSTM representation, and divided attention detection. The results of our experiments on a real driving dataset are presented in Sect. 4. Finally, Sect. 5 presents our conclusions.

2 Related Work

Multiple studies have been conducted examining the relationship between UFOV test performance and driving. These studies have used a variety of outcome measures, including on-road driving performance, crashes, simulated driving performance, and self-reported driving performance that assess components of driving ability that are neither exhaustive nor necessarily unique.

Driving performance can be assessed by cognitive tests, simulation, on-road driving tests, or a combination of these. In the driving activity, people have to respond rapidly to risks with good abilities. Previous research has investigated specific functions and/or deficits for any correlation with safe driving and in order to predict on-road driving performance.

Some physical impairments found frequently among older people may have negative impacts on their driving skills. Among them, a deficit in visual-cognitive functions, and more specifically divided attention, which is a good predictor of driving performance for older drivers [13].

Aging is associated with decreased performance on the UFOV test due to the higher prevalence in visual search, attention, speed of deficit treatment [13], poorer vision and mental status [14]. Poor performance on the UFOV test was associated with increased crash risk. Older drivers with UFOV impairments are twice as likely to be involved in a road accident [5]. The utility of the UFOV measure has been investigated in different studies. However, a link between the number of crashes and UFOV has been examined in the research [5]. Results showed a significant link between visual attention measures and a car crash for the older drivers. Authors highlighted that self-reported accident frequency by older drivers is not an accurate measure of their actual accident frequency. Authors said the use of this dependent measure in earlier studies may have led to erroneous conclusions about vision and driving relationships [15].

A number of studies used a variety of outcome measures. Some of them investigated on-road driving performance, particularly with simulated driving performance and they assessed driving performance and UFOV test performance. Results reported that both decreased with age. Older is the driver, the more errors are reported during the on-road driving assessment with a slower performance during the UFOV test [16]. Willstrand et al. [16] also highlighted an increasing number of driving errors seen and correlated with age-related reduced selective attention. The reduction of selective attention has a negative effect on driving speed, that is driving too fast, which was the most common error in the on-road driving assessment [16]. Baldock et al. [17] emphasized the importance of speed adaptation, especially the “approach speed”, as it can lead to a delay in the needed braking. The third phase of the UFOV test may be an intervention for older drivers to increase their awareness of attentional problems when driving. Reducing speed when appropriate is an important factor to study with older drivers, as it gives them more time for visual search (processing speed and selective attention [16]).

3 Proposed Method

In order to understand how to detect divided attention based on speed data, firstly we describe the UFOV test in detail. Secondly, we will introduce our proposed method based on LSTM model.

3.1 UFOV Test

The UFOV is a computer-administered and computer-scored test of functional vision and visual attention [18], which can be predictive of ability to perform many everyday activities, such as driving a vehicle. The UFOV test lasts about 15 min and is highly recommended for drivers having an age of 55 years or older, particularly those who suffer from health problems including cognitive deficits [18].

UFOV consists in three subtests for assessing speed of visual processing under complex task demands [18]:

1. The first subtest (T1) consists in identifying a target presented in a centrally located fixation box presented for varying lengths of time.
2. The second subtest (T2) consists in identifying a target and localizing a simultaneously displayed target on the periphery of the computer screen.
3. The third subtest (T3) is identical to the second subtest, except that the displayed target is embedded in distractors to make the test more difficult. Each subtest has a threshold score as shown in Table 2.

Table 1 presents an example of UFOV test results (or score) in milliseconds (ms) obtained in real experiments. The range is 17 to 500 ms [18].

Table 1. Example of UFOV test results obtained in real experiments.

	UFOV results		
Participant	Subtest (T1)	Subtest (T2)	Subtest (T3)
1	17	17	197
2	17	23	110
3	17	87	177
4	83	44	287
5	17	23	203
6	20	93	380

The UFOV results can be categorized in different categories called classes of divided attention as shown in Table 2

Table 2. UFOV test values categories

	Classes		
Subtest	Class 1: healthy	Class 2: moderate	Class 3: severe
T1	$\leq$30	>30, and, $\leq$60	>60
T2	<100	$\geq$100, and, <350	$\geq$350
T3	<350	$\geq$350, and, <500	$\geq$500

By using this definition of classes, results (from Table 1) are categorized in Table 3.

Table 3. Example of UFOV test results classes.

	UFOV results		
Participant	Subtest (T1)	Subtest (T2)	Subtest (T3)
1	1	1	1
2	1	1	1
3	1	1	1
4	3	1	1
5	1	1	1
6	1	1	2

Once the classes are defined, we will be able to label the dataset accordingly. Therefore, with driving speed data, we try to predict the corresponding class using the LSTM model described in the next section.

3.2 LSTM Model

This section introduces the LSTM deep learning model we used to predict divided attention.

LSTM models are a type of recurrent neural networks (RNN) for processing, classifying and making predictions based on times-series data. In contrast to other deep learning models such as Convolutional Neural Networks [19,20], LSTM models are able to extract temporal features from data. This is a very important characteristic, particularly in driving context where driving speed tend to change over time due to different environmental factors. Moreover, LSTM models have the property of selectively remembering patterns for long durations of time, which make them advantageous compared to basic RNN models.

All recurrent neural networks have the form of a chain of repeating modules of neural network, normally a single tanh layer [21]. In LSTM models, the repeating modules have different structures so that instead of having one single tanh layer, they have four layers as shown in Fig. 1 (this figure is taken from [21]).

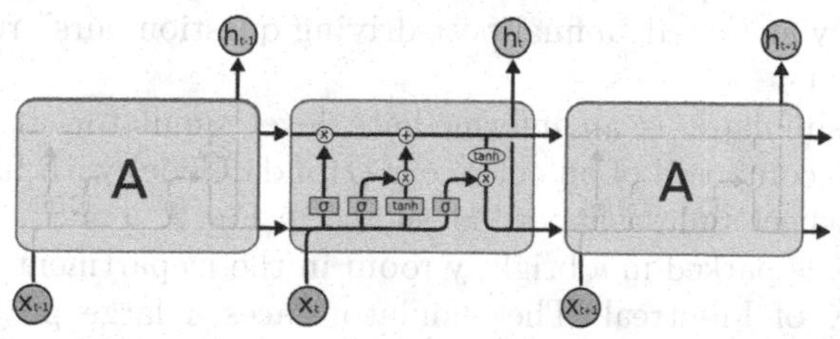

Fig. 1. LSTM structure.

The central component of LSTM model is the cell state presented in Fig. 1 with a horizontal line in the top. Information in the cell state could be added or removed, and this process is regulated by components called gates [21]. In other words, gates have the ability to let or not let information through [21].

To prevent the LSTM model from overfitting, we used the dropout principle [22]. The dropout consists in randomly dropping units with their connections from the neural network during training. Therefore, we randomly dropped 20% of units and their connection after each hidden layer. This percentage is recommended in literature [22]. We experimentally setup the number of units to 256 with a batch size of 128. The number of epochs is experimentally setup to 50. Our LSTM model was implemented in Python programming language using Tensorflow [23].

4 Experimental Study

In this section, we describe our experiments conducted at the University of Montreal for data collection and validation of proposed method.

The UFOV test, as mentioned previously, measures three types of attention: selective, shared and divided attention and detects an attention deficit. It is a 15 min computer test. The requirements increase in complexity between tasks. The purpose is to evaluate the visual processing speed of a person by detecting, identifying and locating targets briefly presented on the screen. This test is recommended to measure driving ability for older drivers [5,18].

Twenty-eight participants (14 women, 14 men) aged between 55 and 79 years old (mean: 63,86 y-o; standard-deviation: 6,20) were recruited. They drive on average five days per weeks. All participants have a valid driving licence and have been driving for several years (mean: 45 y-o, sd: 8,95). Participants did not report sleep disturbance or medication use that may affect driving.

All participants went to the driving simulation laboratory at the University of Montreal. Participants received a financial compensation of 60 CAD. The experiments were carried for 20 days during a two-month period.

The research protocol was to provide participants a consent form followed by a first sociodemographic questionnaire. Then, participants performed the UFOV test before driving in the simulator for about 40 min. Different data were saved with the simulator as speed, acceleration, braking and steering wheel angle. After driving, they answered "a final post-driving questionnaire" regarding their driving experiment.

The driving simulator is an intermediate level simulator. It is interactive with a fixed base, composed of an entire car (Honda Civic) with fully functional pedals, steering wheel and dashboard as shown in Fig. 2.

The simulator is parked in a brightly room in the Department of Psychology at the University of Montreal. The simulator faces a large projection screen (three metres by four metres), which allows a 70- degree view. The road image is computerized and projected by an RGB overhead projector. The location and speed (km/h) of the vehicle on the x, y and z axes are recorded during each simulation. We used these data for our analysis.

Fig. 2. Driving simulator used in our experiments.

5 Classification Results

To evaluate our proposed method for automatic detection of the different classes of drivers' divided attention, we divided the data collected into trainset (70%) and testset (30%). The trainset is used to build and train the LSTM model whereas the testset is used to validate the model. To evaluate the performance of the LSTM model, we used the precision, recall, and F-measure metrics. The classification results obtained are presented in Table 4.

Table 4. Classification results.

	Classification results		
	Subtest (T1)	Subtest (T2)	Subtest (T3)
Precision	0.9645	0.8581	0.8828
Recall	0.9642	0.8559	0.8733
F-Measure	0.9643	0.857	0.8780

As shown in Table 4, our method shows promising results in classifying the three subtests T1, T2 and T3 with high accuracy. More specifically, the highest performance was observed in T1 with an F-measure equals to 0.9645, while T2 represents the lowest performance with an F-measure equals to 0.857. The rational of having lower F-measure for T2 and T3 compared to T1 is the lack of data about the moderate and severe classes in these two categories. More participants should be recruited in the future in order to overcome this limitation. Confusion matrices obtained for the classification of the three subtests are presented in Fig. 3

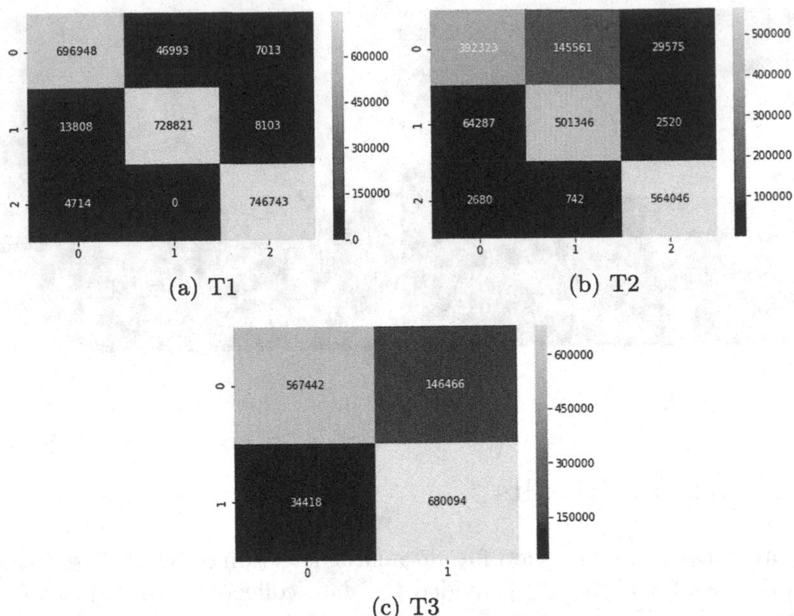

Fig. 3. Confusion matrices.

As shown in Fig. 3(a), some samples of class T3 were misclassified as class T1. This could be explained by the similarity in terms of some driving patterns at the beginning of the driving test as shown in Fig. 4 compared to T2.

We also evaluated the performance of our proposed method compared to the well known state-of-the-art methods of the domain such as decision trees, naive Bayes, Bayesian networks, support vector machines, K-nearest neighbor, and perceptron neural network. The comparison results for the three different subtests are presented in Figs. 5(a), (b), and (c) respectively.

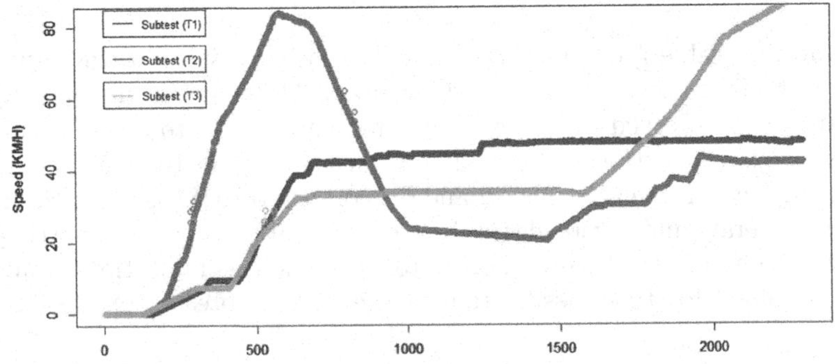

Fig. 4. Speed examples for participants in each class.

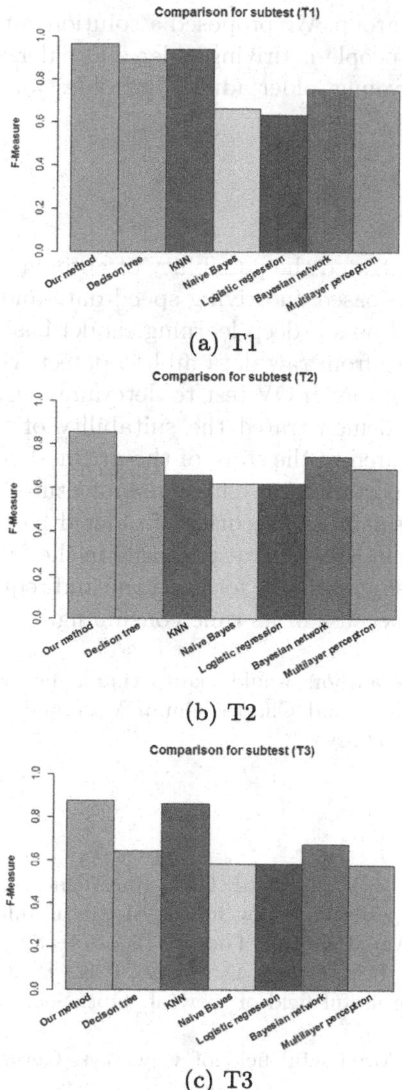

(a) T1

(b) T2

(c) T3

Fig. 5. Classification accuracy using different values of window size.

As shown in Fig. 5, our proposed method outperforms all the existing state-of-the-art methods in terms of classification accuracy followed by the K-NN method and Bayesian networks.

Some limits appear in this study. The first one concerns the number of participants. The sample was convenient with only 28 participants coming from the metropole area of Montreal. A further study has to integrate more participants coming from suburban area or countryside to confirm these results.

Another limit is the age group. We proposed a solution with only one age group (55 to 79 years old). As people is driving older and older, a comparison should be interesting between 'young' older adults and oldest one (55–74 years-old vs 75–100 years-old).

6 Conclusion

In this paper, we demonstrated the possibility of automatically detecting visual attention in older drivers based on driving speed data and their score from the UFOV test. Our method uses a deep learning model based on LSTM to automatically extract features from raw data and to detect with high accuracy the three different subtests of the UFOV test to determine visual attention of older drivers. We empirically demonstrated the suitability of the proposed method and its superiority compared to the state-of-the-art methods. The results of this research are of great importance for vehicle manufacturers who could integrate our finding to improve safety and security of older drivers. Moreover, the outcome of this research could have a great potential in the future to replace UFOV measure which is not easily reachable for everyone and requires human resources and temporal planning because of its time consuming.

Acknowledgement. The authors would like to thank the professors Jacques Bergeron, University of Montreal, and Charles Gouin Vallerand, TELUQ University, to share the data used in this study.

References

1. Crizzle, A.M., Winter, S.M., Lanford, D.N., Sherrilene, C., Wang, Y.: Predicting older driver on-road performance by means of the useful field of view and trail making test part B. Am. J. Occup. Ther. **67**(5), 574–582 (2013)
2. Roenker, D.L., Miller, R.L., Griggs, D.S., Ball, K.K., Beard, B.L.: Age and visual search: expanding the useful field of view. J. Opt. Soc. Am. Opt. Image Sci. **5**, 2210–2219 (1988)
3. Owsley, C., Wood, J.M.: Useful field of view test. Gerontology **60**(4), 315–318 (2014)
4. Sloane, M.E., Roenker, D.L., Bruni, J.R., Ball, K., Owsley, C.: Visual attention problems as a predictor of vehicle crashes in older drivers. Invest. Ophthalmol, Vis. Sci. **34**(11), 3110–3123 (1993)
5. Owsley, C., et al.: Visual processing impairment and risk of motor vehicle crash among older adults. JAMA **279**(14), 1083–1088 (1998)
6. Owsley, C., McGwin, G., Ball, K.: Vision impairment, eye disease, and injurious motor vehicle crashes in the elderly. Ophthalmic Epidemiol. **5**(2), 101–113 (1998)
7. Allman, R.M., Ball, K., Owsley, C., Sims, R.V., McGwin Jr., G.: Exploratory study of incident vehicle crashes among olderdrivers. J. Gerontol. Ser. A **55**(1), 22–27 (2000)
8. Goode, K.T., et al.: Useful field of view and other neurocognitive indicators of crash risk in older adults. J. Clin. Psychol. Med. Settings **5**(4), 425–440 (1998)

9. Vance, D.E., Stavrinos, D., McManus, B., Cox, M.K.: Predicting motor vehicle collisions in a driving simulator in young adults using the useful field of view assessment. Traffic Inj. Prev. **16**(8), 818–823 (2015)
10. Dubinsky, R., McDowd, J.M., Atchley, P.: The role of visual attention in predicting driving impairment in older adults. Psychol. Aging **20**(4), 610–622 (2005)
11. Edwards, J.D., Roth, D.L., Roenker, D.L., Ball, K.K., Clay, O.J., Wadley, V.G.: Cumulative meta-analysis of the relationship between useful field of view and driving performance in older adults: current and future implications. Optom. Vis. Sci. **82**(2), 724–731 (2005)
12. Lacherez, P., Hickson, L., Wood, J.M., Chaparro, A.: Useful field of view predicts driving in the presence of distracters. Optom. Vis. Sci. **89**(4), 373–381 (2012)
13. Roenker, D.L., Miller, R.L., Griggs, D.S., Ball, K.K., Beard, B.L.: Age and visual search: expanding the useful field of view. J. Opt. Soc. Am. Opt. Image Sci. **5**(12), 2210–2219 (1988)
14. Owsley, C., Ball, K.: The useful field of view test: a new technique for evaluating age-related declines in visual function. J. Am. Optom. Assoc. **64**(1), 71–79 (1993)
15. Owsley, C., Ball, K., Sloane, M.E., Roenker, D.L., Bruni, J.R.: Visual/cognitive correlates of vehicle accidents in older drivers. Psychol. Aging **6**(3), 403–415 (1991)
16. Selander, H., Dukic Willstrand, T., Broberg, T.: Driving characteristics of older drivers and their relationship to the useful field of view test. Gerontology **63**(2), 180–188 (2017)
17. Baldock, M.R.J., Berndt, A., Mathias, J.: The functional correlates of older drivers' on-road driving test errors. Top Geriatr. Rehabil. **24**, 204–223 (2008)
18. BrainHQ. Ufov assessment manual. Technical report (2011)
19. Chikhaoui, B., Gouineau, F.: Towards automatic feature extraction for activity recognition from wearable sensors: a deep learning approach. In: 2017 IEEE International Conference on Data Mining Workshops, ICDM Workshops 2017, New Orleans, LA, USA, 18–21 November 2017, pp. 693–702 (2017)
20. Chikhaoui, B., Gouineau, F., Sotir, M.: A CNN based transfer learning model for automatic activity recognition from accelerometer sensors. In: 14th International Conference on Machine Learning and Data Mining in Pattern Recognition, MLDM 2018, New York, NY, USA, 15–19 July 2018, Proceedings, Part II, pp. 302–315 (2018)
21. Olah, C.: Understanding LSTM networks. Technical report (2015)
22. Srivastava, N., Hinton, G., Krizhevsky, A., Sutskever, I., Salakhutdinov, R.: Dropout: A simple way to prevent neural networks from overfitting. J. Mach. Learn. Res. **15**(1), 1929–1958 (2014)
23. Abadi, M., et al.: Tensorflow: a system for large-scale machine learning. In: 12th USENIX Symposium on Operating Systems Design and Implementation (OSDI 2016), pp. 265–283 (2016)

Smart Mat for Respiratory Activity Detection: Study in a Clinical Setting

Samuel Otis[1(✉)], Bessam Abdulrazak[2], Sofia Ben Jebara[3], Francois Tournoux[4], and Neila Mezghani[1,5]

[1] Laboratoire de recherche en imagerie et en orthopédie, CRCHUM, Montreal, Canada
samuel.otis.1@ens.etsmtl.ca

[2] Department of Computer Science, Sherbrooke University, Sherbrooke, Canada
Bessam.Abdulrazak@usherbrooke.ca

[3] COSIM Laboratory, Carthage University, Higher School of Communications of Tunis, Ariana, Tunisia
sofia.benjebara@supcom.tn

[4] Department of Medicine, Centre Hospitalier de l'Université de Montréal, Montreal, Canada
francois.tournoux@umontreal.ca

[5] Centre de recherche LICEF, Université TÉLUQ, Montreal, Canada
neila.mezghani@teluq.ca

Abstract. We discuss in this paper a study of a smart and unobtrusive mattress in a clinical setting on a population with cardiorespiratory problems. Up to recently, the vast majority of studies with unobtrusive sensors are done with healthy populations. The unobtrusive monitoring of the Respiratory Rate (RR) is essential for proposing better diagnoses. Thus, new industrial and research activity on smart mattresses is targeting respiratory rate in an Internet-of-Things (IoT) context. In our work, we are interested in the performances of a microbend fiber optic sensor (FOS) mattress on 81 subjects admitted in the Cardiac Intensive Care Unit (CICU) by estimating the RR from their ballistocardiograms (BCG). Our study proposes a new RR estimator, based on harmonic plus noise models (HNM) and compares it with known estimators such as MODWT and CLIE. The goal is to examine, using a more representative and bigger dataset, the performances of these methods and of the smart mattress in general. Results of applying these three estimators on the BCG show that MODWT is more accurate with an average mean absolute error (MAE) of 1.97 ± 2.12 BPM. However, the HNM estimator has space for improvements with estimation errors of 2.91 ± 4.07 BPM. The smart mattress works well within a standard RR range of 10–20 breaths-per-minute (BPM) but gets less accurate with a bigger range of estimation. These results highlight the need to test these sensors in much more realistic contexts.

Keywords: Smart mattress · Ballistocardiogram · Respiratory rate

This research was supported by the Canada Research Chair on Biomedical Data Mining (950-231214).

J. Pagán et al. (Eds.): ICOST 2019, LNCS 11862, pp. 61–72, 2019.
https://doi.org/10.1007/978-3-030-32785-9_6

1 Introduction

New sensors for the unobtrusive detection of vital signs have to be tested in a clinical setting to assess their potential and limits. These sensors are interesting to propose better treatment and care for subjects having cardiorespiratory problems in an Internet of Things (IoT) context. This is especially important since long term data is required to offer better and more accurate diagnoses [7]. Recently, smart mattresses acquiring the ballistocardiogram (BCG) [24] have proven to be reliable. The BCG is the motion of the body following the mechanical action of the heart. Consequently, the BCG also contains the motion from the respiration. Thus, if a subject rests on a smart mattress, it would be possible to acquire his vital signs in a completely unobtrusive way during in-bed periods.

Still, most studies on a smart mattress are done using a small number of healthy and/or young subjects [10,12–14,20]. Thus, having a few number of subjects or only healthy subjects is not sufficient because the recruited populations are not representative of the targeted users. Most of the potential users of these sensors have contrasted health issues and physiological differences such as being overweight, underweight, young, old, smoker, and non-smoker. All of these parameters have [8] effects on the quality of the acquired BCG. This is an issue since we want to extract important vital signs such as the respiratory rate (RR) from the BCG. The RR has been neglected in the past but is now more and more in use by nurses and doctors. For instance, an abnormal RR is a strong marker of serious illness [6].

In this paper, we test the performance of a smart mattress, the microbend fiber optic sensor (FOS) mattress, during the detection of the RR. This was done through a study, in a clinical setting, involving 100 subjects having a wide range of cardiorespiratory problems. We acquired the BCG and estimated the RRs of the subjects using well-known methods. Maximal Overlap Discrete Wavelet Transform (MODWT) [22] and Continuous Local Interval Estimation (CLIE) [2,4] are the two most used vital signs estimators for the RR in the literature. Although, CLIE hasn't been tested on an unhealthy population and MODWT has limits in the range of frequency phenomenons it can capture. Thus, we propose to enrich the study with a new estimator based on Harmonic plus Noise Models (HNM)[17].

The rest of this paper is organized as follows: In Sect. 2, we will explore in more details the use of the BCG as well as the signal processing tools we selected. In Sect. 3, we detail our experimental methodology study and describe the population that was recruited. In Sect. 4, we present and analyze the results of the study. In Sect. 5, we discuss the relevance of the results and justify the used tools. In Sect. 6, we conclude with a summary of our findings, we show their limits and propose future relevant work in this field.

2 Background

The BCG signal contains vital signs such as the Heart Rate (HR) and Respiratory Rate (RR). It is present in the range of indiscernible motions coming from the human body. The BCG measures the ballistic forces generated by the heart, that is, the mechanical response of the body when the heart ejects the blood into the vascular tree. Notwithstanding the heart activity, it is also possible to retrieve the respiratory activity from the motion of the thorax when a subject inhales and exhales. All other motions present during the sleep also corrupt the signals Fig. 1.

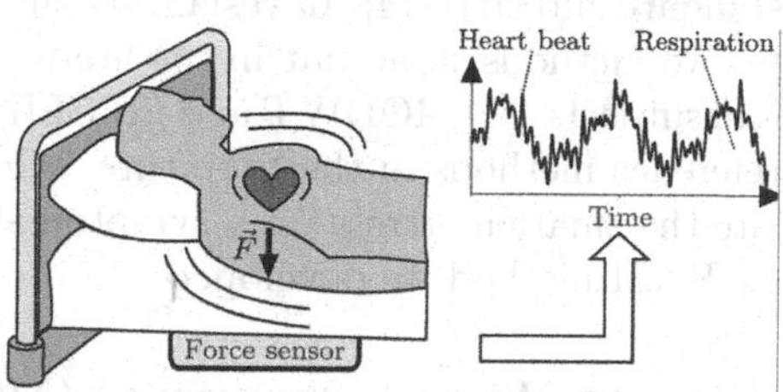

Fig. 1. A raw BCG signal containing heart activity, respiratory activity and general body motions. [5]

To retrieve the respiratory activity from the BCG, we need both a very sensitive force sensor placed under the subject and advanced signal processing techniques to estimate the information. New generations of sensor-based mattress can unobtrusively monitor the BCG by being placed under the sheets or even under the bed mattress.

Recently, an interesting microbend FOS, embedded in a small mattress, has been developed [24]. This microbend FOS provides a new way of acquiring the mechanical activity of the human body. It is achieved through the intensity attenuation of the light passing through an optic fiber in response to a mechanical stimulus on the fiber [26]. Figure 2 shows the principle of the microbend FOS.

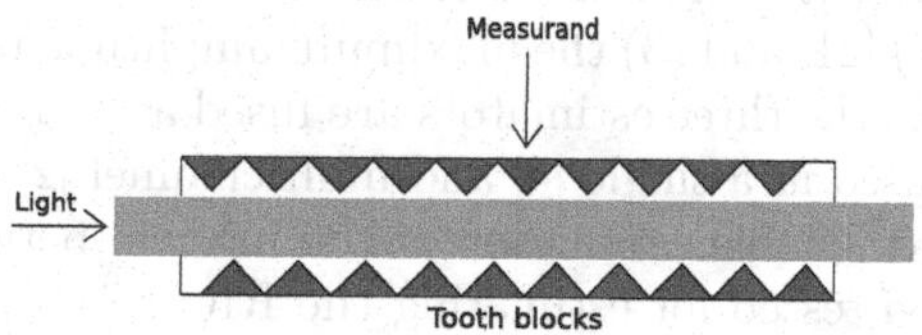

Fig. 2. Microbend FOS principle. The light passing through the microbend FOS is modulated by the deformations in the optical fiber due to the displacement of the micro-benders.

Lau *et al.* [13] used an FOS mattress to monitor the respiration and gait the image in synchrony with said respiration. They obtained high accuracy on the respiration estimation using simple filtering and peak detection on still subjects during functional magnetic resonance imaging (fMRI). Sadek *et al.* [22,28] also used an FOS mattress to acquire the BCG of subjects during headrest on a chair. Research using this sensor has given promising results, showing high accuracy for that technology.

Nevertheless, as it has been mentioned earlier, such sensors also require advanced signal processing algorithms to estimate the vital signs and more precisely the RR from the raw BCG signal. Multiple estimators have been tested like wavelets [22], empirical mode decomposition (EMD) [23], cepstrum analysis [5,27], clustering [3], standard filtering [14], bayesian fusion [4] and fast Fourier transforms (FFT) [11]. Two methods stand out in the literature for having good results on wider groups of subjects: (1) MODWT and (2) CLIE. These algorithms can be considered as reference methods in the literature. We use them not only as a reference to validate the smart mattress on a symptomatic population, but also to validate the new HNM method we developed.

Maximal Overlap Discrete Wavelet Transform (MODWT). It is a method to gain a spectro-temporal representation of studied signal by passing it through multiple and customizable narrow filters at arbitrarily selected levels. It is often used for signal denoising as well as for feature extraction. Jin *et al.* [9] detected the heart rate with a peak searching algorithm and wavelet shrinkage. Sadek *et al.* [22] implemented the Maximal Overlap Discrete Wavelet Transform (MODWT) to extract the BCG signal from a microbend FOS. Previous studies [15,18,22] have shown that wavelets and especially MODWT fare better than other algorithms such as clustering and EMD. DWT's strengths rely on its ability to split the signal into multiple levels of frequency components. It is, however, harder to select the right level of frequency components to represent the desired phenomenons.

Continuous Local Interval Estimation (CLIE). It is developed by Bruser *et al.* [4] and uses the Bayesian fusion of three estimators of the interval between heartbeats. These indicators are respectively *i* a modified version of the autocorrelation method [19], *ii* a modified version of the average magnitude difference function (AMDF) [21] and (3) the maximum amplitude pairs (MAP). Using Bayesian mathematics, the three estimators are fused as seen in Fig. 3. This estimator has also been used in a single [4] and multichannel [2] context. It offers a much more robust and reliable estimation of the interval between heartbeats. It has, however, not been tested for estimating the RR.

Harmonic Plus Noise Models (HNM). It represents a signal as a sum of harmonic parts and a noise part [25]. By using special methods like the one developed by Pantazis *et al.* [17], it is possible to estimate the harmonics of this HNM. This method, known as the iterative estimation of sinusoidal signal parameters, only needs the fundamental frequency of the signal to build a model of it. The goal with HNM is to construct a synthetic representation of the respiration signal. The synthetic signal can be written as follow:

$$\hat{s} = s_h(t) + s_n(t) \tag{1}$$

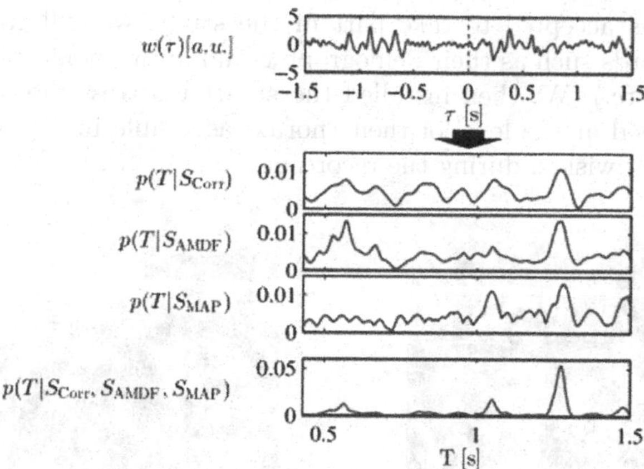

Fig. 3. Example of the fusion of autocorrelation, AMDF and MAP estimators as proposed by Bruser *et al.* [4]. Each of the estimators proposes its probability distribution of the most probable interval between two heartbeats. The fusion of the three of them, in the bottom graph, shows more robustness in the quality of the estimation than the three separate estimators.

The harmonic part is modeled as a sum of harmonics:

$$s_h(t) = \sum_{k=-L}^{L} A_k(t) cos\left(2 * \pi k f_0 t + \phi_k(t)\right), \tag{2}$$

where L denotes the number of harmonics included in the harmonic part, $\phi_k(t)$ is the temporal phase of the kth harmonic, f_0 denotes the fundamental frequency and A_k denotes the amplitude of the sinusoidal components.

The noise part is commonly considered as white Gaussian noise synchronized with the harmonic part.

In the next section, we explain our experimental setup for conducting the study at a hospital as well as the specifics of the population recruited into the study. We also describe the methods we used to extract the RR from an FOS mattress as well.

3 Methodology

Experimental Setup. The study for this work was conducted in the Centre Hospitalier de l'Universite de Montreal (CHUM) at the Cardiac Intensive Care Unit (CICU) in Montreal, Canada. This study was reviewed and approved by the TELUQ, ETS and CHUM institutional review board (IRB). We approached patients already admitted in the CICU who were *i* conscious and able to give informed consent, *ii* french-speaker, *iii* at least the whole night in the CICU and *iv* able to be lightly mobilized for the installation of the smart mattress.

Once patients accepted to take part in the study, we collected data from their health records such as their demographic and anthropomorphic data (age, weight, height, etc.). We then installed the smart mattress directly under the sheets of their bed at the level of their thorax, as visible in Fig. 4. They could still move as they wished during the recording.

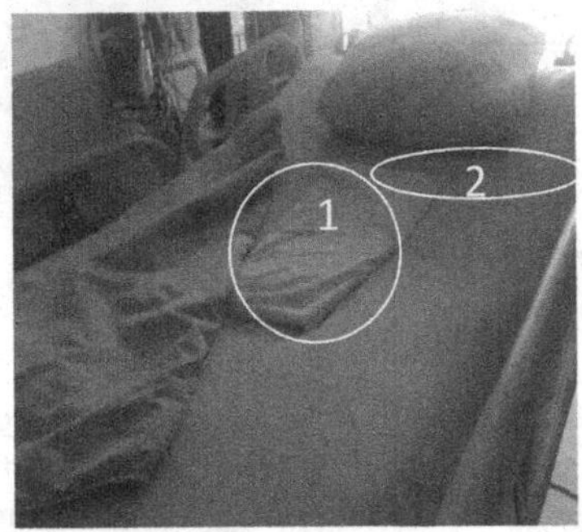

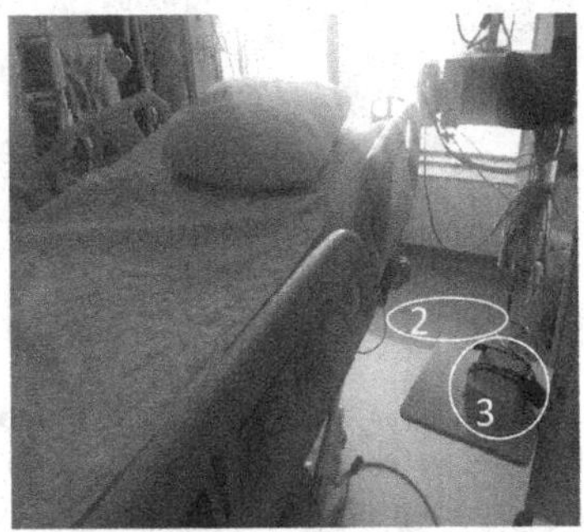

Fig. 4. Positioning of the smart mattress (1) and its acquisition box (3). On the left, we see the smart mattress (1) encased in a waterproof pillowcase. This is to protect it against standard biohazards present in a hospital as well as to meet the sanitary requisites of the hospital. On both images, we see the fiber optic cable (2) going from the smart mattress (1) to the acquisition box (3).

We then started a recording of the movements of the subject which would last more or less 24 h, depending on the length of the stay. After the recording, the smart mattress would be removed from the subject's bed. The data recorded by the system is then extracted on a normal computer as a *.csv file.

The reference values of the hospital, which serve as ground truth for future estimations of our system, were also extracted from the hospital' systems.

Hardware. The microbend FOS technology allowed us to record raw BCGs with their system. The raw data is sampled at 50 Hz by the acquisition module. Through a debug port on the acquisition module, the time serie of the BCG was stored on a Raspberry Pi 3 B+. The reference values of the hospital' systems were acquired through the CARESCAPE Monitor B850 of GE Healthcare. The CARESCAPE monitor recorded, amongst other values, the ElectroCardioGram (ECG), PhotoPlethysmoGraph (PPG) and Impedance PneumoGram (IPG). The CARESCAPE monitor also recorded the time occurrence of anomalous events such as TachyCardia (TC), BradyCardia (BC) and Atrial Fibrillation (AF).

The extracted recordings of the smart mattress and the CARESCAPE monitor were all processed on Intel(R) Core(TM) i7-6700 CPU @ 3.40 GHz computer using Python 3.7.

Dataset. We have recruited 100 patients that were admitted for the night at the CICU. 20 patients were removed from the study because of (1) missing data or (2) unforeseen leave from the CICU. When a patient leaves the hospital, his recordings are automatically deleted from their systems. Thus, it was impossible to compare the recorded BCG with the reference. In total, 80 patients with a maximum of 24 h of recorded data (53 male, 27 female; age 65.58 ± 12.58 years old; height 168.65 ± 9.35 cm; weight 77.94 ± 18.31 kg) are used for RR detection. The available data compiles 1520 h of recordings.

Filtering and Artefacts Removal. The data went first through a bidirectional Butterworth bandpass filter of 5th order with bandpass frequencies of 0.1 to 2 Hz. Moreover, the motions from a subject may quickly decrease the quality of the signal. Therefore, the motions were removed from the raw signals using a simple thresholding technique. We added bottom and upper variance thresholds to remove parts of the recordings where the bed was empty and where there was too much motion. We experimented on the size of the sliding window as well as the values of the thresholds. By looking at samples of performance results, we adjusted these parameters to yield maximal precision during estimations. With a sliding window of 6 s, the bottom threshold was set at 0.01 times the variance of the whole complete recording. The upper threshold was set at 10 times the complete recording. Signal segments with a variance outside of these limits were automatically removed with a mask in the end. These parts of the signal generally include motions like turning over, getting in or out of bed and coughing. Since the sensor is a single motion sensor, it remains hard to detect which position the subject is in. Therefore, we keep every segment of the signal with low variance even if the subject is in an undesirable posture.

3.1 RR Estimation

To estimate the RR, we used each of the RR estimation technique with a sliding window of 800 samples (16 s). Windows overlapped by 50% (8 s). All parameters were optimized, while the others were fixed, by choosing the value yielding the best estimation performance at the end of the processing chain. Optimized parameters, for our study, include the selected wavelet, its coefficient level, the low and high periods of the CLIE method and the number of harmonics used for synthesizing the signal using HNM.

MODWT. It is one of the estimators that yielded good results in the past. The approach we use is similar to that of Sadek *et al.* [22]. We use the Symlet 8 (Sym8) wavelet transform to extract the coefficients of the filtered signal. The 6-th level of the approximation coefficients is selected since it represents best the respiration cycle in the BCG. We then apply a basic peak searching algorithm to extract the mean period between peaks and, thus, the RR.

CLIE. It is implemented as per the work of Bruser *et al.* [4]. Since they used it to detect the heart rate, we adapted some parameters to capture the period range of the RR instead of the HR. The lowest period T_{min} was set to 1 s and the highest period T_{max} was set to 10 s.

HNM. When working with the BCG, the heart, respiration, and noise signals are mixed. It is possible to build a synthetic heart signal from its original version using an HNM. It is critical, though, that we estimate the fundamental frequency f_0 of the heart as close as possible to the truth. We do this using an FFT with Harmonic Artifact Rejection (HAR) as proposed by Beattie *et al.* [1]. A set of heuristics will work to eliminate higher and lower amplitudes harmonics to make sure we extract the true fundamental frequency of the heart. This is more efficient than simply selecting the highest amplitude frequency in the FFT.

We then build an HNM using this frequency by applying the same operations as Pantazis *et al.* [17]. The filtered signal is directly fed to the HNM algorithm and we build an HNM with $L = 6$ harmonics of the fundamental heart frequency. We then subtract this HNM from the original signal. This yielded the estimated true respiration component from which we selected, using the highest spectral peak, the fundamental respiration frequency.

4 Results and Discussion

We extracted the average Mean Absolute Error (MAE), Root Mean Squared Error (RMSE) and Standard Deviation (SD) of the Absolute Error (AE) for every recording on 81 patients. The AE is the absolute difference between an estimate of the RR and the RR from the ground truth. Every metric is expressed in Breaths Per Minute (BPM). This yielded the following results for the HNM, CLIE and MODWT estimators.

Table 1. Performances of estimators in relation to ground truth for different ranges of RR

Estimator	Average MAE (BPM)	RMSE (BPM)	SD (BPM)
All RR estimates			
HNM	6.29	10.29	8.14
CLIE	8.71	12.11	8.37
MODWT	4.57	8.27	6.89
Between 5 and 30 BPM			
HNM	4.64	7.04	5.30
CLIE	7.18	9.17	5.71
MODWT	2.89	4.17	3.01
Between 10 and 20 BPM			
HNM	2.91	5.00	4.07
CLIE	5.38	7.39	5.06
MODWT	1.97	2.89	2.12

We separated the results for 3 ranges of reference values. The top part of Table 1 represents the performances on all possible values of the recorded reference. This allows us to view if the estimators work well for big (>30 BPM) and small (<10 BPM) reference values. The middle part shows results with reference limits between 5 and 30 BPM. Finally, in the bottom part, we look at the performances between 10 and 20 BPM, which are standard values for the RR of healthy subjects. Figure 5 shows the agreement between the methods and the reference equipment using Bland-Altman analyses. Our artifact removal method yielded a mean coverage of 76.62% ± 12.05%.

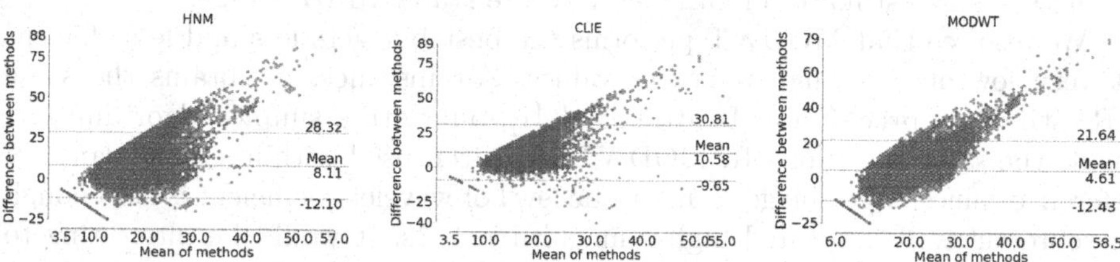

Fig. 5. These 3 Bland Altman graphs represent the agreement of each method during the estimation of the RR. The left graph represents the agreement for HNM, the middle graph is the agreement for CLIE and the right graph is the agreement for MODWT.

It is possible to view the results of Table 1, as good indicators of the caveats of RR and even HR estimators. Most studies preoccupy themselves with performances concerning a healthy population. Thus, the subjects of these studies have vital signs within the standard limits. For instance, Paalasmaa *et al.* [16] had a mean error on the HR of 0.78 BPM for 46 healthy subjects. Our best results, lower than theirs, of 1.97 ± 2.12 BPM is with unhealthy subjects and within a strict range. It drops to 4.57 ± 6.892 BPM with the entire range of RR values. This shows that when facing high variance in the recorded RR values and unhealthy subjects, the quality of the estimations decreases rapidly for estimators that would have similar performances on a similar dataset. An estimator should be able to keep the same performances no matter the reference values and the type of subject. However, we see that previously developed estimators, as well as our HNM estimator, have troubles in finding very high or very low RR values. This especially apparent in every Bland-Altman analyses, where we observe a difference proportional to the mean of the methods. To put it simply, the methods work well between 10 and 20 BPM rates but will overestimate for slower rates and underestimate for faster rates.

Moreover, with every result, we can observe an SD as big or bigger than the average MAE. This means that there are multiple bad estimations but that it is common for the estimator to give results of the right order of magnitude. This is even more apparent with the HNM estimator. Most of the HNM's estimations are directly related to the fundamental frequency estimation, before building the HNM model. The computed fundamental frequency needs to be exactly right if we want to build a high-fidelity model of the respiration. This means that the HAR we used is not as efficient as we thought in finding the right fundamental frequency, thus leading to incorrect models and incorrect true RR estimations.

CLIE is generally seen as the golden standard for estimating the HR. Its performance, however, diminishes in a single channel setup with the RR. It is too sensitive to the heart rate, which we can't remove from the signal perfectly with basic bandpass filtering. With many subjects, the heart signal is often stronger than the respiration signal. In other cases, we see the opposite situation. Thus, during the fusion of the three sub-estimators of CLIE (autocorrelation, AMDF, and MAP), the heart rate will often greatly modify the result. This explains the often very high estimates of CLIE even in the standard RR range.

We also see that MODWT performs the best but gets less and less efficient at very low or very high reference values. For instance, it obtains the same RR estimation precision as Beattie *et al.* [1], but with a simpler algorithm and inside the same range of RR. MODWT was often used within a small range of reference values. With bigger ranges, one level of wavelet coefficient is not enough to represent well lower and higher magnitude RRs. It would be interesting to select the right coefficient to represent the RR during computations. It would lead to much lower RMSE and SD for MODWT.

5 Conclusion

In this work, we discuss a study involving a smart FOS mattress for the detection of the respiratory rate in a clinical setting. This study, including 100 subjects, is done with old subjects having a wide range of cardiorespiratory problems, in opposition with precedent studies using mostly young and healthy subjects. We use previously known methods for estimating the RR from the recordings. These methods were MODWT and CLIE. Since they had shortcomings in their precedent applications, we also proposed a new method based on HNM. Our new HNM algorithm gave good results, but the selection of the fundamental frequency for the computation of the HNM needs to be improved. MODWT gave the best performances, similar to other studies on the RR [1], but only within constrained reference values. It is, however, less accurate than other vital signs tools used in bigger studies [4,16] on the HR. This is most probably due to the subjects of these studies being healthy and younger. It would still be interesting to add a way of selecting the right level of wavelet coefficients to further improve the estimation of the RR with MODWT.

Future work will be on the characterization of this database and its relation to the performances of estimators such as MODWT. We will explore the effects of anthropomorphic parameters on the quality of the estimations.

Acknowledgment. This research was supported in part by the Canada Research Chair on Biomedical Data Mining (950-231214). The authors would like to thank the anonymous reviewers for their valuable comments and suggestions to improve the quality of the paper.

References

1. Beattie, Z.T., Jacobs, P.G., Riley, T.C., Hagen, C.C.: A time-frequency respiration tracking system using non-contact bed sensors with harmonic artifact rejection. In: 2015 37th Annual International Conference of the IEEE Engineering in Medicine and Biology Society (EMBC), pp. 8111–8114, August 2015
2. Brüser, C., Kortelainen, J.M., Winter, S., Tenhunen, M., Pärkkä, J., Leonhardt, S.: Improvement of force-sensor-based heart rate estimation using multichannel data fusion. IEEE J. Biomed. Health Inform. **19**(1), 227–235 (2015)
3. Bruser, C., Stadlthanner, K., Waele, S.d., Leonhardt, S.: Adaptive beat-to-beat heart rate estimation in ballistocardiograms. IEEE Trans. Inf. Technol. Biomed. **15**(5), 778–786 (2011)
4. Brüser, C., Winter, S., Leonhardt, S.: Robust inter-beat interval estimation in cardiac vibration signals. Physiol. Meas. **34**(2), 123–138 (2013)
5. Bruser, C., Antink, C.H., Wartzek, T., Walter, M., Leonhardt, S.: Ambient and unobtrusive cardiorespiratory monitoring techniques. IEEE Rev. Biomed. Eng. **8**, 30–43 (2015)
6. Cretikos, M.A., Bellomo, R., Hillman, K., Chen, J., Finfer, S., Flabouris, A.: Respiratory rate: the neglected vital sign. Med. J. Aust. **188**(11), 657–659 (2008)
7. Donaldson, M.S., Corrigan, J.M., Kohn, L.T., et al.: To Err Is Human: Building a Safer Health System, vol. 6. National Academies Press, Washington, DC (2000)
8. Harrison, W.K., Smith, J.E.: Sex differences in cardiac function of a group of young adults. Cardiology **66**(2), 74–84 (1980)
9. Jin, J., Wang, X., Li, S., Wu, Y.: A novel heart rate detection algorithm in ballistocardiogram based on wavelet transform. In: 2009 Second International Workshop on Knowledge Discovery and Data Mining, pp. 76–79, January 2009
10. Jung, D.W., Hwang, S.H., Yoon, H.N., Lee, Y.J.G., Jeong, D.U., Park, K.S.: Nocturnal awakening and sleep efficiency estimation using unobtrusively measured ballistocardiogram. IEEE Trans. Biomed. Eng. **61**(1), 131–138 (2014)
11. Kortelainen, J.M., Gils, M.v., Pärkkä, J.: Multichannel bed pressure sensor for sleep monitoring. In: 2012 Computing in Cardiology, pp. 313–316, September 2012
12. Kortelainen, J.M., Mendez, M.O., Bianchi, A.M., Matteucci, M., Cerutti, S.: Sleep staging based on signals acquired through bed sensor. IEEE Trans. Inf. Technol. Biomed. **14**(3), 776–785 (2010)
13. Lau, D., et al.: Intensity-modulated microbend fiber optic sensor for respiratory monitoring and gating during MRI. IEEE Trans. Biomed. Eng. **60**(9), 2655–2662 (2013)
14. Mack, D.C., Patrie, J.T., Suratt, P.M., Felder, R.A., Alwan, M.: Development and preliminary validation of heart rate and breathing rate detection using a passive, ballistocardiography-based sleep monitoring system. IEEE Trans. Inf. Technol. Biomed. **13**(1), 111–120 (2009)
15. Otis, S., Mezghani, N., Abdulrazak, B.: Comparative study of heart rate extraction methods for a novel intelligent mattress. In: 2018 9th International Symposium on Signal, Image, Video and Communications (ISIVC), pp. 93–98, November 2018
16. Paalasmaa, J., Toivonen, H., Partinen, M.: Adaptive heartbeat modeling for beat-to-beat heart rate measurement in ballistocardiograms. IEEE J. Biomed. Health Inform. **19**(6), 1945–1952 (2015)
17. Pantazis, Y., Rosec, O., Stylianou, Y.: Iterative estimation of sinusoidal signal parameters. IEEE Signal Process. Lett. **17**(5), 461–464 (2010)

18. Pino, E.J., Chávez, J.A.P., Aqueveque, P.: Noninvasive ambulatory measurement system of cardiac activity. In: 2015 37th Annual International Conference of the IEEE Engineering in Medicine and Biology Society (EMBC), pp. 7622–7625, August 2015
19. Rabiner, L.: On the use of autocorrelation analysis for pitch detection. IEEE Trans. Acoust. **25**(1), 24–33 (1977)
20. Rosales, L., Skubic, M., Heise, D., Devaney, M.J., Schaumburg, M.: Heartbeat detection from a hydraulic bed sensor using a clustering approach. In: Conference Proceedings of IEEE Engineering in Medicine and Biology Society 2012, pp. 2383–2387 (2012)
21. Ross, M., Shaffer, H., Cohen, A., Freudberg, R., Manley, H.: Average magnitude difference function pitch extractor. IEEE Trans. Acoust. **22**(5), 353–362 (1974)
22. Sadek, I., Biswas, J., Abdulrazak, B., Haihong, Z., Mokhtari, M.: Continuous and unconstrained vital signs monitoring with ballistocardiogram sensors in headrest position. In: 2017 IEEE EMBS International Conference on Biomedical Health Informatics (BHI), pp. 289–292, February 2017
23. Sadek, I., Biswas, J., Fook, V.F.S., Mokhtari, M.: Automatic heart rate detection from FBG sensors using sensor fusion and enhanced empirical mode decomposition. In: 2015 IEEE International Symposium on Signal Processing and Information Technology (ISSPIT), pp. 349–353, December 2015
24. Sadek, I.: Ballistocardiogram signal processing: A literature review, July 2018
25. Stylianou, Y.: Concatenative speech synthesis using a harmonic plus noise model. In: The Third ESCA/COCOSDA Workshop (ETRW) on (1998)
26. Udd, E.: An overview of fiber-optic sensors. Rev. Sci. Instrum. **66**(8), 4015–4030 (1995)
27. Zhu, Y., et al.: Heart rate estimation from FBG sensors using cepstrum analysis and sensor fusion. In: 2014 36th Annual International Conference of the IEEE Engineering in Medicine and Biology Society, pp. 5365–5368, August 2014
28. Zhu, Y., Zhang, H., Jayachandran, M., Ng, A.K., Biswas, J., Chen, Z.: Ballistocardiography with fiber optic sensor in headrest position: a feasibility study and a new processing algorithm. In: 2013 35th Annual International Conference of the IEEE Engineering in Medicine and Biology Society (EMBC), pp. 5203–5206, July 2013

Non-invasive Classification of Sleep Stages with a Hydraulic Bed Sensor Using Deep Learning

Rayan Gargees[1(✉)], James M. Keller[1], Mihail Popescu[2], and Marjorie Skubic[1]

[1] Electrical Engineering and Computer Science Department, University of Missouri, 201 Naka Hall, Columbia, MO 65211, USA
{rsgxc9,kellerJ,skubicm}@missouri.edu

[2] Health Management and Informatics Department, University of Missouri, CE707 Clinical Support and Education Building, DC006.00, Columbia, MO 65212, USA
popescuM@missouri.edu

Abstract. The quality of sleep has a significant impact on health and life. This study adopts the structure of hierarchical classification to develop an automatic sleep stage classification system using ballistocardiogram (BCG) signals. A leave-one-subject-out cross validation (LOSO-CS) procedure is used for testing classification performance. Convolutional Neural Networks (CNNs), Long Short-Term Memory (LSTM), and Deep Neural Networks DNNs are complementary in their modeling capabilities; while CNNs have the advantage of reducing frequency variations, LSTMs are good at temporal modeling. A transfer learning (TL) technique is used to pre-train our CNN model on posture data and then fine-tune it on the sleep stage data. We used a ballistocardiography (BCG) bed sensor to collect both posture and sleep stage data to provide a non-invasive, in-home monitoring system that tracks changes in health of the subjects over time. Polysomnography (PSG) data from a sleep lab was used as the ground truth for sleep stages, with the emphasis on three sleep stages, specifically, awake, rapid eye movement (REM) and non-REM sleep (NREM). Our results show an accuracy of 95.3%, 84% and 93.1% for awake, REM and NREM respectively on a group of patients from the sleep lab.

Keywords: Sleep stages · Transfer learning · BCG bed sensor · Deep learning

1 Introduction

Sleep is a critical physiological phenomenon for recovery from mental and physical fatigue. Lately, there has been much interest in the quality of sleep, and research is actively underway. In particular, it is vital to have a repetitive and regular sleep cycle for good sleep. Nevertheless, it takes much time to determine

J. Pagán et al. (Eds.): ICOST 2019, LNCS 11862, pp. 73–82, 2019.
https://doi.org/10.1007/978-3-030-32785-9_7

sleep stages using physiological signals by experts. A person with a sleep disorder such as apnea will stop breathing for a while throughout sleep. If it regularly happens, sleep disorders can be risky for health. An early step in diagnosing these disorders is the classification of sleep stages [4,13].

Unfortunately, sleep disorders have been affecting many people around the world in different ways. Whatever the cause of these disorders, the consequences can be severe. The quality of sleep depends on the number and order of these stages. The names of these stages, are Wake, Non-REM1, Non-REM2, Non-REM3, and REM. Detection of any sleep disorder, such as sleep apnea, insomnia, or narcolepsy, requires a correct staging of sleep [2,18].

Classification of sleep stages is also essential for managing the quality of sleep. Sleep studies depend on manual scoring of sleep stages from raw polysomnography signals, which is a tedious visual task. Thus, research efforts to develop an automatic sleep stage scoring based on machine learning techniques have been carried out in the last several years [19]. Convolutional neural networks (CNN) [14] and Long-Short Term Memory Recurrent Neural Networks (LSTM) [15] provide an interesting framework for automated classification of sleep based on raw waveforms. In the past few years, Deep Neural Networks (DNNs) have accomplished tremendous success for time series tasks compared to traditional machine learning systems. Recently, further improvements over DNNs have been obtained with alternative types of neural network architectures. CNNs, LSTMs, and DNNs are individually limited in their modeling capabilities, and we believe that time series data classification can be improved by combining these networks in a unified framework. The classification of time series signals presents many challenges that make it a uniquely difficult problem in machine learning. Many feature extraction approaches in time series face issues related to the non-stationary nature of the signal when the probability distribution does not change over time. Accordingly, features such as mean and variance will not change. Furthermore, the physiological signals are very noisy, being susceptible to factors such as posture, mood, physical movement, and external noise [8]. Lack of comparability between experiments is another issue that can be faced in this field. Unlike in image classification, there are no standard time series datasets used as performance benchmarks [16,20]. Some approaches use models for individuals, while others try to make a general model, training, and testing with samples from all individuals at one time.

In this paper, we propose a method for classifying sleep stages based on the CNN, LSTM and DNN with the help of transfer learning. More specifically, we use a transfer learning technique to train our network model with sleep posture data for 56 subjects (source dataset) and use it for sleep stage classification (target data). The sleep data was obtained from 5 subjects and it was collected in the Boone Hospital Center (BHC) in Columbia, MO, USA under the University of Missouri IRB approval, project number 2008526. The main contribution of this work is developing a new deep model architecture that utilizes CNNs and LSTMs to classify sleep stage data. The CNNs are trained to learn filters that extract time-invariant features from the BCG signals while the LSTMs are trained to encode temporal information such as sleep stage transition rules.

2 Sensors and Datasets

A home monitoring system using a ballistocardiography (BCG) hydraulic sensor has been developed to monitor sleep at home (see Fig. 1). The hydraulic bed sensor has been developed at the Center for Eldercare and Rehabilitation Technology (CERT) at the University of Missouri. A BCG device provides a noninvasive, low-cost, and robust solution for capturing physiological parameters such as heart rate and respiration rate, during sleep [6,10,11]. The BCG sensor has four transducers. Each transducer is composed of a water tube with a pressure sensor placed at one end. The water tube is 50 cm long and 6 cm wide and it is filled with about 0.4 liters of water. The BCG sensor is placed under the mattress, parallel to the body direction, to provide sleeping comfort and not to disturb a person's normal sleep pattern.

The pressure outputs are coupled to a Maxim MAX7401 which is a filtering circuit that consists of a 741 operational amplifier and an 8th-order integrated Bessel filter [3,9]. The four-channel signal is sampled and quantized to 12-bit precision. The BCG signal acquired from the sensor is superimposed over the respiration signal. The four matching transducers are independent; consequently, the data quality collected by those transducers might vary depending on the subject's sleeping position, type of bed (*e.g.*, material, thickness, *etc.*) and the physical characteristics of the subject such as age and body mass index (BMI). In this study, two kinds of datasets have been collected utilizing our bed sensor: sleep posture and sleep stages.

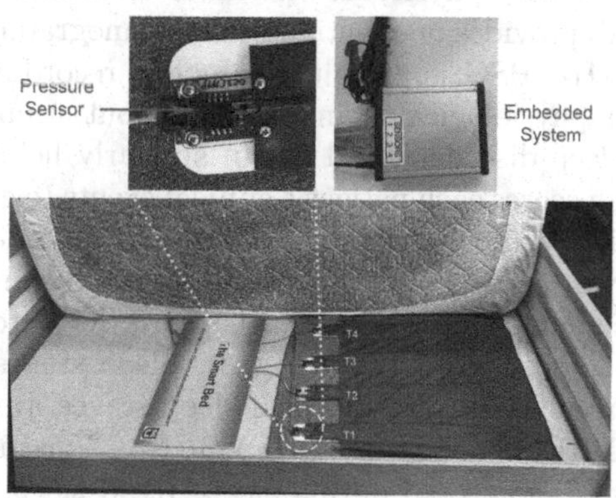

Fig. 1. Hydraulic bed sensor system.

2.1 Posture Dataset

A total of 56 young healthy subjects (About 75.8% of males and 24.2% of females) were asked to lie still in our lab for one minute on each of the four main postures, supine, prone, left lateral and right lateral. The data collection procedure was approved by the University of Missouri Institutional Review Board (MUIRB). The bed sensor produced data sampled at 100 Hz. The subjects age ranged between 18 and 49 years (mean 29.27 years); the weight ranged between 48 and 184 kg (mean 77.40 kg); the height ranged between 100 and 190 cm (mean 173.04 cm); the average body mass index was 27.34 kg/m^2, ranged between 18.1 and 184 kg/m^2.

2.2 Sleep Stage Dataset

Sleep stage data was collected from consenting patients by a sleep-credentialed physician during the regularly scheduled PSG studies conducted in the sleep lab of the Boone Hospital Center (BHC) in Columbia, MO, USA. In addition to the regular PSG equipment, we placed our hydraulic bed sensor under the study bed mattress. The scoring system for staging the sleep was based on the American Academy of Sleep Medicine Manual (AASM) [1], which is the standard for scoring sleep stages and it provides guidelines for associated events during sleep. Sleep stage scoring in 30-second epochs is required for the AASM protocol. A program produced by Natus SleepWorks (Natus Medical Inc., San Carlos, CA, USA) was used in the BHC sleep lab to assist the staff in monitoring a patient throughout the night. SleepWorks not only collects the PSG data but also performs a video recording of the entire night. The technician can view the patient's sleep video if they have any uncertainty about the data. SleepWorks can also provide an initial analysis of the collected data and can generate a report, which helps the sleep physicians who make treatment recommendations.

The BHC sleep lab provides de-identified polysomnography (PSG) data with a sample rate of 256 Hz. PSG is a multiparametric recording method used in sleep labs to monitor physiological changes throughout sleep. It is a consistent tool for diagnosing sleep disorders, and it can similarly help adjust treatment. Moreover, a technician scores each patient's clinical events (e.g., limb movements, respiratory and cardiac events, and arousals) using the American Academy of Sleep Medicine (AASM) standards. PSG is used in this research as ground truth for our bed sensor signals. The hypnogram is one PSG outcome that displays the sleep stages as a function of time (Fig. 2). Sleep stages are annotated in 30-second epochs. From top to bottom, the sleep stages are Wake (W), REM (R), NREM1 (N1), NREM2 (N2), and NREM3 (N3). For the patient shown in Fig. 2, 742 epochs were monitored during sleep. REM sleep happened between epoch 392 and epoch 485, also highlighted in red.

Those who participated in the sleep study are likely to have a sleep disorder. The partial and the complete collapse of the airways are called hypopnea and apnea, respectively. Lack of airflow will affect breathing patterns and then influence sleep stage sequence. The Apnea-hypopnea index (AHI) represents the number of apnea and hypopnea events per hour during sleep. Based on the AASM, the mild sleep apnea AHI is between 5 and 15. In this study, we did not use the data collected from patients with severe apnea symptoms. For this study, we selected five sleep lab patients with a low Apnea-hypopnea index (AHI), so

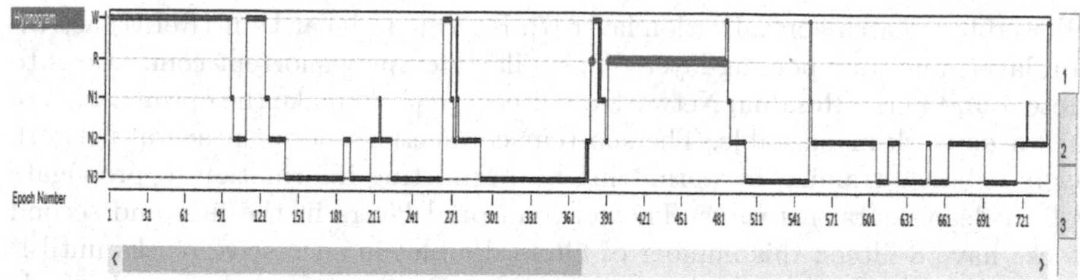

Fig. 2. Hypnogram of an entire night exported from a PSG system. (Color figure online)

that each one has sufficient REM, NREM, and Wake sleep stages during the night.

2.3 Data Preprocessing

We present the preprocessing steps for our data. For the posture data, we truncate the signals utilizing the percentile method [21] to remove any noise that was introduced due to the desynchronization between the time of leaving the bed and stopping recording the signal. After denoising, we normalize the data by utilizing standard score normalization technique. Then we down-sample the data to 100 Hz and shuffle it to prepare it for net training. To account for the varying length of the signals, we divide the preprocessed bed sensor signals into 5-second segments with 80% overlap. Each output label corresponds to a segment of the input. Together the output labels cover the full sequence. The above two algorithms are applied on posture and sleep stage data. Another algorithm is applied for sleep stages only, which are the rules from [22] that help to improve the accuracy about 1%. These rules can be illustrated as followed:

- For three consecutive 30s epochs, if the center one is not the same as the other two and the other two are the same, change the center one to the same stage as the other two epochs. However, the center epoch is not changed if it is an Awake stage.
- For every three 30s epochs, if the sleep stages are all different, the center epoch is removed from the recording. Similarly, this rule does not apply to the Awake stage.
- If REM stages show up in the first hour, these stages are removed from the recording.

3 Architecture Design

We propose a new architecture to classify BCG bed sensor data (see Fig. 3.). The network takes as input the windows of time series of filtered BCG signal and outputs a sequence of label predictions. The basic block is a convolution layer followed by a batch normalization layer [7], Rectified Linear Unit (ReLU) activation layer, and max-pooling layer. We similarly employ shortcut connections to those found in the Residual Network architecture [5] to make the optimization of such a network manageable. The shortcut connections between neural network layers enhance training by permitting by permitting information to propagate well in deep neural networks. The convolutional layers in the first and second blocks have 8 filters; this number of filters doubles in successive blocks until it reaches 32 in the last block. Moreover, the Max Pooling layer helps to subsample the input to become one-fourth of the input sample at the top layer since Max Pool is set to size two. When a block subsamples the input, the corresponding shortcut connections also subsample their input using a Max Pooling operation with the same subsample size. We next pass the CNN block output to LSTM layers with 128 units, which are appropriate for modeling the signal in time.

Regularization techniques are employed in our architecture to reduce overfitting effects during training. Regularization techniques help keep the model from becoming too complex and specific to the training data, thus reducing the tendency to overfit. In this paper, two regularization techniques were used. The first technique was a dropout, which randomly sets the input value to zero with a certain probability [17]. A probability of 0.5 was used in the dropout layer after LSTM, as shown in Fig. 3. The second technique was L2 weight decay, which adds a penalty term into the loss function. L2 regularization is a typical technique used in many optimization methods, in which the squared sum of the weights is applied as a penalty to the optimization function. In essence, this weighs the advantage of increased classification of the training data against model complexity. By preventing the model from becoming too complicated, memorization of the training data is reduced, and a more generalizable model is developed.

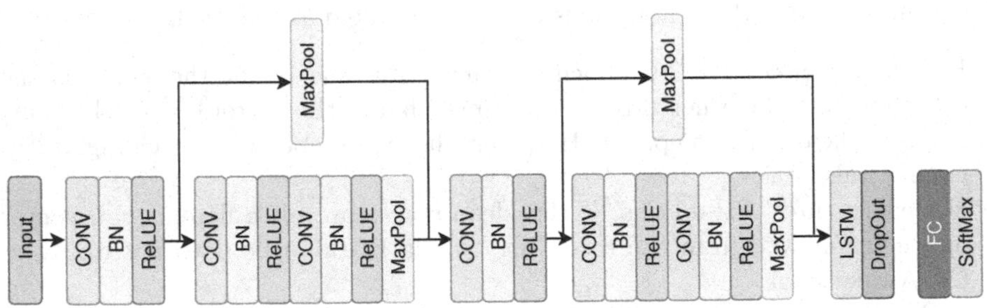

Fig. 3. The proposed architecture of the network

4 Training and Experimental Results

Transfer learning is employed in the experiments of this paper to classify sleep stages. Transfer learning is a technique wherein the knowledge gained from training a model on a dataset (source) can be reused as a starting point, when fine-tuning the model on another dataset (target). This is usually done when the target dataset is not as rich as the source, and hence, a complex deep network would have more trouble training only on the target. Consequently, we split the network model training into two distinct phases. First, our model is trained on the class-balanced training posture dataset of 56 people using five-fold cross-validation. Then, the network weights obtained in the first phase are used as an initialization for the second phase of training on sleep stage data subjects.

We conducted LOSO-CS to fine-tune the sleep stage data. Each time (fold), one patient was left out for testing while the remaining four patients were used to train the DNN networks. In the testing part, we utilize a hierarchical classification scheme for our automatic sleep stage classification system. This structure is composed of two layers. The first layer separates wake from the sleep, which is a union of REM and NREM, in a binary classification problem. Next, all the epochs classified as sleep are fed into the next layer to classify the REM and NREM epochs further. The last block of the architecture, shown in Fig. 3 is used to fine-tune the sleep stage data. In the first phase, the optimal hyperparameters for the model are carefully chosen for a given dataset. The model is at that time fine-tuned on the given dataset with these hyperparameter settings.

Training overnight raw sleep stage data using DNN is time-consuming. Moreover, the ground truth of the posture data is more reliable than the ground truth of sleep stage data. Deep learning models with transfer learning can, however, successfully converge on short-time data (sleep posture data) split across multiple subjects. By training a model over multiple posture data subjects, we obtained an initialization that is then used for fine-tuning our model on the sleep stage data. Based on Williams *et al.* [20], this process is hypothesized to make convergence on an individual's data more likely; it should also provide stronger general filters in the first layers of the neural network.

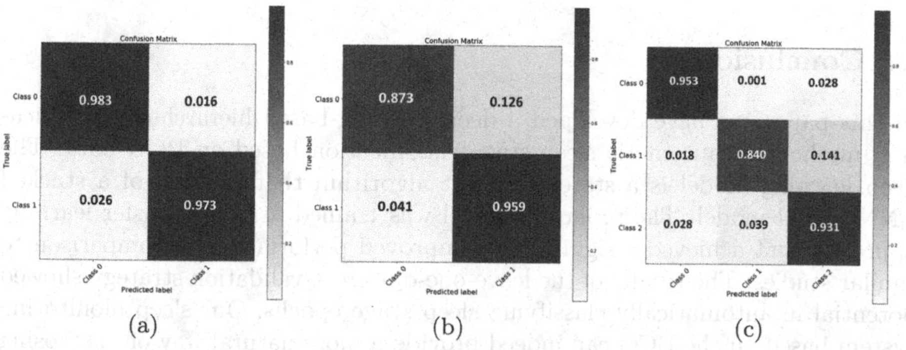

Fig. 4. Confusion matrix of leave-one-subject-out hierarchical sleep stages classification utilizing posture data knowledge (a) Training phase, Class 0: Wake, Class 1: Sleep (b) Training phase, Class 0: REM, Class 1: NREM (c) Hierarchical testing phase Class 0: Wake, Class 1: REM, Class 2: NREM

Figure 4(a) and (b) show the average of fine-tuned training five-fold LOSO-CS sleep stage data to classify wake from sleep and to classify REM from NREM respectively. Figure 4(c) shows the average of hierarchical fine-tuned testing five-fold LOSO-CS sleep stage data. Clearly, our model was able to classify the sleep stage classes better than the results reported by Yi, *et al.* [23] which were 79.9%, 78.8%, and 88.8% sensitivity for wake, REM, and NREM respectively; the previous work has been done using the same data and the same sensor, but with traditional machine learning algorithms. Table 1 shows the percentage of epochs that are correctly classified for each class Wake, REM, and NREM comparing to the percentage ground truth. The sleep stage agreement was 3.64%, 2.76%, and 8.920% for the Wake, REM, and NREM, respectively. This agreement result is much better than the agreement reported by Rosenberg *et al.* [12], which was 82.6% as the highest agreement averaged for REM and 63.0% as the lowest agreement averaged for NREM. From the results shown in Fig. 4, and Table 4, it is worth to mention the misclassification of the Wake as Sleep in the first layer in the hierarchical method is fed into the second layer, which has a cumulative impact on the second layer classification.

Table 1. Selected five sleep lab patients with a low Apnea-hypopnea index (AHI).

Information			Ground truth			Predicted labels		
Subject	Gender	Age	Wake (%)	REM (%)	REM (%)	Wake (%)	REM (%)	NREM (%)
1	F	69	21.57	14.13	64.29	19.13	11.54	54.32
2	M	66	14.95	16.61	68.44	13.53	13.39	57.14
3	M	68	33.76	12.3	53.94	29.83	10.04	45.03
4	F	66	46.98	7.32	45.7	42.01	6.03	39.07
5	F	62	29.85	19.53	50.63	25.58	15.75	43.74

5 Conclusion

In this paper, we have developed a deep learning-based hierarchical classification method for automatic sleep stage classification based on BCG data. The deep learning model is a state-of-the-art algorithm that consists of a stacked CNN-LSTM model. The proposed model was trained using a transfer learning approach that achieved a significantly improved performance in comparison to similar studies. The results of the leave-one-out cross-validation strategy showed potential in automatically classifying sleep stage epochs. Our sleep monitoring system based on the BCG can indeed provide a more natural way of diagnosing sleep problems, and make long-term sleep monitoring possible. However, to validate our algorithms we used a selected, balanced dataset with a reduced level of noise. We are currently working to increase the robustness of our methodology and validate it for patients with reduced REM and high AHI.

Acknowledgments. We would like to show our gratitude to all staff of Boone Hospital Center Sleep Center at Columbia, Missouri, with a special thanks to Mr. Custer for his patient and helpful advice.

References

1. Berry, R.B., Brooks, R., Gamaldo, C.E., Harding, S.M., Marcus, C.L., Vaughn, B.V., et al.: The AASM manual for the scoring of sleep and associated events. Rules, Terminology and Technical Specifications. American Academy of Sleep Medicine, Darien, Illinois, vol. 176 (2012)
2. Dursun, M., Gunes, S., Ozsen, S., Yosunkaya, S.: Comparison of artificial immune clustering with fuzzy c-means clustering in the sleep stage classification problem. In: 2012 International Symposium on Innovations in Intelligent Systems and Applications, pp. 1–4. IEEE (2012)
3. Gargees, R., Keller, J., Popescu, M.: Early illness recognition in older adults using transfer learning. In: 2017 IEEE International Conference on Bioinformatics and Biomedicine (BIBM), pp. 1012–1016. IEEE (2017)
4. Giri, E.P., Arymurthy, A.M., Fanany, M.I., Wijaya, S.K.: Sleep stages classification using shallow classifiers. In: 2015 International Conference on Advanced Computer Science and Information Systems (ICACSIS), pp. 297–301. IEEE (2015)
5. He, K., Zhang, X., Ren, S., Sun, J.: Deep residual learning for image recognition. In: Proceedings of the IEEE Conference on Computer Vision and Pattern Recognition, pp. 770–778 (2016)
6. Heise, D., Rosales, L., Sheahen, M., Su, B.Y., Skubic, M.: Non-invasive measurement of heartbeat with a hydraulic bed sensor progress, challenges, and opportunities. In: 2013 IEEE International Instrumentation and Measurement Technology Conference (I2MTC), pp. 397–402. IEEE (2013)
7. Ioffe, S., Szegedy, C.: Batch normalization: accelerating deep network training by reducing internal covariate shift. In: Proceedings of the 32nd International Conference on Machine Learning, vol. 37, pp. 448–456 (2015)
8. Kevric, J., Subasi, A.: Comparison of signal decomposition methods in classification of EEG signals for motor-imagery BCI system. Biomed. Signal Process. Control **31**, 398–406 (2017)
9. Lydon, K., et al.: Robust heartbeat detection from in-home ballistocardiogram signals of older adults using a bed sensor. In: 2015 37th Annual International Conference of the IEEE Engineering in Medicine and Biology Society (EMBC), pp. 7175–7179. IEEE (2015)
10. Rosales, L., Skubic, M., Heise, D., Devaney, M.J., Schaumburg, M.: Heartbeat detection from a hydraulic bed sensor using a clustering approach. In: 2012 Annual International Conference of the IEEE Engineering in Medicine and Biology Society, pp. 2383–2387. IEEE (2012)
11. Rosales, L., Su, B.Y., Skubic, M., Ho, K.: Heart rate monitoring using hydraulic bed sensor ballistocardiogram 1. J. Ambient. Intell. Smart Environ. **9**(2), 193–207 (2017)
12. Rosenberg, R.S., Van Hout, S.: The american academy of sleep medicine interscorer reliability program: sleep stage scoring. J. Clin. Sleep Med. **9**(01), 81–87 (2013)
13. Sadek, I., Biswas, J., Abdulrazak, B.: Ballistocardiogram signal processing: a review. Health Inf. Sci. Syst. **7**(1), 10 (2019)

14. Sainath, T.N., Vinyals, O., Senior, A., Sak, H.: Convolutional, long short-term memory, fully connected deep neural networks. In: 2015 IEEE International Conference on Acoustics, Speech and Signal Processing (ICASSP), pp. 4580–4584. IEEE (2015)
15. Sak, H., Senior, A., Beaufays, F.: Long short-term memory recurrent neural network architectures for large scale acoustic modeling. In: Fifteenth Annual Conference of the International Speech Communication Association (2014)
16. Schmidt, S., Eich, G., Hanquinet, S., Tschäppeler, H., Waibel, P., Gudinchet, F.: Extra-osseous involvement of langerhans' cell histiocytosis in children. Pediatr. Radiol. **34**(4), 313–321 (2004)
17. Srivastava, N., Hinton, G., Krizhevsky, A., Sutskever, I., Salakhutdinov, R.: Dropout: a simple way to prevent neural networks from overfitting. J. Mach. Learn. Res. **15**(1), 1929–1958 (2014)
18. Tuominen, J., Peltola, K., Saaresranta, T., Valli, K.: Sleep parameter assessment accuracy of a consumer home sleep monitoring ballistocardiograph beddit sleep tracker: a validation study. J. Clin. Sleep Med. **15**(03), 483–487 (2019)
19. Vilamala, A., Madsen, K.H., Hansen, L.K.: Deep convolutional neural networks for interpretable analysis of eeg sleep stage scoring. In: 2017 IEEE 27th International Workshop on Machine Learning for Signal Processing (MLSP), pp. 1–6. IEEE (2017)
20. Williams, J.M.: Deep learning and transfer learning in the classification of EEG signals (2017)
21. Wu, M.H., Chang, E.J., Chu, T.H.: Personalizing a generic ECG heartbeat classification for arrhythmia detection: a deep learning approach. In: 2018 IEEE Conference on Multimedia Information Processing and Retrieval (MIPR). IEEE (2018)
22. Yang, J., Keller, J.M., Popescu, M., Skubic, M.: Sleep stage recognition using respiration signal. In: 2016 38th Annual International Conference of the IEEE Engineering in Medicine and Biology Society (EMBC), pp. 2843–2846. IEEE (2016)
23. Yi, R., Enayati, M., Keller, J., Popescu, M., Skubic, M.: Non-invasive in-home sleep stage classification using a ballistocardiography bed sensor. In: 2019 IEEE International Conference on Bioinformatics and Biomedicine (BIBM). IEEE (2019)

Biomedical and Health Informatics

A Convolutional Gated Recurrent Neural Network for Epileptic Seizure Prediction

Abir Affes[1(✉)], Afef Mdhaffar[1,2], Chahnez Triki[3], Mohamed Jmaiel[1,2], and Bernd Freisleben[4]

[1] University of Sfax, ENIS, ReDCAD Laboratory, B.P. 1173, Sfax, Tunisia
abir.affes@stud.enis.tn
[2] Digital Research Center of Sfax, 3021 Sfax, Tunisia
{afef.mdhaffar,mohamed.jmaiel}@redcad.org
[3] Department of Child Neurology, Hospital Hedi Chaker, 3029 Sfax, Tunisia
chahnezct@gmail.com
[4] Department of Mathematics and Computer Science, Philipps-Universität Marburg, Marburg, Germany
freisleb@informatik.uni-marburg.de

Abstract. In this paper, we present a convolutional gated recurrent neural network (CGRNN) to predict epileptic seizures based on features extracted from EEG data that represent the temporal aspect and the frequency aspect of the signal. Using a dataset collected in the Children's Hospital of Boston, CGRNN can predict epileptic seizures between 35 min and 5 min in advance. Our experimental results indicate that the performance of CGRNN varies between patients. We achieve an average sensitivity of 89% and a mean accuracy of 75.6% for the patients in the data set, with a mean False Positive Rate (FPR) of 1.6 per hour.

Keywords: Epilepsy · Elecroencephalogram · Spectrogram · STFT · CNN · GRU · Seizure prediction

1 Introduction

Epilepsy is a complex neurological disorder, manifested by unexpected and unprovoked seizures due to abnormally excessive or synchronous neuronal activity in the brain. There are various forms of epileptic seizures, and the symptoms differ from one person to another. Epileptic seizures can be accompanied with a loss of consciousness that leads to serious injuries with residual disabilities and even to death. Also, people with epilepsy are socially discriminated due to a widespread lack of knowledge, negative public attitudes, and misconceptions about the disease that reduce their self-esteem.

Therefore, it is crucial to predict epileptic seizures before they happen. This is a challenging problem attracting researchers from several disciplines. Existing approaches [3,8,10–12,17,19–21,23] can be divided into two categories. The first

J. Pagán et al. (Eds.): ICOST 2019, LNCS 11862, pp. 85–96, 2019.
https://doi.org/10.1007/978-3-030-32785-9_8

category [3,6,8,16,19,20,23] includes seizure detection approaches that are usually used by health professionals to improve diagnostic capabilities. In fact, they do not allow us to prevent the consequences of epileptic seizures. The second category [10–12,17,21] focuses on seizure prediction to improve a patient's quality of life. One approach [17] is based on a combination of a convolutional neural network (CNN) and a long short-term memory network (LSTM). It achieves promising results. Other approaches are essentially based on the use of a single type of deep learning network, such as a CNN or a recurrent neural network (RNN) variant (e.g., RNN vanilla, LSTM, gated recurrent unit (GRU)). GRU networks have shown good results in temporal sequence modeling and especially in the detection of different seizure phases [12,19,22].

In this paper, we present a novel convolutional gated recurrent neural network (CGRNN) to predict epileptic seizures. It is a combination of CNN and GRU. The proposed approach is a patient-specific predictor that allows us to predict epileptic seizures on the basis of the electrical activity of the brain (EEG signals). Our CGRNN takes into consideration the temporal aspect as well as the frequency aspect of the EEG signal. Using a data set collected in the Children's Hospital of Boston, CGRNN can predict epileptic seizures between 35 min and 5 min in advance. Our experimental results indicate that the performance of CGRNN varies between patients. We achieve an average sensitivity of 89% and a mean accuracy of 75.6% for the 13 patients in the data set, with a FPR ranging from 0 to 6.57 per hour.

The paper is organized as follows. Section 2 explains basic concepts of epilepsy disorder. Related work is discussed in Sect. 3. In Sect. 4, we present our proposed approach. Section 5 discusses the experimental setup and our obtained results. Section 6 concludes the paper and outlines areas for future research.

2 Background

2.1 Epilepsy

Epilepsy is a chronic neurological disease that affects people of all ages and has a worldwide distribution [4]. It affects approximately 65 million people in the world [14] and is considered as the fourth most common neurological disease [4]. The cardinal manifestations of epilepsy are epileptic seizures, i.e., recurrent paroxysmal events characterized by stereotyped behavioral alterations reflecting the neural mechanisms involved in the epileptic process [5]. The recurrence of seizures and their unpredictability cause major concerns for patients and their family and have physical and psychological consequences. Therefore, epilepsy is a burdensome neurological disorder. Despite the growing number of antiepileptic drugs, almost 30% of epilepsy cases are intractable with uncontrolled epileptic seizures. These events have several phases that may not be visible or easily distinguishable from each other [4]:

- **The pre-ictal phase** refers to the period just before a seizure [15].
- **The ictal phase** lasts from the initial symptoms of the seizure (including an aura) until the end of the abnormal activity.
- **The post-ictal phase** occurs when the seizure ends. It is the period of recovering from the seizure's symptoms [4].
- **The inter-ictal phase** is the normal state for people with epilepsy (99% of their life). In this phase, these persons have abnormal waveforms in EEG records that are not associated with seizure symptoms [15].

2.2 EEG

Epileptic seizures are related to the electrical activity of the brain. Therefore, electroencephalography (EEG) is the most effective way to determine the epileptogenic cortex. EEG [2] is an electrophysiological exploration method to measure the electrical activity of the brain using electrodes fixed on the scalp. Since EEG can detect any abnormal brain activity, it is mainly used for epilepsy diagnosis and seizure analysis. Figure 1 shows the EEG signal of a patient that has experienced a seizure. It is evident that a seizure can be visually distinguished from a normal brain signal.

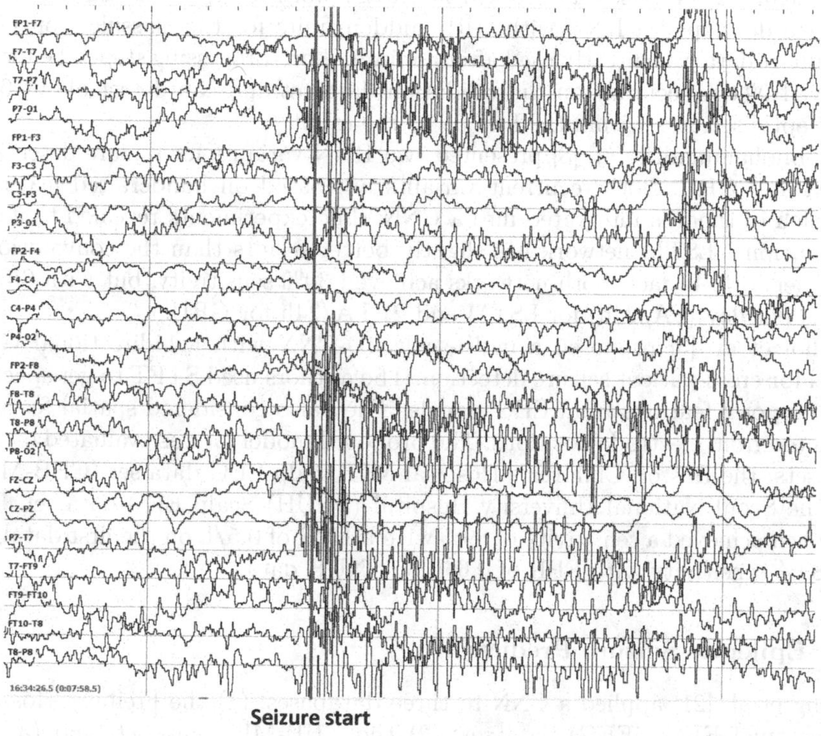

Fig. 1. Exemple of normal and seizure EEG recordings

3 Related Work

In this section, different approaches related to seizure detection and prediction are presented.

3.1 Epileptic Seizure Detection

Thodoroff et al. [20] proposed patient-specific and cross-patient epileptic seizure detectors. Both are based on features extracted from spatial, temporal, and frequency information of the EEG recordings. EEG data was first transformed into an image representation that integrates spatial domain knowledge (i.e., electrode's positions). Then, the data was fed into a recurrent convolutional neural network that combines CNN and LSTM networks.

The method presented by Yuan et al. [23] detects epileptic seizure onsets. It combines features extracted from handcrafted engineering methods and deep learning approaches. The authors used short-time Fourier transforms (STFT) for image based representation and a stacked sparse denoising autoencoders (SSDA) for data classification. An SSDA-based channel selection procedure was adopted to reduce the dimension of features by considering the correlation of EEG channels.

Talathi [19] proposed a deep learning framework for epileptic seizure detection. He developed a RNN with GRU hidden units for the classification task. Raw input data was directly used after a minimal pre-processing step. The model achieved 99.6% accuracy on the validation data set and can detect about 98% of epileptic seizures within the first 5 s of the event.

Golmohammadi et al. [8] presented two RNN variants for seizure detection: LSTM and GRU. Both recurrent variants are based on handcrafted features, and each of them is integrated into a CNN. The experiments revealed that the convolutional LSTM network has slightly better results than the convolutional GRU network. In fact, both networks achieved 30% sensitivity, but with 6 false alarms per day (FA/24h) for LSTM and 21 FA/24h for GRU.

Choi et al. [3] proposed a multi-scale 3D-CNN with a bidirectional GRU model for cross-patient seizure detection. The authors used STFT to get spectral and temporal features from EEG signals. They also considered spatial features extracted from electrode positions. The proposed model [3] was evaluated on two data sets: the Boston Children's Hospital MIT scalp EEG data set (CHB-MIT) and the Seoul National University Hospital (SNUH) Scalp EEG data set. The approach achieved a sensitivity of 89% with a FPR of 0.5/h on the first database and 89% sensitivity with FPR of 0.6/h on SNUH data.

3.2 Epileptic Seizure Prediction

Truong et al. [21] applied a CNN to three databases: (1) the Freiburg Hospital intra-cranial EEG (iEEG) data set, (2) the CHB-MIT data set, and (3) the American Epilepsy Society (AES) Seizure Prediction Challenge data set. They considered only data from 13 patients over 24 cases when considering the CHB-MIT database. These patients have less than 10 seizures per day and at least 3 h of inter-ictal signals. STFT has been applied on raw data to build spectrograms. The proposed model is patient-oriented. It achieved a sensitivity of 81.4%, 81.2%, and 75% and a FPR of 0.06/h, 0.16/h, and 0.21/h, for the 3 data sets mentioned above, respectively.

In the context of the AES Seizure Prediction Challenge organised by Kaggle, Korshunova [11] implemented two models for seizure prediction. She proposed a CNN architecture and also explored a classifier based on logistic regression and linear discriminant analysis. The iEEG data used in the competition was recorded from 5 dogs and 2 humans. It was transformed into spectrograms by applying a discrete Fourier transform (DFT) before being fed to the models.

Larmuseau [12] compared three RNNs for seizure prediction: vanilla RNN, GRU, and LSTM. iEEG data of four subjects was used. He concluded that GRU layers outperform other networks and are also faster than LSTM. RNNs are effective in analyzing the sequential iEEG data, but the results were not better than those of other methods used from the state of the art.

Hosseini et al. [10] proposed a cloud-based approach for real-time seizure prediction. This work followed three main steps: (1) dimensionality reduction to reduce algorithmic computational complexity and get faster response, (2) a stacked autoencoder as a deep learning approach for automatic feature extraction and classification, and (3) a cloud computing system for real-time analysis of iEEG signals. The authors achieved 94% of accuracy and a FPR of 0.05/h.

Shahbazi and Aghajan [17] proposed an approach based on CNN-LSTM and STFT for raw data transformation. A seizure is anticipated only if at least 8 of 10 successive samples are detected as pre-ictal signals. This model was evaluated on the CHB-MIT data set. It achieved an average sensitivity of 98.21% with a FPR of 0.13/h and a mean 44.74 min as the prediction time.

Seizures are events demarcated in time with several successive phases. During this event, EEG segments are correlated. Therefore, the recurrent aspect in a neural network was shown to be important in seizure prediction. In fact, RNNs are usually used when output at time t depends on the previous one. Regarding different proposed networks [3,8,12,19], GRU was demonstrated to be efficient for EEG data analysis.

4 CGRNN

To predict epileptic seizures on the basis of EEG signals in a patient-oriented manner, we propose a deep learning model based on the combination of CNN and GRU networks, called convolutional gated recurrent neural network (CGRNN). As shown in Fig. 2, our approach follows two steps: data preparation and data analysis.

The data preparation step consists of refining the data and transforming raw EEG into spectrograms, which allows us to capture spectral and temporal patterns representing a seizure. The data analysis step includes the deep learning

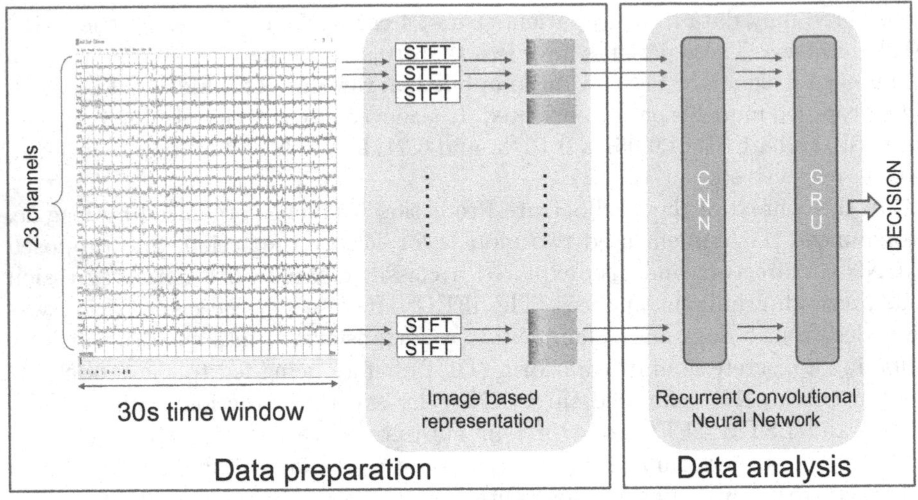

Fig. 2. The proposed approach

model composed of a CNN and a GRU. The convolutional network plays the role of a feature extractor. It takes as input the image-based representation of EEG and reduces the image into an easier form to process, without losing essential features. The GRU learns from the extracted features the epileptic seizure patterns to make the final decision.

4.1 Data Preparation

Epileptic seizure prediction can be modeled as a binary classification problem. Therefore, after introducing the used data set (CHB-MIT Scalp EEG database), we select the two appropriate classes. We also exclude the unused signals from our data set before data transformation.

Database: The CHB-MIT Scalp EEG database is used in this paper. It was collected by an MIT team in partnership with the pediatric hospital in Boston and can be downloaded from the Physionet platform [7]. The data set is composed of approximately 1136 h of brain activity recordings and 198 seizures. It includes many types of seizures and was collected from both genders with different ages. One fifth of the data was recorded from men aged from 3 to 22 years. The remaining data concerns females aged from 1.5 to 19 years [18]. In a few records, other non-EEG signals were also recorded, such as electrocardiogram (ECG) or vagal nerve stimulus (VNS). Furthermore, we used electrode positions and nomenclature different from the International 10–20 system in some records. Consequently, one step to do was data refitting to get the same channels for all files. The data sampling rate is 256 samples per second [7].

Data Refinement: Litt et al. [13] demonstrate that complex epileptiform discharges are common 7 h before seizures and an activity similar to a seizure becomes more frequent 2 h before the actual onset. Also, the accumulated energy increases during the 50 min before the ictal state [13]. Most of the existing studies consider the pre-ictal phase as one hour before a seizure begins. In our work, we consider the inter-ictal and the pre-ictal signals, shown in Fig. 3, as the two most relevant categories to classify. The inter-ictal signal is defined as the period between 1 h after the end of a seizure and 1 h before the onset of the next one. Based on Truong et al. [21], the pre-ictal signal is extracted from 35 min to 5 min before the epileptic seizure, which enables us to take the necessary precautions. Furthermore, considering that seizures can happen very close to each other, we are interested in predicting the leading crisis, which is about less than 30 min away from the next one.

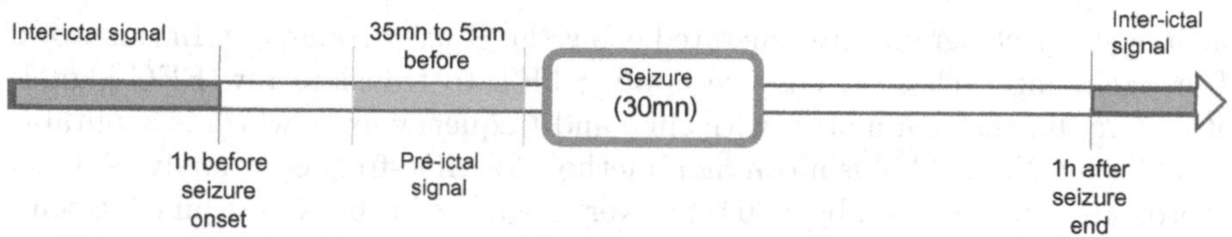

Fig. 3. Inter-ictal and pre-ictal signals as the two classification categories

After considering the two categories, we get different ratios between pre-ictal and inter-ictal data for every patient due to the number of recorded seizures. Considering that seizures are rare events, the number of inter-ictal recordings is higher than the number of pre-ictal ones. Consequently, we get an unbalanced data set for all cases. Most machine learning algorithms assume that data from different classes is equally distributed. If we have unbalanced data, we get biased classifiers towards classes with more instances over other classes [9]. Therefore, to deal with this issue, we use an overlapped sampling technique with the training data to get more pre-ictal segments. For every patient, we calculate the ratio between the pre-ictal and inter-ictal hours. Then, we slide a 30 s window by the calculated factor along the time axis over all the pre-ictal records.

Raw Data Transformation: Abnormal brain activity is detected on the basis of the cerebral rhythms in the EEG recordings. These are classified according to their frequency range hence the importance of the frequency aspect with the temporal aspect in EEG data analysis. Time-frequency features are usually studied using the signal spectrogram [1]. This is a tool used to visualize the change in the frequency spectrum of a signal over time. It represents in one two-dimensional diagram three parameters. The time and frequency are the two axes of the graph. The third parameter indicates the amplitude of a particular frequency at a particular time and is distinguished by the color of each point in

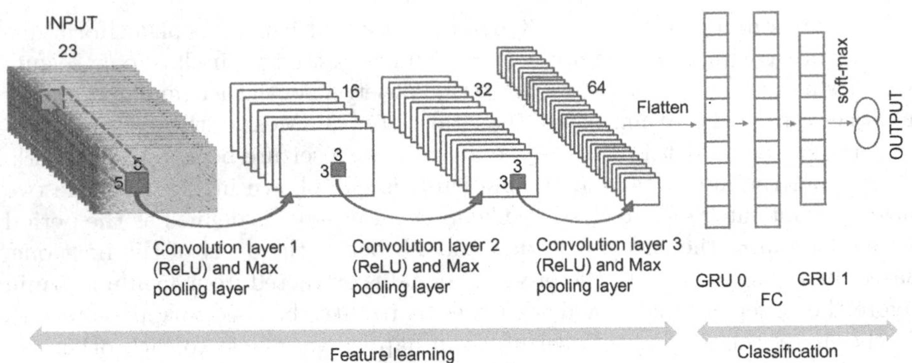

Fig. 4. The CGRNN architecture

the image. Spectrograms are generated using the Fourier transform. In this work, after excluding useless signals, we apply STFT to translate raw EEG signals into a two-dimensional matrix with time and frequency axes, which is a suitable input for a CNN. STFT is a common method for time-frequency analysis. EEG records are contaminated by a 60 Hz power line noise in the American continent. Therefore, a bandpass filter for frequency ranges of 57–63 Hz and 117–123 Hz is used. The 0 Hz component is also excluded.

4.2 Data Analysis

We use our CGRNN model illustrated in Fig. 4 for data analysis. The first part of the model is a CNN with 3 convolution blocks. Each block includes a convolution layer with a rectified linear unit activation (ReLU). Max pooling layers are used to reduce the number of calculations and prevent the model from overfitting during the training. We also use batch normalization between layers to ensure that the input distribution is the same for each layer no matter the changes in the previous one. The data is then flattened and reshaped to be piped into a first gated recurrent layer with 256 units. The next fully connected layer uses a sigmoid activation function. It is followed by a second gated recurrent layer with 100 units. The output of this layer is fed into the softmax layer to predict the class probabilities of the input data. The gated recurrent layer has a dropout rate of 0.5 to reduce overfitting.

5 Experimental Evaluation

The proposed CGRNN was implemented in Python 3.5 using Tensorflow 1.9.0 backend and Keras 2.2. Models for different patients were configured to run on an NVIDIA GeForce GTX 1080 GPU.

We used 25% of the data for validation and 75% for training. Categorical cross-entropy was adopted as our loss function and the ADAM optimization

Table 1. Seizure prediction results obtained with CHB-MIT. CNN is our implementation of the approach of Truong et al. [21]. Sen: percentage of sensitivity, FPR: false positive rate per hour, Acc: percentage of accuracy.

Patient	[21]		CNN		CGRNN		
	Sen	FPR	Sen	FPR	Acc	Sen	FPR
Patient 1	85.7	0.24	87.5	0	94.46	87.59	0
Patient 2	33.3	0	100	0	83.61	100	0
Patient 3	100	0.18	100	0.66	87.72	82.26	0
Patient 5	80 ± 20	0.19 ± 0.03	18.6	0	57.53	92.85	3.6
Patient 9	50	0.12 ± 0.12	100	2.5	73.57	79.13	0
Patient 10	33.3	0.00	53.7	7.428	48.57	59.33	6.57
Patient 13	80	0.14	46.6	2.5	51.67	100	5.5
Patient 14	80	0.40	93.3	9.0	60.79	92.21	3.33
Patient 18	100	0.28 ± 0.02	91.6	3.5	71.83	100	0.5
Patient 19	100	0.00	100	10.0	97.23	100	0
Patient 20	100	0.25 ± 0.05	24.8	0	76.47	96.36	1.33
Patient 21	100	0.23 ± 0.09	84.3	0	87.11	83.98	0
Patient 23	100	0.33	100	0	92.45	84.26	0
Average	80.01	0.18	76.95	2.73	75.6	89.07	1.6

algorithm was used for model optimization. It is an extension of stochastic gradient descent.

To test our model, we consider that one signal clip is preceding a seizure only if at least 8 of 10 successive samples of this sequence are detected as pre-ictal. The calculated metrics are accuracy, sensitivity, and FPR. We also implemented a CNN model with the same architecture as proposed by Truong et al. [21]. This model considers the same defined classes in [21]: the inter-ictal signal which is about 4 h before and after a seizure and the pre-ictal signal as the period from 35 min to 5 min before the ictal phase. Thus, both implemented CGRNN and CNN models can predict epileptic seizures between 35 min and 5 min in advance.

For the seizure prediction task, the most crucial part is to determine all of the positive cases. Missing a patient who has a seizure but goes undetected will be critical. Furthermore, the less we get false alarms, the better will be the solution. Therefore, our model evaluation is mainly based on sensitivity and also FPR values.

The obtained results on the 13 patients considered by Truong et al. [21] are shown in Table 1. The differences between metrics presented by Truong et al. [21] and the results obtained with the implemented CNN is due to data pre-processing step and also to the random initialization of weights in neural networks.

The model performance varies from one patient to another. In fact, for the patients 1, 2, 10, 18 and 19, our CGRNN achieves better classification results. For the three patients 3, 13, and 20, we obtain better sensitivity values than the CNN approach, but we get a higher FPR. Our model achieves comparable results for the patients 14 and 21 and lower sensitivity values for the patients 3, 9, and 23. An average of 75.6% accuracy and an average sensitivity of 89% are reached for the 13 patients. The FPR ranges between 0 and 6.57 per hour, with a mean FPR of 1.6 per hour. The differences in the performance for each patient are related to the characteristics of the available data, namely the number of recorded seizures and the time periods between the events.

6 Conclusion

We presented a novel convolutional gated recurrent neural network (CGRNN) to predict epileptic seizures. The proposed approach is a patient-specific predictor that allows us to predict epileptic seizures on the basis of EEG signals, taking into account the temporal aspect as well as the signal frequency content. The publicly available data set CHB-MIT was used in our experimental evaluation. Our CGRNN can predict epileptic seizures between 35 min and 5 min in advance and achieved an average sensitivity of 89% and a mean accuracy of 75.6% for the 13 patients in the data set, with a mean FPR of 1.6 per hour. This demonstrates the efficiency of the proposed approach in the epileptic seizure prediction task.

There are several areas for future work. First, we want to investigate whether techniques of weight initialization and regularization of the implemented neural network have effects on the evaluation metrics, such as zero and He initializations. Furthermore, we plan to train the model on large-scale data sets to achieve higher performance, such as the Freiburg Hospital iEEG data set and the TUH EEG Seizure Corpus. Also, we plan to build a real database by recording EEG signals from the university hospital of Sfax, Tunisia. Finally, we also intend to investigate channel selection techniques and design neural architectures based on attention mechanisms.

Acknowledgements. This work is supported by the German Academic Exchange Service (DAAD) (Transformation Partnership: Theralytics Project).

References

1. Bashivan, P., Rish, I., Yeasin, M., Codella, N.: Learning representations from EEG with deep recurrent-convolutional neural networks. In: 4th International Conference on Learning Representations, ICLR 2016, San Juan, Puerto Rico, 2–4 May 2016, Conference Track Proceedings (2016). http://arxiv.org/abs/1511.06448
2. Blinowska, K., Durka, P.: Electroencephalography (EEG). American Cancer Society (2006). https://doi.org/10.1002/9780471740360.ebs0418. https://onlinelibrary.wiley.com/doi/abs/10.1002/9780471740360.ebs0418

3. Choi, G., et al.: A novel multi-scale 3D CNN with deep neural network for epileptic seizure detection. In: 2019 IEEE International Conference on Consumer Electronics (ICCE), pp. 1–2, January 2019. https://doi.org/10.1109/ICCE.2019.8661969
4. Fisher, R.S., et al.: Epileptic seizures and epilepsy: definitions proposed by the international league against epilepsy (ILAE) and the international bureau for epilepsy (IBE). Epilepsia **46**(4), 470–472 (2005). https://doi.org/10.1111/j.0013-9580.2005.66104.x. https://onlinelibrary.wiley.com/doi/abs/10.1111/j.0013-9580.2005.66104.x
5. Fisher, R.S., et al.: Operational classification of seizure types by the international league against epilepsy: Position paper of the ilae commission for classification and terminology. Epilepsia **58**(4), 522–530 (2017). https://doi.org/10.1111/epi.13670. https://onlinelibrary.wiley.com/doi/abs/10.1111/epi.13670
6. Fukumori, K., Thu Nguyen, H.T., Yoshida, N., Tanaka, T.: Fully data-driven convolutional filters with deep learning models for epileptic spike detection. In: ICASSP 2019–2019 IEEE International Conference on Acoustics, Speech and Signal Processing (ICASSP). pp. 2772–2776, May 2019. https://doi.org/10.1109/ICASSP.2019.8682196
7. Goldberger, A., et al.: Physiobank, physiotoolkit, and physionet : components of a new research resource for complex physiologic signals. Circulation **101**, E215–E220 (2000). https://doi.org/10.1161/01.CIR.101.23.e215
8. Golmohammadi, M., et al.: Gated recurrent networks for seizure detection. In: 2017 IEEE Signal Processing in Medicine and Biology Symposium (SPMB), pp. 1–5, December 2017. https://doi.org/10.1109/SPMB.2017.8257020
9. Guo, X., Yin, Y., Dong, C., Yang, G., Zhou, G.: On the class imbalance problem. In: 2008 Fourth International Conference on Natural Computation. vol. 4, pp. 192–201, October 2008. https://doi.org/10.1109/ICNC.2008.871
10. Hosseini, M., Soltanian-Zadeh, H., Elisevich, K., Pompili, D.: Cloud-based deep learning of big EEG data for epileptic seizure prediction. In: 2016 IEEE Global Conference on Signal and Information Processing (GlobalSIP), pp. 1151–1155, December 2016. https://doi.org/10.1109/GlobalSIP.2016.7906022
11. Korshunova, I.: Epileptic Seizure Prediction using Deep Learning. Master's thesis, Universiteit Gent, Belgique (2014–2015)
12. Larmuseau, M.: Epileptic Seizure Prediction using Deep Learning. Master's thesis, Universiteit Gent, Belgique (2015–2016)
13. Litt, B., et al.: Epileptic seizures may begin hours in advance of clinical onset. Neuron **30**, 51–64 (2001). https://doi.org/10.1016/S0896-6273(01)00262-8
14. Moshe, S., Perucca, E., Ryvlin, P., Tomson, T.: Epilepsy: new advances. Lancet **385**, 884–898 (2014). https://doi.org/10.1016/S0140-6736(14)60456-6
15. Mula, M., Monaco, F.: Ictal and peri-ictal psychopathology. Behav. Neurol. **24**, 21–25 (2011). https://doi.org/10.3233/BEN-2011-0314
16. Roy, S., Kiral-Kornek, I., Harrer, S.: ChronoNet: a deep recurrent neural network for abnormal EEG identification. arXiv e-prints arXiv:1802.00308, January 2018
17. Shahbazi, M., Aghajan, H.: A generalizable model for seizure prediction based on deep learning using CNN-LSTM architecture, pp. 469–473 (2018). https://doi.org/10.1109/GlobalSIP.2018.8646505
18. Shoeb, A.H., Guttag, J.V.: Application of machine learning to epileptic seizure detection. In: Proceedings of the 27th International Conference on Machine Learning (ICML 2010), Haifa, Israel, 21–24 June 2010, pp. 975–982 (2010). https://icml.cc/Conferences/2010/papers/493.pdf
19. Talathi, S.S.: Deep recurrent neural networks for seizure detection and early seizure detection systems. arXiv e-prints arXiv:1706.03283, June 2017

20. Thodoroff, P., Pineau, J., Lim, A.: Learning robust features using deep learning for automatic seizure detection. In: Doshi-Velez, F., Fackler, J., Kale, D.C., Wallace, B.C., Wiens, J. (eds.) Proceedings of the 1st Machine Learning in Health Care, MLHC 2016, JMLR Workshop and Conference Proceedings, Los Angeles, CA, USA, 19–20 August 2016, vol. 56, pp. 178–190. JMLR.org (2016). http://proceedings.mlr.press/v56/Thodoroff16.html
21. Truong, N.D., et al.: Convolutional neural networks for seizure prediction using intracranial and scalp electroencephalogram. Neural Netw. **105**, 104–111 (2018). https://doi.org/10.1016/j.neunet.2018.04.018. http://www.sciencedirect.com/science/article/pii/S0893608018301485
22. Xu, Y., Kong, Q., Huang, Q., Wang, W., Plumbley, M.: Convolutional gated recurrent neural network incorporating spatial features for audio tagging (2017). https://doi.org/10.1109/IJCNN.2017.7966291
23. Yuan, Y., Xun, G., Jia, K., Zhang, A.: A multi-view deep learning method for epileptic seizure detection using short-time Fourier transform. In: Proceedings of the 8th ACM International Conference on Bioinformatics, Computational Biology, and Health Informatics, ACM-BCB 2017, pp. 213–222. ACM, New York (2017). https://doi.org/10.1145/3107411.3107419. http://doi.acm.org/10.1145/3107411.3107419

Ubiquitous Healthcare Systems and Medical Rules in COPD Domain

Hicham Ajami[1(✉)], Hamid Mcheick[1], and Karam Mustapha[2]

[1] Department of Computer Sciences and Mathematics,
University of Québec at Chicoutimi, Chicoutimi, QC G7H 2B1, Canada
{hicham.ajamil,Hamid_mcheick}@uqac.ca

[2] Polytechnic of Montreal, Station Centre-Ville, Montreal H3C 3A7, Canada
Karam.mustapha@gmail.com

Abstract. Chronic Obstructive Pulmonary Disease (COPD) is a severe lung illness that causes a progressive deterioration in the function and structure of the respiratory system. Recently, COPD became the fifth cause of mortality and the seventh cause of morbidity in Canada. The advancement of context-aware technology creates a new and important opportunity to transform the standard shape of healthcare services into a more dynamic and interactive form. This research project design and validates a rule-based ontology-reasoning framework that provides a context-aware system for COPD patients. The originality of the proposed approach consists in its methodology to prove the efficiency of this model in simulated examples of real-life scenarios based on collaborative data analysis, recognized by specialized medical experts.

Keywords: Data analysis · Ontology · Context-aware system · COPD · Healthcare systems

1 Introduction

COPD has a significant impact on individuals and society. Moreover, COPD represents an economic burden on the health care system. Statistics Canada [1], ranked COPD as the fifth cause of death in the country. Studies show that people with COPD are vulnerable to many natural events, environmental factors, and sudden worsening of the common signs and symptoms. Recent years have witnessed a widespread increase in the number of telemedicine projects in this domain. This kind of intervention will help COPD patients to avoid severe problems and lengthy hospital admissions [2]. Most research focuses on post exacerbation reactions, but what if we took a step back, and look for ways to avoid exacerbation as much as possible. This task requires working on three different levels, first, find the safe range of environmental factors, second, adjust the normal limits of relevant biomarkers, and third, figure the external influences (e.g. excessive physical effort, climatic factors) on the patient's body. The originality of this approach resides in the intelligent monitoring and control of persistent changes in the physiological parameters and the ambient environment. This work was part of a concentrated effort to create safe adaptive ranges for the personalized biomarkers where the normal values of these vital signs are often affected by the medical profile, the type

J. Pagán et al. (Eds.): ICOST 2019, LNCS 11862, pp. 97–108, 2019.
https://doi.org/10.1007/978-3-030-32785-9_9

of current exercise, the place, and the weather. Environmental factors are also one of the COPD irritants, where cumulative exposure to the multitude of climate hazards such improper humidity levels or extreme weather temperatures, both indoor and outdoor air pollution, in addition to the abnormal concentrations of oxygen in the atmosphere may threaten patient lung health. Developing dynamic alarm thresholds is an important contribution because that would promote the services provided and increase the value of telemonitoring in self-management. Moreover, a customized threshold will help to decrease the proportion of false alarms and differentiate between true exacerbation and normal variation. To achieve these goals, there is an important need to develop a comprehensive representation of knowledge to capture the real context of the patient to avoid misdiagnosis and allow dynamic reconfiguration of health disorders threshold. Rule-based ontology to support context-aware systems offers potential solutions to the multi-scale nature of COPD. In a previous work [3] we designed an ontological reasoning framework that provides a rules-driven context-aware system for COPD patients. In this article, we will present the validation process of that proposition, proving its results by specialized medical experts, and demonstrating its efficiency in simulated examples of real-life scenarios through empirical data about environment, activities, symptoms and physiological parameters.

2 Related Works

Almost two decades ago, the use of medical ontologies was no longer limited to define medical terminologies such as Systematized Nomenclature of Medicine - Clinical Terms (SNOMED CT) or Unified Medical Language System (UMLS), but also it has become one of the powerful solutions to tackle serious health problems and support the management of complex and large data. The ontologies have been also used in hundreds of research projects concerned with medical issues such as diagnosis, self-management, and treatment [4]. The ontological approach proved its effectiveness in the remote healthcare arena, for instance, Lasierra et al. [5] and Larburu et al. [6] have presented robust examples of ontology usage in the telemonitoring domain for generic and specific chronic diseases. Lasierra proposed an autonomic computing ontology for integrated management at home using medical sensors. Rubio provides a formal representation of knowledge to describe the effect of technological context variations in the clinical data quality and its impact on a patient's treatment. Another example can be found in [7], Benyahia developed a generic ontology for monitoring patients diagnosed with chronic diseases. The proposed architecture aims to detect any anomalies or dangerous situations by collecting physiological and lifestyle data. Hristoskova et al. [8] presented an ontology-based ambient intelligence framework that supports real-time physiological monitoring of patients suffering from congestive heart failure. Ryu [9] proposed a ubiquitous healthcare context model using an ontology; the model extracts the contextual information for implementing the healthcare service taking into consideration the medical references and environments. Kim [10] has designed an interactive healthcare system with wearable sensors that provides personalized services with formal ontology-driven specifications. In the same setting, an ontology-based context-aware framework for customized care has been presented by Ko et al. [11] as a form of wearable biomedical technology. An interesting projection of ontology in this domain can be found in [12] that builds a context-aware mobile service aiming at supporting mobile caregivers and sharing information to improve quality of life of people living with chronic diseases. In addition to this obvious interest in ontology, most of health care projects related to computer-assisted medical decision-making, are often modelled using rule-based approaches. The Semantic Web Rule Language (SWRL) has emerged over existing OWL axioms to promote expressiveness of Semantic Web. In the medical environment, there are several uses of rules, for example, but not limited, the IF-THEN rules can be used for chaining or mapping ontology properties to achieve Knowledge Integration. By applying rules, the pattern of behaviors of all entities can be expressed, which would produce new facts and tailored services. The use of the ontology in COPD is only restricted to certain aspects of patients' lives. For example, authors in [13] developed an ontology inspired by the autonomic computing paradigm that provides configurable services to support home-based care. Authors in [6] proposed a predictive model to extract relevant attributes and enable the early detection of deteriorations but the proposed ontology aims at describing the basic structure of the application. Although a significant amount of research has been done studying the importance of telehealth in COPD, the concept of integrated care services is still in its infancy. The use of semantic mapping between the physiological parameters, environmental factors, symptoms, physical activity and patient-specific data to construct a telemonitoring system for COPD using ontologies was not found in the literature. This work will be the first building block for creating a comprehensive primary e-health care delivery system, capable of organizing various daily life scenarios for COPD patients in a healthy and safe environment.

3 Proposed System

In our previous work, we proposed an ontology-based approach to keep track of the physical status of patients, suggest recommendations and deliver interventions in a timely manner. The proposed system provides an intelligent monitoring infrastructure guided by rules. This process involves observing and controlling the behavior of physiological parameters and the surrounding environment. Consequently, the system adapts the safe ranges for the vital signs in proportion to demographic factors, medical profile, physical activity, and external ambiance. The main contribution of that work consists in proposing a specific domain architecture for COPD. This architecture is designed and implemented in four distinct layers: the acquisition layer is dedicated for collecting and properly transmitting different sorts of data, such as the medical profile of COPD patient, biomarkers and environmental information whether gathered from wearable or fixed monitoring sensors. The semantic layer or the ontological schema has been used to interpret complex information and translate the real context of the patient into machine-understandable and accessible language. At the macro level, the telemonitoring system aims to detect all the possible hazardous events that could influence COPD patient. Since OWL has expressivity limitations on representing many types of contextual information, especially IF-THEN statement, our ontologies have been extended with forward-chaining rules. These rules were expressed in the Semantic Web

Rule Language (SWRL) to describe all implications and consequences. The proposed rules are extracted from data analysis, existing medical guidelines and opinions of pneumologists. Practically, these rules are used by an inference engine to derive new facts, detect events, and predict the potential risk. The novelty of these rules lies in its dynamic structure, which has the capacity to configure and re-configure the secure boundaries according to the current circumstances and contexts.

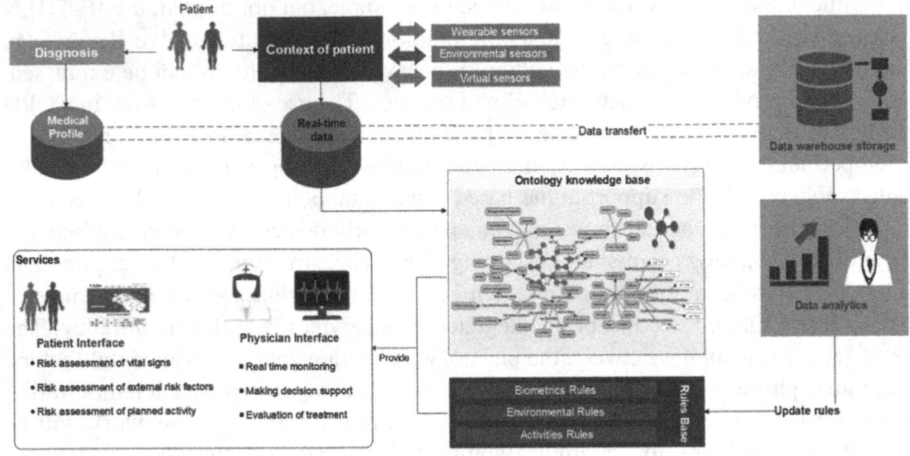

Fig. 1. General architecture

Figure 1 above provides an explanation of the relationships between the constituent entities of the system in a simplified manner. In the next section, we will learn about the methods of extracting the medical rules of COPD.

4 COPD Rules

In preparation for rules extraction, we performed data analysis, reviewed medical guidelines, interviewed experts and examined published sources to map biomarkers of COPD patients to various real-life patterns. A rule, on the other hand, is a description of how a patient is affected by internal bodily characteristics and external environmental factors.

4.1 Biomarkers Rules

In clinical therapy, each patient must be recognized as individuals with a unique health state. However, grouping patients with a similar medical profile is an excellent solution to treat diseases. Unlike previous works and based on this scientific principle, we studied all relevant factors according to the personal and medical profile, which includes the demographic information and the clinical chart of patients. Hurst et al. [14] and Rajeh et al. [15] identified the main physiological parameters and symptoms to be monitored. Understanding the maximum possible extent of change for each variable in different scenarios is a crucial need for the early detection of pulmonary exacerbations. In the next section, we will try to find out how these parameters change with COPD patient in different medical profiles and during common daily life activities. Profile differences help to explain discrepancies in medical care received by COPD patients. Having considered the guidelines, it is recommended dividing the population of patients into groups or quartiles according to age, gender, stage, BMI, smokers, medication, and comorbidity. Identifying factors that may indicate if something is wrong with COPD patients is about to happen was a daunting task and took a long time. This study has established 11 physical parameters must be monitored namely, body temperature, blood pressure, heart rate, partial pressure oxygen (PaO2), oxygen saturation (SpO2), partial pressure carbon dioxide (PaCO2), oxygen consumption (VO2), respiration rate, PH, HCO3, and FEV1. Understanding the role of these biomarkers and their normal ranges in the stable COPD patients with all potential scenarios grants us the ability to sense imminent danger. Patients were separated horizontally by gender, age and stage, these groups have been then reclassified vertically according to the effects of BMI, smoking, medication, and comorbidities on the vital signs. To illustrate this point, we will provide an example to explain changes in heart rate with different profiles.

4.1.1 Heart Rate Rules

Analysis of data obtained from medical records [16, 17, and 18] finds that heart rate in women can be slightly different from men. Figure 2 shows that females have a higher heart rate compared with males at all ages, as this difference increases in the early middle age and decreases in late adulthood. In contrast, the overall analysis shown a remarkable decline in the normal resting heart rate (Fig. 3).

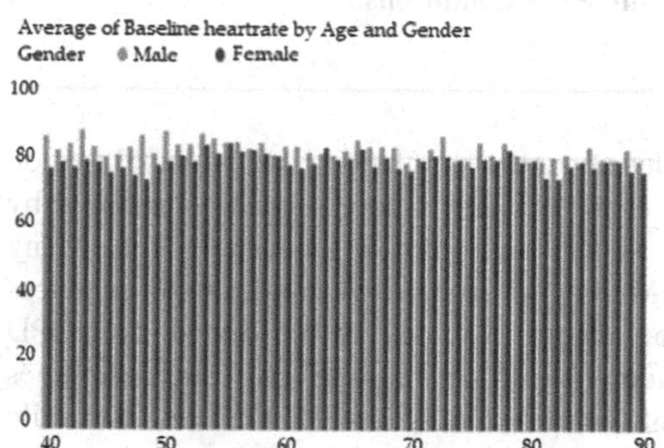

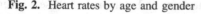

Fig. 2. Heart rates by age and gender

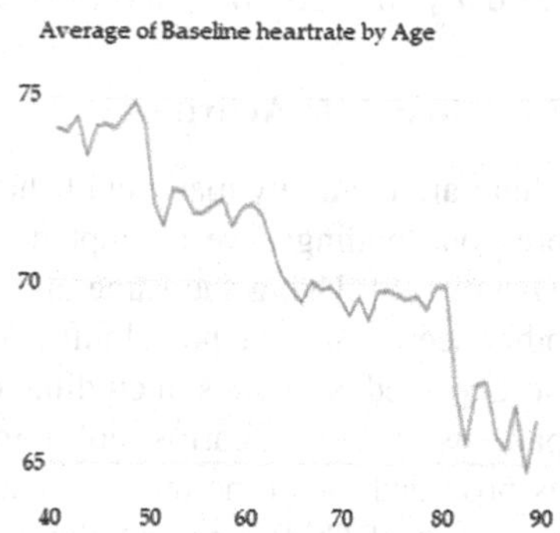

Fig. 3. Heart rates by age

Resting heart rate was also associated with both obese and all inhaler medication across all stages of COPD ($p < 0.004$ and $p < 0.003$). The change in heart rate was only associated with four comorbidities, CHF, anemia, PH, and asthma. One of the key factors that change heart rate is activity. Heart rate differs from person to person during exercise or when doing any physical effort, this variation is determined by mathematical equations with an acceptable degree of accuracy. In summary, this evidence-based analysis proves that heart rate varies depending on the medical profile of the patient, which in turn will affect the stable ranges of this vital sign during physical activities. The same analytical methodology has been used on the other physiological parameters mentioned above.

4.2 Indoor and Outdoor Rules

According to Healthy Environments and Consumer Safety Branch (HECSB), Canadians spend approximately 90% of their life indoors [19] often, due to the extreme nature of the climate conditions. Therefore, it's very important to pay attention to the quality of that indoor air, temperature, humidity, and pressure, especially as COPD patients must fully live in a safe environment, away from any kind of exacerbation irritants. Unlike the internal environment, we cannot control the external environmental factors. There are six main factors that affect the patient outside of the ordinary indoor ambient, these factors must include outdoor temperature, humidity, wind speed, precipitation, atmospheric pressure, and air quality but in terms of air compounds and outdoor pollutants. The proposed rules must provide customized protection against all the inappropriate environmental factors.

5 Dataset

Gatherings such different kinds of data from real sensors are subject to some practical limitations such as ethical approval, financial costs, and deployment time. Hence, researchers suggest an alternative experimental method using intelligent simulation. There are three basic data sources to build such scenarios, (1) medical information, (2) daily life activities, and (3) the environmental conditions.

5.1 Real-Life Activities

There are relatively many published studies about the simulation of activities. Based on previous findings, we attempted to extend the existing indoor scenarios proposed by Mshali [20]. Using the same approach which is built upon Markovian models. Many other scenarios have been built upon the Markovian models, we created new sequences of expected activities including outdoor actions that can be performed by COPD patients. These scenarios took into consideration the levels of severity and disabilities as provided for in the international classification of functioning (ICF). These daily life activities of COPD patients have been divided into six successively sequences associated with six-time periods from sunrise to sunset. Each one of these sequences consists of a set of coordinated activities with a random duration created through transition probabilities matrices.

5.2 Environmental Conditions

Unlike the patient activity dataset, challenges in assembling environmental data were easier, where we found many open sources that describe environmental conditions of indoor and outdoor spaces at long intervals. One of the most interesting outdoor datasets for environmental information is published by the ministry of environment and climate change strategy in British Columbia in Canada [21]. These data sets contain continuous readings of meteorological and pollutants index from air quality monitoring stations across the province from 1980 till the end of 2017. Simulation of the internal environment is also important where the patient spends most of his time at home. The indoor data is tracked via GAMS indoor air quality monitor [22].

5.3 Medical Records

Medical profiles are a vital asset in ensuring the validation process. In this context, we have collected thousands of electronic medical records, hospital admission data, and measures of the outcome in clinical studies from different medical sources ([16] Al-Sahel hospital and MIR clinic [17]).

6 Implementation

The experimental dataset consists of the activities that have been generated using the MATLAB, the environmental conditions which are captured by real sensors and the biomarkers that obtained from medical sources. The simulated scenarios revolve around creating sequential records over 12 months period for COPD patients with different levels of disease severity and autonomy. In this section, we briefly describe the implementation steps of this project using protégé (Fig. 4).

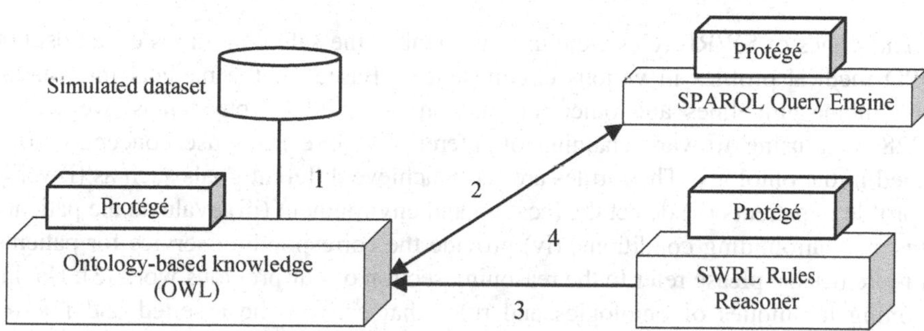

Fig. 4. Flow in the implemented system

The initial implementation of the project will be done in the following manner: (1) the simulated data stored in Excel spreadsheet files will be uploaded directly to Ontology-based knowledge using Cellfie plugin. (2) The SPARQL query engine accesses to the Knowledge Base to retrieve information of patient's profile, current location, and activity, etc. (3) SWRL rule reasoner adds additional information such as normal ranges, and appropriate environment to the Knowledge Base. Moreover, SWRL rule reasoner performs reasoning on the updated Knowledge Base of COPD domain and new inferred facts are added to the Knowledge Base. (4) The SPARQL query engine accesses to the Knowledge Base to retrieve the notifications and the recommendations according to the patient's context. We constructed eight ontologies for monitoring COPD patient to represent machine-understandable Knowledge Base. The developed ontologies consist of concepts related to personal and medical profile, physical examinations, laboratory tests, location, activity, environment, time, recommendations, and disease [3] (Fig. 5).

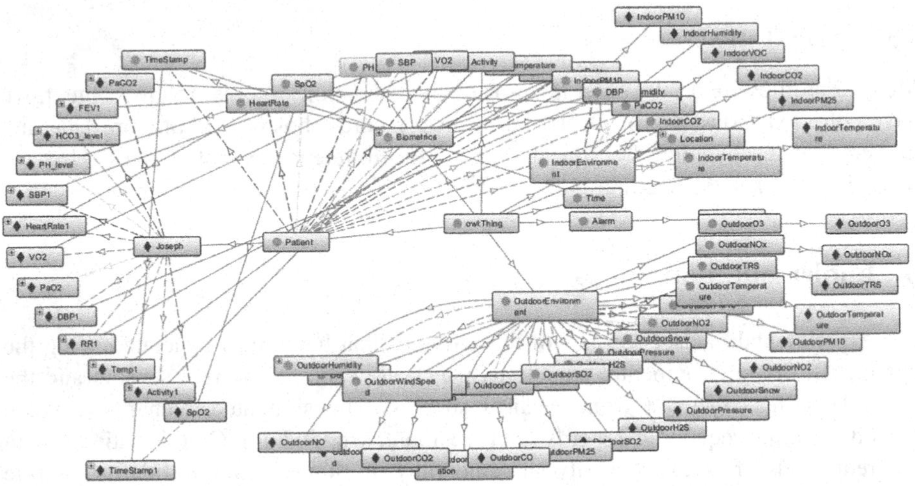

Fig. 5. Part of the ontology

Thousands of SWRL rules were used to manage the safe conditions of almost 600 COPD medical profiles in various circumstances. Based on the medical information found in the guidelines and other information provided by physicians, we created 20,328 rules using forward chaining of inference. These rules use concepts/axioms defined in our ontology. These rules are set to achieve different goals such as (i) verify the profile of patients (ii) detect the location and environment (iii) evaluate the patient's status and surrounding conditions, (iv) provide the corresponding service for patients. For more details, please refer to the reasoning section of our previous work [3]. Having reasoning techniques of ontologies and rules that contain the asserted and inferred statements, we used SPARQL to retrieve, and derive contextual information from the knowledge base. The aim of this query is to retrieve any information relating to an identified instance, such as a sign, symptom, treatment, alarm, recommendation, decision, etc. To illustrate the use of the model, we will present some examples. Let's consider the scenario of a COPD patient being remotely monitored after diagnosis. The patient vital signs, activity, and environmental parameters are continuously monitored (Fig. 6).

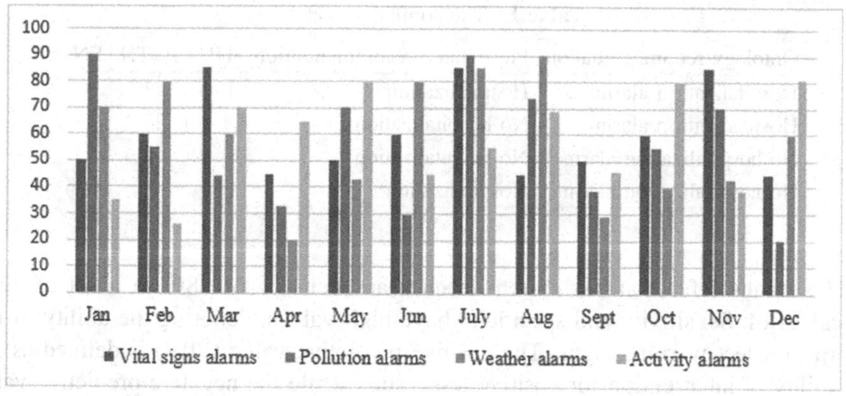

Fig. 6. Number of alarms by months

The presented simulations have handled a great amount of data of possible situations. The generated alarms have been classified into four main categories: vital signs, activity, pollution, and weather. The system applies continuous monitoring and detects a total of 2,817 abnormal situations.

7 Evaluation

This section will explore partially the performance of our system using a confusion matrix. Performance measurement refers to information that quantifies accuracy, sensitivity, specificity, and the probability of predicting a dangerous change in physiological parameters in COPD patients. The purpose of this evaluation is to measure the diagnostic performance of technical and clinical accuracy.

A master file was created in MS Excel® that contains 1200 patients records, biometric readings for each patient have been extracted from the results inferred from ontology in different scenarios. This information was presented to physicians. This data is used to calculate the confusion matrices for the physician's report outcomes. There are four possible outcomes, true positive (TP), true negative (TN), false positive (FP), and false-negative (FN). The confusion matrix contains information about the predicted classifications identified by our ontology and the opinions of medical experts. Categories in this research are defined as follows (Table 1):

1. TP is an alarm with a hospitalization.
2. FN has no alarm with a hospitalization.
3. TN has no alarm and no hospitalization.
4. FP has an alarm with no hospitalization.

Table 1. The confusion matrix

Ontology recommendation	Physicians' recommendation	TP	FP	TN	FN
Hospitalization alarm	Hospitalization	1			
Hospitalization alarm	No hospitalization		1		
No hospitalization alarm	No hospitalization			1	
No hospitalization alarm	Hospitalization				1

The results refer that our system reaches an accuracy of 88% in a set of 1200 clinical cases. Sensitivity and specificity have high values, denoting the ability of the system to detect warning signs. The positive predictive value (PPV) is defined as the probability of intervention for positive test results while the negative predictive value (NPV) describes the probability of being healthy for negative test results (Table 2).

Table 2. Standard reference and results for the clinical decision support system

	Intervention present	Intervention absent	Total
Index test positive	True positive (TP) = 512	False positive (FP) = 88	TP + FP = 600
Index test negative	False negative (FN) = 56	True negative (TN) = 544	TN + FN = 600
Total	TP + FN = 568	TN + FP = 632	
1. Accuracy = 88%			
2. Sensitivity = 91.14%			
3. Specificity = 86.07%			
4. Positive predictive value (PPV) = 85.33%			
5. Negative predictive value (NPV) = (TN)/(FN + TN) = 90.66%			

8 Conclusion

The proposed model involves a qualitative leap in the healthcare systems that supports COPD because it establishes new obligations that will limit many of the potential hazards at different levels, both physiological and environmental. The system can recognize any important changes in biometrics and environment based on a personalized threshold. The protection process aims to adjust the thresholds around the normal state to avoid exacerbation triggers. Our findings proved that dynamic thresholds can enhance the existing telemonitoring systems and make a valuable contribution identify the health status of COPD patients. Many conclusions can be drawn from this experimental simulation. Firstly, the ontology-based system can provide a more efficient way to deal with medical data. Secondly, adding an SWRL layer of experts' rules on top of OWL can handle various types of context and suggest reliable recommendations. Thirdly, the results support the importance of context where it demonstrates that context variables have a strong influence on the accuracy of decisions. For future research, this study will have to be evaluated through real implementation and crossover trial to assess patients' experiences and measure their effectiveness and usability.

References

1. Public Health Agency of Canada Report from the Canadian Chronic Disease Surveillance System: Asthma and Chronic Obstructive Pulmonary Disease (COPD) in Canada, Ottawa (2018). ISBN 978-0-660-09274-4
2. Segrelles, G., Gómez-Suárez, C., Soriano, J.B., Zamora, E., Gónzalez-Gamarra, A., et al.: A home telehealth program for patients with severe COPD: the PROMETE study. Respir. Med. **108**, 453–462 (2014)
3. Ajami, H., Mcheick, H.: Ontology-based model to support ubiquitous healthcare systems for COPD patients. Electronics **7**, 371 (2018)
4. Button, K., van Deursen, R.W., Soldatova, L., Spasić, I.: TRAK ontology: defining standard care for the rehabilitation of knee conditions. J. Biomed. Inform. **46**(4), 615–625 (2013). https://doi.org/10.1016/j.jbi.2013.04.009. [PMID: 23665300]
5. Lasierra, N., Alesanco, A., Guillen, S., Garcia, J.: A tree stage ontology-driven solution to provide personalized care to chronic patients at home. J. Biomed. Inform. **46**, 516–529 (2013)
6. Larburu, R., Bults, R.G., Van Sinderen, M.J., Hermens, H.J.: An ontology for telemedicine systems resiliency to technological context variations in pervasive healthcare. IEEE J. Transl. Eng. Health Med. **3**, 10 (2015). https://doi.org/10.1109/JTEHM.2015
7. Benyahia, A.A., Hajjam, A., Hilaire, V., Hajjam, M.: E-care ontological architecture for telemonitoring and alerts detection. In: 5th IEEE International Symposium on Monitoring & Surveillance Research (ISMSR): Healthcare-Safety-Security (2012)
8. Hristoskova, A., Sakkalis, V., Zacharioudakis, G., Tsiknakis, M., De Turck, F.: Ontology-driven monitoring of patient's vital signs enabling personalized medical detection and alert. In: Nikita, K.S., Lin, J.C., Fotiadis, D.I., Arredondo Waldmeyer, M.-T. (eds.) MobiHealth 2011. LNICST, vol. 83, pp. 217–224. Springer, Heidelberg (2012). https://doi.org/10.1007/978-3-642-29734-2_30
9. Ryu, J.-K., et al.: Ontology based context information model for u-healthcare service. In: 2011 International Conference on Information Science and Applications, pp. 1–6 (2011)
10. Kim, J., Lee, D., Chung, K.: Ontology driven interactive healthcare with wearable sensors. Multimed. Tools Appl. **71**, 827–841 (2012)
11. Ko, E.J., Lee, H.J., Lee, J.W.: Ontology-based context modeling and reasoning for U-HealthCare. IEICE Trans Inf. Syst. **E90-D**(8), 1262–1270 (2007)
12. Paganelli, F., Giuli, D.: An ontology-based system for contextaware and configurable services to support home-based continuous care. IEEE Trans. Inf. Technol. Biomed. **15**, 324–333 (2011)
13. Valls, A., Gibert, K., Snchez, D., Batet, M.: Using ontologies for structuring organizational knowledge in home care assistance. Int. J. Med. Inform. **79**(5), 370–387 (2010)
14. Hurst, J.R., et al.: Susceptibility to exacerbation in chronic obstructive pulmonary disease. New Engl. J. Med. **363**, 1128–1138 (2010)
15. Al Rajeh, A., Hurst, J.: Monitoring of physiological parameters to predict exacerbations of chronic obstructive pulmonary disease (COPD): a systematic review. J Clin. Med. **5**, 108 (2016)
16. AL Sahel Hospital. Beirut, Lebanon (2018)
17. Medical International Research (MIR), clinical laboratory. Beirut, Lebanon (2018)
18. Simulated patient cases, training and validation dataset. https://doi.org/10.1371/journal.pone.0188532.s004

19. Ventilation and the Indoor Environment. Water and Air Quality Bureau Healthy Environments and Consumer Safety Branch, March 2018. http://publications.gc.ca/collections/collection_2018/sc-hc/H144-54-1-2018-eng.pdf
20. Mshali, H., Lemlouma, T., Magoni, D.: Context-aware adaptive framework for e-health monitoring. In: IEEE International Conference on Data Science and Data Intensive Systems, Sydney, Australia, pp. 276–283, December 2015
21. Outdoor air quality dataset. https://catalogue.data.gov.bc.ca/dataset/air-quality-monitoring-verified-hourly-data
22. GAMS Indoor Air Quality Dataset. https://github.com/twairball/gams-dataset

DL4DED: Deep Learning for Depressive Episode Detection on Mobile Devices

Afef Mdhaffar[1,2(✉)], Fedi Cherif[3], Yousri Kessentini[1], Manel Maalej[4], Jihen Ben Thabet[4], Mohamed Maalej[4], Mohamed Jmaiel[1,2], and Bernd Freisleben[5]

[1] Digital Research Center of Sfax, Sfax, Tunisia
afef.mdhaffar@gmail.com
[2] National School of Engineering of Sfax, University of Sfax, Sfax, Tunisia
[3] Geeks Data Consulting, Tunis, Tunisia
[4] Department of Psychiatry "C", Hedi Chaker University Hospital, Faculty of Medicine of Sfax, University of Sfax, Sfax, Tunisia
[5] Department of Mathematics and Computer Science, University of Marburg, Marburg, Germany

Abstract. This paper presents a deep learning approach for depressive episode detection on mobile devices, called DL4DED. It is based on a convolutional neural network and a long short-term memory network to identify the status of a patient's voice extracted from spontaneous phone calls. To run DL4DED on mobile devices, two neural network model compression techniques are used: quantization and pruning. DL4DED protects data privacy, since it can be executed on a patient's smartphone. Our proposal is validated on the DAIC-WOZ database. The obtained results show that the accuracy of DL4DED with model compression is only slightly lower than the accuracy of DL4DED without model compression. Furthermore, our experiments indicate that the power consumption of DL4DED is reasonably low.

Keywords: Deep learning · Mobile application · Depression · Pruning · Quantization · Optimization

1 Introduction

According to the World Health Organization (WHO), 800 000 people die every year due to suicide[1], which is the second leading cause of death in people aged between 15 and 29 years. However, many suicides can be prevented. Indeed, mental disorders, such as depression, contribute to many of them around the world. Hence, early detection and appropriate management are key to ensuring that people receive the care they need[2]. Therefore, patients suffering from Major

[1] https://www.who.int/news-room/fact-sheets/detail/depression.
[2] https://apps.who.int/iris/bitstream/handle/10665/131056/9789241564779_eng.pdf.

J. Pagán et al. (Eds.): ICOST 2019, LNCS 11862, pp. 109–121, 2019.
https://doi.org/10.1007/978-3-030-32785-9_10

Depressive Disorder (MDD) and Bipolar Disorders (BD) should be continuously monitored, since they might experience frequent depressive episodes.

Several mental health monitoring approaches using mobile devices have been proposed. Most of them [1–3,5–11,13,14] are based on (1) collecting and analyzing smartphone features such as activity, localization, and phone calls, and (2) launching interactive questionnaires such as PHQ-9[3] and BDI[4]. "Active" monitoring approaches (i.e., requiring a patient's intervention) are less used and less effective than "passive" ones (i.e., not requiring a patient's intervention) in practice. Actually, patients do not like to answer questionnaires every day, and even if they answer them, we cannot be sure about the honesty of their answers.

Passive monitoring approaches [3,5–8,10,11,13,14] can be divided into two categories. The first category tries to use most of the smartphone's sensors, such as accelerometer and camera, to collect related features [5–7,11,14]. These approaches require special environmental conditions to ensure the precision of collected data. For instance, Maxhuni et al. [11] require the smartphone to be held in a special position to accurately capture the patient's activity. This makes these approaches difficult to use in practice. The second category of approaches [3,8,10,13] focuses on analyzing "only" voice sounds, recorded from phone calls. Indeed, acoustic changes in speech allow us to detect depressive episodes [8]. Most of these approaches are based on the use of complex algorithms for speech analysis, such as deep learning approaches. Typically, these approaches require significant computational resources. Therefore, this category of approaches sends recorded phone calls to an external server for analysis, since running complex algorithms on smartphones is still a challenging task [12]. This reduces the chances of using these mobile applications, because they do not protect data privacy. Actually, many patients do not accept that external servers process their recorded phone calls.

In this paper, we present a novel deep learning approach that can be loaded and executed on a patient's smartphone to allow real-time detection of depressive episodes. Our proposal, called DL4DED (Deep Learning for Depressive Episode Detection), is based on optimizing and compressing a deep learning model to be integrated in our mobile application. DL4DED (1) records phone calls, (2) executes our deep learning model, and (3) triggers alerts if a depressive episode is detected. DL4DED does not send recorded phone calls to an external server and consequently preserves data privacy. To evaluate our approach, two groups of experiments have been conducted. The first one illustrates the efficiency of DL4DED in terms of accuracy. The second one demonstrates that the power consumption of DL4DED is reasonable when compared to baseline approaches.

The paper is organized as follows. Section 2 discusses related work. DL4DED and its implementation are detailed in Sects. 3 and 4, respectively. Section 5 presents experiments and results. Section 6 concludes the paper and outlines areas for future research.

[3] Patient Health Questionnaire (PHQ-9).

[4] Beck's Depression Inventory.

2 Related Work

A comprehensive survey reviewing existing mobile applications for mental health diseases (e.g., BD, MDD, schizophrenia) has been published by Cornet et al. [1]. This survey explains different parameters that have been used throughout the years to detect mental health diseases. These parameters are usually extracted from smartphone sensors, such as microphone (i.e., phone calls), accelerometer (i.e., movement data), and GPS (i.e., localization). The authors also describe the used analysis algorithms, where the most advanced ones are based on deep learning networks. Moreover, the authors discuss data privacy issues related to all reviewed approaches, since all extracted smartphone features are sent to an external server for analysis.

Haque et al. [6] present a deep learning model to measure the severity of depression symptoms. The proposed approach is based on analyzing 3D facial expression and spoken language. It has been evaluated on the DAIC-WOZ dataset [4]. The proposed approach requires an active intervention from the patient, which makes it unusable in some cases. Actually, it is hard to ask a patient to daily record videos, due to privacy issues. In contrast, our approach is passive, analyzes spontaneous phone calls, and preserves data privacy.

Su et al. [14] present a diagnosis assistance system that is based on deep learning and fusion techniques. The proposed system makes use of two deep learning models. The first one is used for speech classification, while the second one processes facial expression. This work is aimed at assisting doctors to avoid misdiagnosis in the case of BD. Actually, BD is usually confused with MDD. The results are quite promising, but the system architecture cannot not be applied in a spontaneous manner. Indeed, the system requires special environmental conditions to be applied, such as a camera.

Huang et al. [7] propose an attention-based convolutional neural network (CNN) and long short-term memory (LSTM) approach for distinguishing between MDD and BD. The proposed approach identifies mood disorders on the basis of responses given to 6 video sequences. Consequently, it can be applied to depressive episode detection. The analysis includes speech processing and facial recognition to extract emotional state. In contrast to our approach, this work cannot be applied in a spontaneous manner and does not protect data privacy. Actually, recording responses to 6 particular videos cannot be expected on a daily basis and without the intervention of a psychiatrist.

Grunerbl et al. [5] present a smartphone-based approach for mood status identification in BD. The proposed approach makes use of smartphone features (e.g., location, phone call sounds, phone light) to detect depressive and maniac episodes. Features are extracted manually, and data privacy is not protected.

Maxhuni et al. [11] define an analysis approach that identifies manic and depressive episodes on the basis of activity data and phone calls. To monitor activities, the authors mention that the phone has to be held in a special position. Moreover, phone calls are recorded, stored in the phone's memory card and sent to another server for analysis. This means that this approach does not protect data privacy and requires special environmental conditions to generate accurate results.

Khorram et al. [10] propose a machine learning (ML) approach for depression detection in BD. The proposed approach is based on the analysis of acoustic features of the patient's voice. The paper shows the effectiveness of speech features in detecting depression. However, features are extracted manually due to the use of ML techniques. Moreover, a patient's voice is sent to an external server for analysis, which does not protect data privacy. Therefore, we propose a deep learning model that allows us to automatically extract features and preserve data privacy.

Gideon et al. [3] discuss the impact of a recorded voice on the identification of depressive and manic episodes in BD. Only phone calls recorded during clinical trial are considered. Other phone calls are removed to protect data privacy. This means that this work does not analyze naturalistic and spontaneous voice, which might alter the detection results. However, our work is based on the analysis of spontaneous phone calls (i.e., recorded on a daily basis), thanks to our deep learning model that is locally running on a patient's smartphone.

Huang et al. [8] define two speech features based on speech landmark bigrams (i.e., bigram count and LDA bigram) for depression detection. Both features could be extracted from naturalistic phone calls including 6 elicitation tasks such as measuring the diadochokinetic rate. Landmarks are extracted using the SpeechMark® toolbox[5], which is a Matlab tool that runs under Windows 7, Windows XP, Apple OSX (Lion or Mountain Lion), as mentioned on their web page. This means that the proposed work needs to send recorded phone calls to an external server for feature extraction. However, our work allows us to locally extract features on the smartphone.

Pan et al. [13] propose analysis approaches for detecting manic episodes in BD. The proposed approaches are based on the use of Support Vector Machines (SVM) and Generalized Markov Models (GMM). They record spontaneous phone calls and send them to an external server for analysis. This approach does not protect data privacy.

3 DL4DED

This section presents our novel approach, called DL4DED. It is a mobile voice analysis approach that:

1. monitors patients suffering from BD and MDD;
2. detects depressive episodes by locally analyzing their phone calls without storing them;
3. alerts patients, their family members, and their psychiatrists if a depressive episode is detected.

[5] https://speechmrk.com/speechmark-products-downloads/the-speechmark-matlab-toolbox/.

DL4DED is based on the use of deep learning methods applied to spontaneous speech, recorded from phone calls, to identify depressed voice. The proposed deep learning model is locally running on a patient's smartphone to preserve data privacy. Indeed, recorded phone calls are "temporarily" stored on the smartphone until the analysis is accomplished. Once the decision is sent to our external server, the recorded phone call is discarded. The architecture of DL4DED, the proposed deep learning model, and our optimizations are described below.

3.1 Architecture

Figure 1 shows the architecture of DL4DED. Our approach (1) records spontaneous phone calls, (2) stores them temporarily in a buffer belonging to the local memory of a patient's phone, (3) processes them via our "mobile" deep learning model, (4) identifies the state of the recorded voice (i.e., depressed or not depressed), (5) discards the recorded voice (i.e., phone call), and finally (6) sends and stores the obtained decision to a database that is installed on a cloud server. The communication links between the smartphone and the cloud server are enabled via the HTTP protocol. A web dashboard is available for both patients and psychiatrists. It is used to display the patient's mood on the basis of the voice status.

To identify the status of the voice, we use a novel deep learning model that is described in Sect. 3.2.

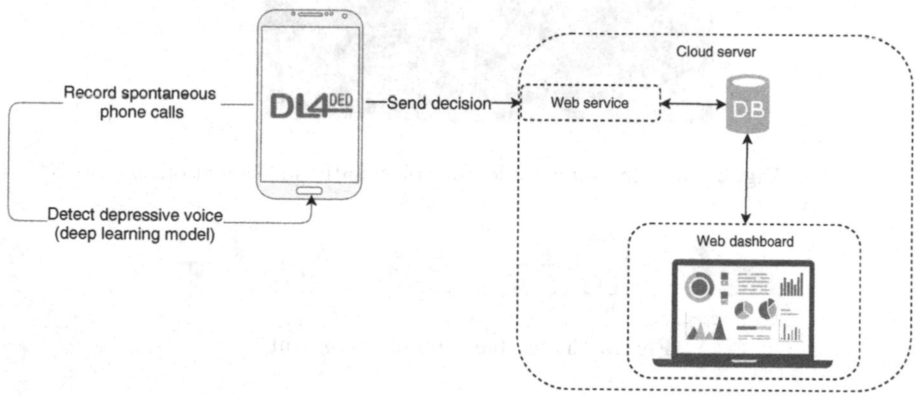

Fig. 1. Architecture of DL4DED

3.2 Deep Learning for Voice Status Identification

Figure 2 shows our deep learning model. It processes recorded phone calls and detects depressed voice. The proposed model takes as input a spectrogram. To obtain a spectrogram, a Short-Time Fourier Transform (STFT) is applied to the recorded phone calls. A spectrogram, also called voiceprint, represents the

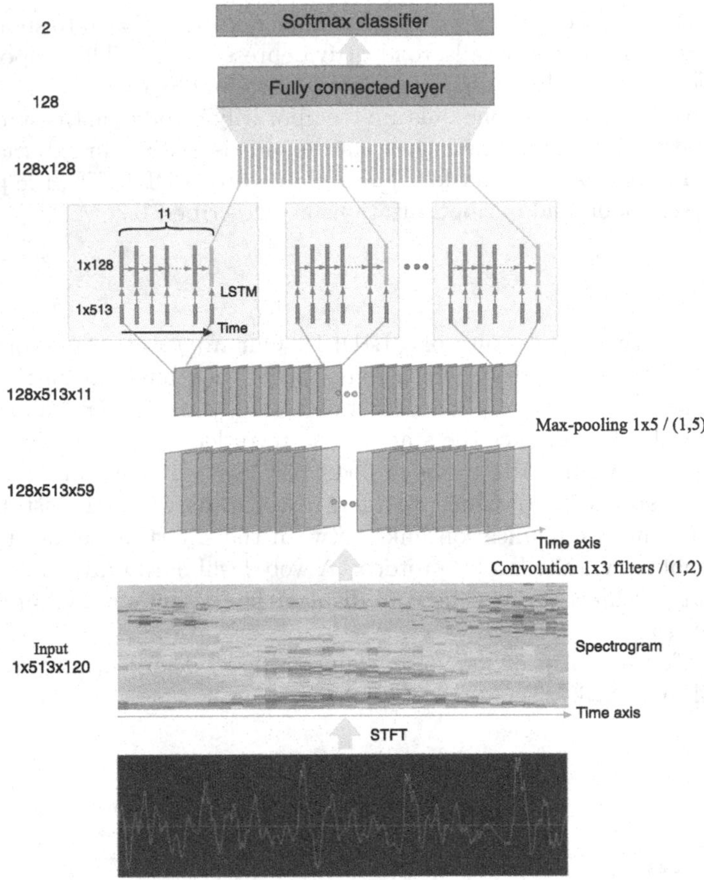

Fig. 2. Deep learning model for voice status identification

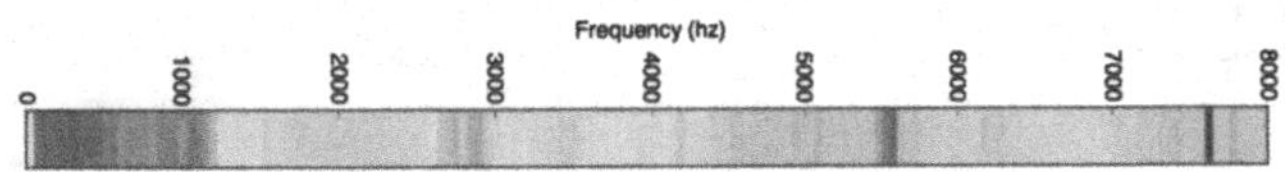

Fig. 3. Energy bar: an audio segment

spectrum of frequencies of the recorded phone call, as a function of time. It is composed of a set of frequency bars. Each bar corresponds to a time-stamp t. It is a vector, having the dimension 513 corresponding to the quantities of energy, expressed in decibels (see Fig. 3).

In our case, the spectrogram is a matrix having the dimensions 513 (frequencies) and 120 (times). The temporal dimension has been experimentally chosen. However, the frequency dimension has been obtained by applying STFT on audio segments, recorded with a frequency of 16 kHz (standard frequency for human voice recording). The intensity of colors represents the intensity of the energy of the recorded voice at the instant t, which might be useful for the identification of the patient's mood. Once the spectrogram is built, it is processed by a CNN network, having one convolution layer and one max-pooling layer. The convolution layer applies a $(1 * 3)$ filter/$(1, 2)$, allowing us to keep all frequencies (i.e., all energy quantities describing the voice) and preserve the temporal continuity. The max-pooling layer applies a $(1 * 5)$ filter /$(1, 5)$, to extract medium-term features, while keeping all frequencies. The output of the max-pooling layer is processed by an LSTM that includes memory cells to save long-term information. A fully connected layer is applied afterwards, to transform the obtained matrix into a 128-dimensional vector. The latter is processed by a softmax classifier allowing a binary classification (i.e., depressed voice or not depressed voice). The parameters of our CNN model have been identified experimentally.

To run the proposed deep learning model on mobile devices, we considered two compression methods: quantization and pruning. These methods allow us to reduce the size of our deep learning model by removing weights or operations that are least useful for prediction.

4 Implementation Issues

Figure 4 shows the technical architecture of DL4DED. The smartphone is in charge of recording and analyzing phone calls, while running our deep learning model that has been implemented using the Keras[6] library. Generated decisions are then sent to a Flask RESTful API 1.0.2, a web service platform that stores received decisions in a RethinkDB 2.3.6 0xenial (GCC 5.3.1) database. A nodeJS v4.2.6 server is installed to build a real-time web application. It is composed of a set of dashboards, displaying analysis results and an estimation of the patient's mood/status.

To predict depressed voice, recorded phone calls are pre-processed first. Afterwards, the deep learning model is loaded into a mobile application to trigger predictions. Implementation details are presented below.

4.1 Data Processing

To process a phone call by a CNN model, a spectrogram is built. For this purpose, the recorded voice (i.e., voice signal) is processed by a pre-emphasis filter. A pre-emphasis filter allows us to (1) improve the Signal-to-Noise Ratio (SNR); (2) avoid numerical problems that might appear during the Fourier Transform operation and (3) balance the frequency spectrum. Actually, high frequencies usually have smaller magnitudes compared to lower frequencies.

[6] https://keras.io.

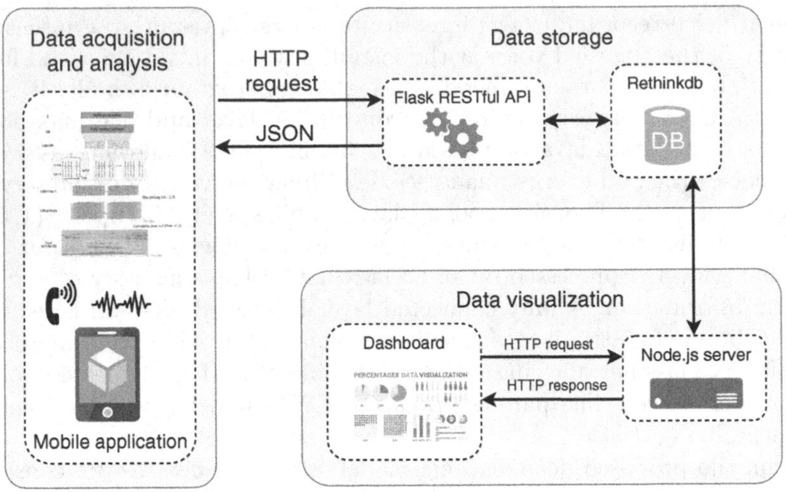

Fig. 4. DL4DED implementation

After applying the pre-emphasis filter, the signal is decomposed into short-time and overlapping frames. This step allows us to avoid applying the STFT across the entire signal and consequently losing the frequency contours of the signal over time. In this case, STFT will be applied on short-term frames allowing us to obtain a good approximation of the frequency contours of the signal by concatenating adjacent frames.

A window function (e.g., Hamming window) and a STFT are applied to each frame. This allows us to compute the power spectrum that is used to extract the frequency bands by applying triangular filters on a mel scale. The mel scale aims to mimic the non-linear human ear perception of sound, by being more discriminative at lower frequencies and less discriminative at higher frequencies.

After applying the filter bank to the power spectrum (i.e., periodogram) of the signal, we obtain the spectrogram that is processed by our CNN.

All steps described above were implemented in Android studio to create our mobile application (see first step of Fig. 5).

4.2 Implementation on Mobile Devices

To implement our deep learning model on mobile devices, we followed three steps (see Fig. 5). First, our Keras-based deep learning model is converted to Tensorflow. Actually, Tensorflow allows an easier integration of deep learning models on mobile devices (i.e., Android or IOS). For this purpose, we use a method called "Keras_to_Tensorflow" provided by the Tensorflow library. This method converts a Keras model file into a Tensorflow file which contains both the network architecture and its associated weights. Second, we optimize the generated model by removing weights and operations that are least useful for predictions by applying pruning and quantization methods. Third, we load our model (i.e.,

*.pb file including weights and architecture) into our mobile application to allow real-time detection of depressed voice.

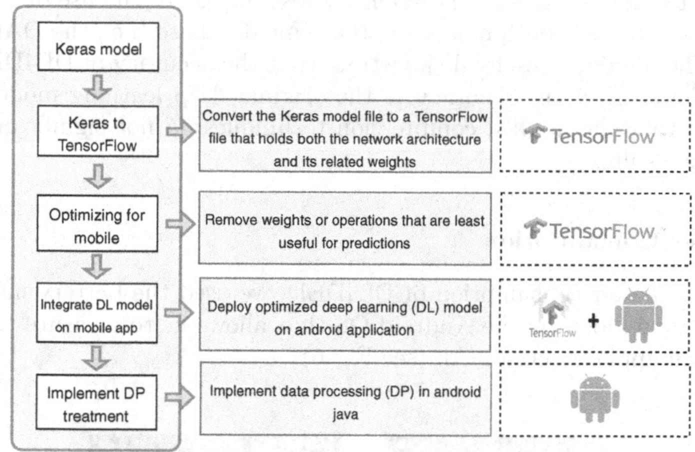

Fig. 5. Implementation of our deep learning model on mobile devices

5 Experimental Results

Our experiments were conducted on (1) an Ubuntu Server 16.04.5 LTS, with 2 GPUs Nvidia GeForce GTX1080 Ti Turbo 11 GB GDDR5X-RAM PCIe x16 HDMI and (2) a OnePlus A6003 Smartphone, running under an Android OS 8.1.0, with 8 GB of RAM and 128 GB of storage. We use the DAIC-WOZ data set[7] to evaluate DL4DED. The DAIC-WOZ dataset was compiled by the USC Institute of Creative Technologies and published as part of the Audiovisual Emotional Challenge 2016 (AVEC 2016). The DAIC WOZ data set includes 189 sessions, with an average duration of 16 min, between a participant and a virtual interviewer, controlled by a human interviewer in another room via a "Wizard of Oz" approach. Prior to the interview, each participant completed a psychiatric questionnaire (PHQ-8), from which a binary classification (depressed, non-depressed) was derived [4]. To evaluate DL4DED, we conducted two groups of experiments. The first group is used to evaluate the performance of our approach in terms of accuracy. The second group aims to assess the power consumption of DL4DED on mobile devices.

5.1 Performance

The main objective of this group of experiments is to compare our "optimized deep learning model" (i.e., with model compression, running on a smartphone)

[7] http://dcapswoz.ict.usc.edu.

and the "original deep learning model" (i.e., the originally created deep learning model without compression and optimization), in terms of accuracy that has been calculated using Tensorflow libraries. This experiment does not depend on the used data since it assesses the accuracy loss related to the use of DL4DED. Therefore, we evaluate both models on the same database (i.e., the DAIC-WOZ dataset). The obtained results demonstrate that the accuracy of DL4DED (0.5) is slightly lower than the accuracy of the original deep learning model (0.52). This means that the applied compression techniques do not significantly alter the analysis results.

5.2 Power Consumption

To assess the power consumption of DL4DED, we used the battery monitoring functionality provided by the Android OS that allows us to measure the power usage of each application in mAh (see Fig. 6).

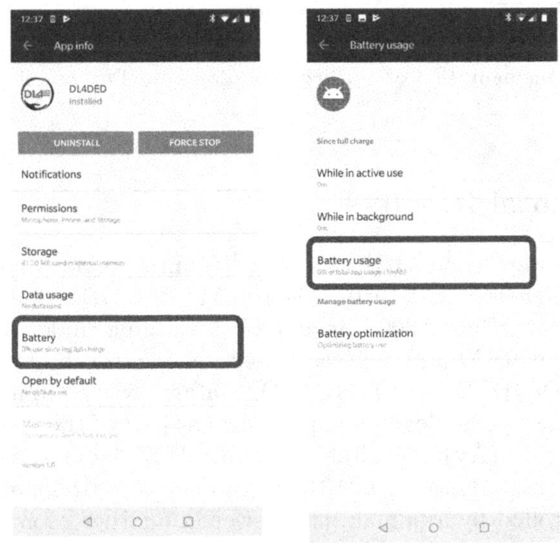

Fig. 6. Power monitoring functionality of Android OS

mAh stands for milli-Ampere-hours and expresses the number of milliampere (i.e., electric charge quantity), the mobile application has used per hour. Actually, the battery capacity is usually expressed in mAh.

We measured the power consumption of (1) DL4DED and (2) a baseline mobile application, while varying the duration of phone calls (from 1 min to 16 min). The baseline mobile application only records phone calls and sends them to an external server that loads and runs our "original deep learning model" (i.e., without compression and optimization) to detect depressed voice. Due to the throughput of our communication links, the baseline approach does not send the whole duration of the phone call. However, DL4DED processes the whole duration of the recorded phone call to allow better classification. The obtained results show that the average power consumption of DL4DED (5 mAh) is higher than the power consumption of the baseline mobile application (1 mAh), for a phone call duration of 4 min. This is quite plausible. Actually, DL4DED records phone calls, saves it to a temporary buffer and loads a deep learning model on the smartphone, to allow real-time prediction of the depressed voice. Loading an optimized deep learning model on a smartphone should logically increase power consumption. Our experiments show that the average difference of power usage (4 mAh) for a phone call of 4 min is reasonably low and therefore acceptable. As shown in Fig. 7, it is clear that the power consumption of DL4DED increases when the duration of the phone call increases. This is related to the fact that we process the whole duration of the phone call in contrast to the baseline approach. This issue will be solved in future work by processing only pertinent parts of the recorded phone call.

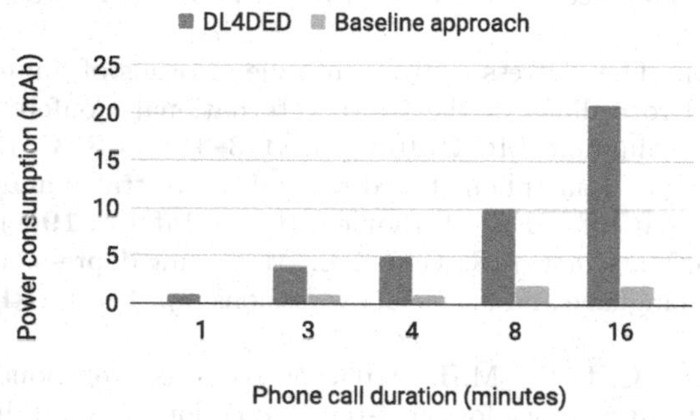

Fig. 7. Power consumption: DL4DED vs. baseline approach

6 Conclusion

We presented a novel mobile deep learning approach for depressive episode detection, called DL4DED. It is a combination of CNN and LSTM networks. The proposed deep learning model was optimized using compression techniques to be loaded onto smartphones. DL4DED records spontaneous phone calls on a daily basis, stores them temporarily locally on a smartphone, and loads our optimized deep learning model to allow real-time detection of depressed voice. DL4DED preserves data privacy since recorded phone calls are not sent to external servers. DL4DED was evaluated on the DAIC-WOZ database. The results demonstrated the efficiency of DL4DED in terms of accuracy and power consumption.

There are several directions for future research. First, we aim to consider the number of recorded phone calls in our study to improve analysis results.

Actually, the absence of phone calls could be seen as a severe sign of depression. Second, we plan to extend our deep learning approach to detect manic episodes in BD. Third, we aim to build a realistic and balanced database to improve the performance of DL4DED. Finally, further optimization methods should be investigated to improve our implementation on mobile devices.

Acknowledgment. This work is supported by the German Academic Exchange Service (DAAD) (Transformation Partnership: Theralytics Project).

References

1. Cornet, V.P., Holden, R.J.: Systematic review of smartphone-based passive sensing for health and wellbeing. J. Biomed. Inform. **77**, 120–132 (2018)
2. Eralp, A., Orhan, Z., Kabil, M.: Psychodroid: a mobile psychological disorder detection application by dynamic question generation and content analysis. Proc. - Soc. Behav. Sci. **159**, 691–696 (2014)
3. Gideon, J., Provost, E.M., McInnis, M.G.: Mood state prediction from speech of varying acoustic quality for individuals with bipolar disorder. In: 2016 IEEE International Conference on Acoustics, Speech and Signal Processing (ICASSP), pp. 2359–2363 (2016)
4. Gratch, J., et al.: The distress analysis interview corpus of human and computer interviews. In: Proceedings of the Ninth International Conference on Language Resources and Evaluation, LREC 2014, pp. 3123–3128. LREC, Reykjavik (2014)
5. Grünerbl, A., et al.: Smartphone-based recognition of states and state changes in bipolar disorder patients. IEEE J. Biomed. Health Inform. **19**(1), 140–148 (2015)
6. Haque, A., Guo, M., Miner, A.S., Fei-Fei, L.: Measuring depression symptom severity from spoken language and 3D facial expressions, pp. 1–7. CoRR abs/1811.08592 (2018)
7. Huang, K.Y., Wu, C.H., Su, M.H.: Attention-based convolutional neural network and long short-term memory for short-term detection of mood disorders based on elicited speech responses. Pattern Recogn. **88**, 668–678 (2019)
8. Huang, Z., Epps, J., Joachim, D.: Speech landmark bigrams for depression detection from naturalistic smartphone speech. In: 2019 IEEE International Conference on Acoustics, Speech and Signal Processing (ICASSP), ICASSP 2019, pp. 5856–5860 (2019)
9. Jiménez-Serrano, S., Tortajada, S., García-Gómez, J.M.: A mobile health application to predict postpartum depression based on machine learning. Telemed. J. E-Health: Off. J. Am. Telemed. Assoc. **21**(7), 567–574 (2015)
10. Khorram, S., Gideon, J., McInnis, M.G., Provost, E.M.: Recognition of depression in bipolar disorder: leveraging cohort and person-specific knowledge. In: INTERSPEECH, pp. 1215–1219 (2016)
11. Maxhuni, A., Muñoz-Meléndez, A., Osmani, V., Perez, H., Mayora, O., Morales, E.F.: Classification of bipolar disorder episodes based on analysis of voice and motor activity of patients. Pervasive Mob. Comput. **31**, 50–66 (2016)
12. Mohammadi, M., Al-Fuqaha, A., Sorour, S., Guizani, M.: Deep learning for IoT big data and streaming analytics: a survey. IEEE Commun. Surv. Tutor. **20**(4), 2923–2960 (2018)

13. Pan, Z., Gui, C., Zhang, J., Zhu, J., Cui, D.: Detecting manic state of bipolar disorder based on support vector machine and gaussian mixture model using spontaneous speech. Psychiatry Invest. **15**(7), 695–700 (2018)
14. Su, M., Wu, C., Huang, K., Yang, T.: Cell-coupled long short-term memory with L-skip fusion mechanism for mood disorder detection through elicited audiovisual features. IEEE Trans. Neural Netw. Learn. Syst. 1–12 (2019)

ICT-Based Health Care Services for People with Spinal Cord Injury: A Pilot Study

Wanho Jang[1], Dongwan Kim[1], Jeonghyun Kim[2], Seungwan Yang[3], Yunjeong Uhm[4], and Jongbae Kim[5](✉)

[1] Department of Occupational Therapy, The Graduate School, Yonsei University, Seoul, South Korea
crewano@gmail.com, dwan3303@naver.com

[2] Usability Center, Enabling Science Technology Research Center, Yonsei University, Seoul, South Korea
otrehab486@gmail.com

[3] Yonsei Enabling Science and Technology Research Center, Seoul, South Korea
shilover0@gmail.com

[4] Department of Ergonomic Therapy, The Graduate School of Health and Environment, Yonsei University, Seoul, South Korea
uyjot@naver.com

[5] Department of Occupational Therapy, College of Health Science, Yonsei University, Seoul, South Korea
jongbae@yonsei.ac.kr

Abstract. People with Spinal cord injuries are having difficulty in health care, and complications cause physical, social and economic losses. In severe cases, complications lead to death and require systematic management. In this study, ICT-based health care service was developed to manage the respiratory function and urinary function of the people with spinal cord injuries and to help adapt to daily living activities and social participation through home visit occupational therapy. A pilot study was conducted with five clients with spinal cord injuries to investigate the effectiveness of the intervention services. As a result, it was confirmed that satisfaction, importance, and difficulty were appropriate. In the future, RCT clinical studies will be needed to diversify intervention services and expand the number of patients.

Keywords: ICT-based health care service · Spinal cord injury · Health · Complication

1 Introduction

People with spinal cord injuries have impaired motor and sensory function and have difficulty in daily activities and social participation [1–3]. They participate in rehabilitation treatment in hospitals, and after discharge, suffer from complications [4]. Pressure ulcers may occur due to sensory impairment, and various complications such as respiratory diseases occur due to respiratory muscle function deterioration [5]. This can lead to difficulties in activity and participation and, in severe cases, to death [6, 7].

J. Pagán et al. (Eds.): ICOST 2019, LNCS 11862, pp. 122–127, 2019.
https://doi.org/10.1007/978-3-030-32785-9_11

Complications, therefore, lead to many losses physically, socially, and economically [8]. In the Republic of Korea, 90.5% of those with spinal cord injuries reported complications. The main complications were cystitis, pressure sores, and pain. Most spinal cord injuries also report that complications are a major detriment to a healthy life [9]. Therefore, it is essential to prevent and systematically manage these complications. Traditionally, complications are managed regularly by a doctor at a hospital. However, people with spinal cord injuries have difficulty in accessing medical services due to the inconvenience of movement due to physical impairment and the economic burden on hospital expenses [10, 11]. Therefore, recently, a service for managing health by using a remote system has been provided [12, 13]. Telerehabilitation using information and communication technology refers to providing comprehensive medical services to patients who have difficulty in moving to medical facilities or who wish to rehabilitate at home [14, 15]. Therefore, this study aims to verify the effectiveness of health management by providing ICT-based health care services for people with spinal cord injuries.

2 Method

2.1 Participants

From June 2019 to July 2019, we visited five families with spinal cord injury in the community and provided an ICT-based complication management system. The characteristics of the subjects were five males, and the mean onset duration was 21.8 years, four thoracic level injury and one lumbar level injury. The level of paralysis is five complete injuries.

2.2 ICT-Based Health Care Services

After using respiratory and urinary devices, and applying home visit occupational therapy, enter the data into a smart device or a desktop computer. If the doctor

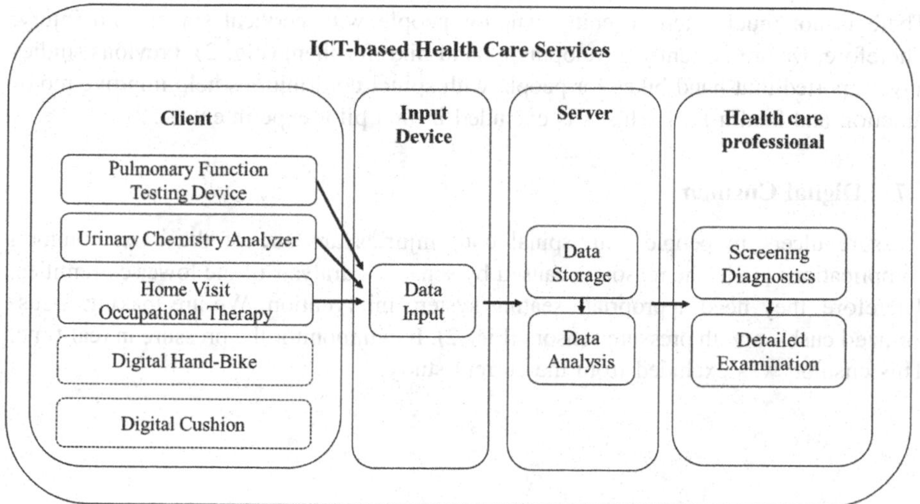

Fig. 1. ICT-based health care services

determines that there is a problem with the patient, he or she will request a hospital visit. Digital hand bikes and digital cushions are currently in development (Fig. 1).

2.3 Pulmonary Function Testing Device

It is a device that can measure FEV1 (Forced Expiratory Volume in one second), PEF (Peak Expiratory Flow), and these are typical indicators of respiratory function [16]. The patient can measure it directly. Occupational therapists can be visited, trained, and assisted with the measurement as needed. This data will be stored on the server. If the doctor or occupational therapist determines that the client have a problem with a pulmonary function, ask to visit the hospital.

2.4 Urinary Chemistry Analyzer

A urine chemistry analyzer can be used to screen a total of 10 components, including glucose, protein, and white blood cells. The client's urine will be examined, or an occupational therapist will be available to help if needed. Data is stored on the server and can be accessed by doctors and occupational therapists. If an outlier is found, the client will be referred for a detailed examination.

2.5 Home Visit Occupational Therapy

The occupational therapist visits the home and performs occupational therapy to the client. Occupational therapy interventions consist of interventions in daily living activities, home environment modifications, self-exercise training, and range of motion exercises, assistive technology services, and community service information. The result data of the evaluation and treatment is input to the smart device, and the data is stored in the server.

2.6 Digital Hand-Bike

There is not much exercise equipment for people with cervical spinal cord injury. Therefore, we are currently developing a hand-bike for them (Fig. 2). Previous studies have reported that hand-bikes for people with spinal cord injuries help improve motor function and health [17]. This was excluded in this pilot experiment.

2.7 Digital Cushion

Pressure ulcers in people with spinal cord injuries are one of the most common complications [18]. The reason is caused by sensory paralysis of the lower extremities. Therefore, they need appropriate seating system intervention. We are making a customized cushion with pressure sensors (Fig. 2). It can monitor the pressure in real-time. This cushion was excluded from the current study.

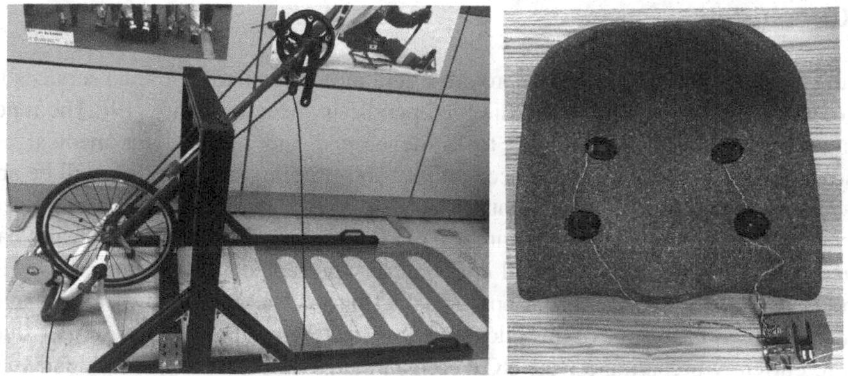

Fig. 2. Digital hand-bike and digital cushion

3 Results

Each intervention was evaluated with satisfaction, necessity, and difficulty, and the scale was 5 points. The results of experiments with five spinal cord injuries are as follows. Satisfaction was high at 4.8 for urinary function test and 4.4 for respiratory intervention and home visit occupational therapy. Necessity was high with interventional function test (4.4), respiratory function intervention (4.2), and home visit occupational therapy (4.2). The difficulty was not severe, all reported as 1.4 (Fig. 3).

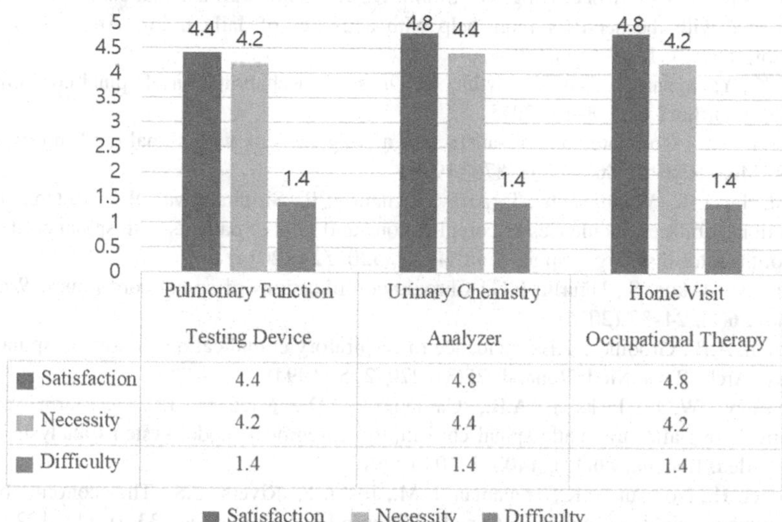

	Pulmonary Function Testing Device	Urinary Chemistry Analyzer	Home Visit Occupational Therapy
Satisfaction	4.4	4.8	4.8
Necessity	4.2	4.4	4.2
Difficulty	1.4	1.4	1.4

Fig. 3. Results

4 Conclusion

World Health Organization (WHO) provides guidance on technologies and services for improving the health of elderly and disabled people in the community [19]. The report recommends that new technologies to be developed and serviced for medical and assistive devices should have good accessibility and usability and that they will be able to use quality and effective services at a low cost. Above all, the emphasis was placed on meeting the needs of local communities and consumers. The ICT-based health care service model for community spinal cord injuries presented in this study shows the appropriate level of satisfaction in both satisfaction and need, as shown in the study results. Based on the results of this pilot study, we recognized the need for further study and are currently preparing for the RCT clinical study. Improvements to products and services will require constant updates. In addition, we are designing exercise equipment to improve body function and developing products to prevent a pressure ulcer. If so, this service could be more helpful in health care and prevention of complications, and it can be expected to be reflected in the health insurance system.

Acknowledgments. The research was supported by a grant of the Korea Health Technology R&D Project through the Korea Health Industry Development Institute (KHIDI), funded by the Ministry of Health & Welfare, Republic of Korea (grant number: HI18C0552).

References

1. Liem, N.R., McColl, M.A., King, W., Smith, K.M.: Aging with a spinal cord injury: factors associated with the need for more help with activities of daily living. Arch. Phys. Med. Rehabil. **85**(10), 1567–1577 (2014)
2. Nas, K., Yazmalar, L., Şah, V., Aydın, A., Öneş, K.: Rehabilitation of spinal cord injuries. World J. Orthop. **6**(1), 8–16 (2015)
3. Dijkers, M.P.: Correlates of life satisfaction among persons with spinal cord injury. Arch. Phys. Med. Rehabil. **80**(8), 867–876 (1999)
4. Amatachaya, S., Wannapakhe, J., Arrayawichanon, P., Siritarathiwat, W., Wattanapun, P.: Functional abilities, incidences of complications and falls of patients with spinal cord injury 6 months after discharge. Spinal Cord **49**(4), 520–524 (2011)
5. Sezer, N., Akkuş, S., Uğurlu, F.G.: Chronic complications of spinal cord injury. World J. Orthop. **6**(1), 24–33 (2015)
6. Jackson, A.B., Groomes, T.E.: Incidence of respiratory complications following spinal cord injury. Arch. Phys. Med. Rehabil. **75**(3), 270–275 (1994)
7. McKinley, W.O., Jackson, A.B., Cardenas, D.D., Michael, J.: Long-term medical complications after traumatic spinal cord injury: a regional model systems analysis. Arch. Phys. Med. Rehabil. **80**(11), 1402–1410 (1999)
8. Krueger, H., Noonan, V.K., Trenaman, L.M., Joshi, P., Rivers, C.S.: The economic burden of traumatic spinal cord injury in Canada. Chronic Dis. Injuries Can. **33**(3), 113–122 (2013)
9. Korea Spinal Cord Injury Association. http://www.kscia.org/board/list/menu03_05?init
10. Hossain, M.S., et al.: A pilot randomised trial of community-based care following discharge from hospital with a recent spinal cord injury in Bangladesh. Clin. Rehabil. **31**(6), 781–789 (2017)

11. White, B.A., et al.: The economic burden of urinary tract infection and pressure ulceration in acute traumatic spinal cord injury admissions: evidence for comparative economics and decision analytics from a matched case-control study. J. Neurotrauma **34**(20), 2892–2900 (2017)
12. Sechrist, S., Lavoie, S., Khong, C.M., Dirlikov, B., Shem, K.: Telemedicine using an iPad in the spinal cord injury population: a utility and patient satisfaction study. Spinal Cord Ser. Cases **4**(1), 71 (2018)
13. Martinez, R.N., et al.: Sociotechnical perspective on implementing clinical video telehealth for veterans with spinal cord injuries and disorders. Telemed. e-Health **23**(7), 567–576 (2017)
14. Wellbeloved-Stone, C.A., Weppner, J.L., Valdez, R.S.: A systematic review of telerehabilitation and mHealth interventions for spinal cord injury. Curr. Phys. Med. Rehabil. Rep. **4**(4), 295–311 (2016)
15. Phillips, V.L., Vesmarovich, S., Hauber, R., Wiggers, E., Egner, A.: Telehealth: reaching out to newly injured spinal cord patients. Public Health Rep. **116**, 94–102 (2016)
16. Tiftik, T., et al.: Does locomotor training improve pulmonary function in patients with spinal cord injury? Spinal Cord **53**(6), 467–470 (2015)
17. Kim, D.I., Lee, H., Lee, B.S., Kim, J., Jeon, J.Y.: Effects of a 6-week indoor hand-bike exercise program on health and fitness levels in people with spinal cord injury: a randomized controlled trial study. Arch. Phys. Med. Rehabil. **96**(11), 2033–2040 (2015)
18. Byrne, D.W., Salzberg, C.A.: Major risk factors for pressure ulcers in the spinal cord disabled: a literature review. Spinal Cord **34**(5), 255–263 (1996)
19. WHO: Consultation on Advancing Technological Innovation for Older Persons in Asia. https://extranet.who.int/kobe_centre/sites/default/files/summary_report_innovation_feb2013.pdf

Smart Environment Technology

An Interconnected Smart Technology System for Individuals with Mental Illness Living in the Community and Transitional Hospital Apartments

Cheryl Forchuk[1,2(✉)], Jonathan Serrato[1], Abraham Rudnick[3], Deborah Corring[2], Rupinder Mann[1], and Barbara Frampton[4]

[1] Lawson Health Research Institute, London, ON, Canada
cforchuk@uwo.ca
[2] Western University, London, ON, Canada
[3] Dalhousie University, Halifax, NS, Canada
[4] CONNECT for Mental Health, London, ON, Canada

Abstract. The overall objective of this research was to develop and test the use of smart technology in delivering safe, effective mental health services before expanding into community homes. A system was created that linked multiple screen devices such as smartphones and tablets and health monitoring devices with a central secure database for data to be funneled and stored for monitoring and tracking. In order to assess the feasibility of this technological innovation, the research team installed equipment in two prototype apartments at two inpatient psychiatric hospitals and in up to eight community homes operated by the Canadian Mental Health Association and London Middlesex Community Housing. The results indicate that most participants found the technology acceptable, and that the system was successfully able to export data securely.

Keywords: Smart technology · Mental illness · Health management · Housing · Data management

1 Introduction

In Canada, the Mental Health Commission of Canada estimates that 20% of the population will experience a mental illness during their lifetime while the remaining 80% will be affected by the mental illness of others [1]. Mood and psychotic disorders have also been linked with polydipsia [2] and cardiovascular disease [3]. It is therefore important for comorbidities to be observed in order to understand the complete health status of the individual. This is of particular importance given the patient-specific issues in Canada such as travel-related barrier for accessing community mental health care as well as long wait-times, lack of information, and stigma [4]. Furthermore, previous research has revealed increased mortality rates among individuals with severe mental illness due to a lack of self-management for acute and chronic illnesses [5]. Impairment in activities of daily living, function (e.g. inability to maintain a healthy diet, lifestyle, etc.) and cognition can result in missed medications, appointments, or self-care activities. Individuals

J. Pagán et al. (Eds.): ICOST 2019, LNCS 11862, pp. 131–142, 2019.
https://doi.org/10.1007/978-3-030-32785-9_12

with these types of impairments may not realize their self-care is declining therefore causing greater declines in mental and physical health. Symptom tracking and monitoring, enhanced awareness of pre-symptoms, and greater access to informational resources through smart technology may also aid patient well-being and beneficence [6].

In previous studies conducted by this research team, correlations between mental health and housing have been demonstrated but housing alone is not enough to promote stabilization [7]. While mental illness is often conceptualized as a problem between the individual and their environment, mental health care is almost entirely focused on "fixing" the individual rather than the environment they are in. To that end, previous research has demonstrated promising findings from the implementation of mobile and web-based technologies in a population of individuals experiencing mood or psychotic disorders [8–11]. Forchuk et al. revealed a 48.6% reduction in hospitalizations and 57% fewer outpatient visits after 18 months using mobile phones for prompts and reminders along with access to a personal health record [12]. This current project therefore reflects a logical extension of these studies by developing a "high-dose" smart technology intervention for those with severe mental illnesses; first by starting in hospital prototype apartments before extending further into community homes. Two reviews have revealed that there is a lack of evaluation of smart technology within a health care context [13, 14]. One of which, a Cochrane review, revealed no health-related smart technology studies that met the Cochrane Handbook criteria for inclusion and none of the identified studies evaluated effectiveness [14].

The groundwork of this project, laid by Corring, Campbell and Rudnick [8], aims to provide supportive systems within an individual's environment, be it within one's home or a hospital transitional apartment to promote community integration, to facilitate chronic illness management, and support independence. Furthermore, this project will attempt to establish the use of smart technology in assisting individuals with mental illness and cognitive impairment in a hospital apartment setting first before progressing and expanding into community homes. The objective of these phases was to develop and test smart technology in delivering safe, effective mental health services. As such, we hypothesize that this smart technology intervention will result in:

1. An increase in participants' level of community integration.
2. An increase in participants' housing stability.
3. A decrease in excessive health and social service utilisation.
4. An improvement in the participants' overall health.

At present, the hospital prototype phase has been ongoing for approximately 7 months. The community phase has seen equipment installed in five homes and is continuing to enroll participants.

2 Materials and Methods

Design

This quasi-experimental project is separated into two phases. The hospital prototype phase is employing a within-group, mixed-methods, descriptive pilot design in order to ascertain the feasibility of the smart technology in a hospital setting as well as testing the system as a whole. Data was collected upon discharge from the hospital apartment and at 6-month follow-up.

As the project moves from the hospital prototype phase, the community phase is adopting a more longitudinal approach in testing the project's hypotheses. This involves a within-group, mixed-methods, repeated-measures design. Data is being collected over three assessments conducted at baseline, 6-month and 12-month follow-ups. Comparisons regarding levels of community integration, health, housing stability and service usage throughout the intervention will be observed. Ethical approval was obtained through Western University's Research Ethics Board and Lawson Health Research Institute.

Description of the Settings

Health Care Providers (HCPs) at two inpatient psychiatric facilities and HCPs in community homes coordinated with the research staff to set up various smart technologies in the apartments for individuals with mental illness. The prototype apartments within the psychiatric facilities are available to individuals who were being discharged into the community in order to provide a transitional experience. The community homes are operated by the Canadian Mental Health Association (CMHA) and London Middlesex Community Housing (LMCH). These include group homes, family homes and individual apartments with staff members providing in-home care and support on a need-to-need basis.

The System

This project has sought to incorporate real-time integration of data in order to provide HCPs with notifications and monitoring capabilities. The system links multiple smart technology devices and funnels the data into one database. This system has been comprised of two software innovations; the Lawson Integrated Database (LIDB) and the Collaborative Health Record (CHR).

The LIDB is an information management platform that collates and manages client health information behind the St. Joseph's Health Care hospital firewall. The LIDB keeps health data segregated in its own database schema but is capable of matching patient data across HCPs. With funds from the Canada Health Infoway, the research team was able to ensure the security of the LIDB through a third-party Privacy Impact Analysis and Threat Risk Assessment. Encrypted incremental data backups are performed on a nightly basis and full backups performed weekly with both stored securely off-site. The LIDB also utilizes virtual servers to move from one server to another to enable continuous operations with no impact to users. Weekly meetings with software engineers and monthly meetings with the hospital I.T. and Privacy departments have been held since the commencement of the project to address any data security concerns and ensure the integrity of the system. HCPs are able to log-in to the LIDB to view data from the health monitoring devices and the CHR, and also to set the reminders to be transmitted to the screen devices.

The CHR allows for both synchronous and asynchronous communication between patients and HCPs to deliver team-based, longitudinal health care. The CHR operates on the screen devices offered to the participants. The specific functions of the CHR include:

1. Access to personal health information and self-assessments to enhance early identification of concerns related to symptoms.
2. A comprehensive patient-record system that provides workflows for a diverse group of HCPs.
3. Prompts and reminders that can support care planning for symptoms and comorbidities (e.g. medication reminders and activity prompts).
4. Secure communication between HCPs and participants including videoconferencing and messaging.

This functionality aids the complex care of people with severe mental illnesses by creating an enhanced secure connection between them and their circle of care. This helps overcome barriers to care such as mobility, transportation, or lack of resources readily available, and reduces the number of in-person appointments necessary. Self-assessments (known in the software as "Qnaires©") are also completed within the CHR by the participant which allows the HCP and care team to monitor changes and potential crises. These self-assessments can include standardised tools used such as Patient Health Questionnaire (PHQ-9) and fully customisable tools created by the HCP within the CHR. The data from these assessments are then backed up to the participant's profile in the LIDB. In the event of a crisis (e.g. a participant indicates suicidal ideation on a Qnaire), an alert is sent to the care team so that they can act accordingly.

Equipment

Participants residing in the hospital prototype apartments can select a variety of screen devices including smartphones, tablets, and touch-screen monitors. These devices provide prompts and reminders generated by the LIDB to assist participants with cognitive deficits and facilitate self-care. The touch-screen monitors are developed in-house by the research team's programmer. The monitor is programmed so that prompts and reminders on the screen can be "acknowledged" by the user by pushing the "Got It" button. This sends an automated message back to the HCP who set the reminder to inform them the reminder was received. Furthermore, a "Help" button was added after initial discussions with HCPs which sends a message to the participant's care team requesting them to provide support. This exhaustive approach of ensuring all devices were able to connect to each other and allowed for ease of data exporting to the LIDB was completed after weekly meetings and thorough testing.

In addition to the screen devices, the participants are offered a choice of adjunct health monitoring devices. In the hospital prototype phase, these include weigh scales, blood pressure monitors, glucometers, and a wearable activity tracker (smartwatch). These devices account for the comorbidities that may be present and will support chronic illness management. Data from these devices is pushed to the LIDB via encrypted authentication keys and SSL connectivity. The weigh scale exports data via WiFi whereas the glucometer, weigh scale and activity tracker utilize Bluetooth connectivity.

The screen devices on offer for individuals residing in the community homes differ slightly. Participants in this phase are offered smartphones and touch-screen monitors only. This was done to further refine the intervention and allow for an additional health adjunct health monitoring device to be offered.

For participants in the community homes, their choice of health monitoring equipment also differs slightly with an automated medication dispenser being made available for selection but the blood pressure monitor and glucometer are not. The medication dispenser was not available for the hospital prototype phase due to medication protocols within the hospital. This addition of a medication dispenser represents the tailoring and refinement of the intervention for individuals living in the community. This was implemented to help participants with self-medication (if appropriate) and save time by reducing the need for participants and/or HCPs to collect medications from the pharmacy.

In both phases, participants are given the choice of devices they can use and are able to refuse any device with which they were not comfortable with. Participants recruited into the study are also allowed to refuse all devices but are still expected to complete a full semi-structured interview in order to acquire their opinions and attitudes as to why.

Recruitment

For all participants in both phases, the research team first recruited HCPs who then referred participants to the research team. For the hospital prototype phase of the project, the study is recruiting up to 20 participants and for the community phase, we are recruiting up to 13 participants. Participants are excluded from the study if they do not reside in the hospital prototype apartment for a minimum of one week.

Additional inclusion criteria for participants to participate in the community phase of the study include:

1. Must be on a caseload of a participating HCP.
2. Able to understand English to the degree necessary to participate.
3. Living in, eligible for, and wanting, housing provided by the CMHA housing program or LMCH.
4. Diagnosed with a psychotic or major mood disorder.
5. Identified by the clinical team to require prompting/reminding to complete activities of daily living and self- assessments as indicated by a score between 70 and 20 on the Social and Occupational Functioning Assessment Scale [15].
6. Must be between the ages of 18–85 years old and able to provide informed consent.

For both phases, this represents an opportunity sample as enrollment entirely depended on whether the participant is currently residing in the hospital or in the community. All participants have provided capable informed consent.

Procedure

The initial hospital prototype phase includes two hospital apartments located in two psychiatric inpatient facilities. Upon consenting to participate in the study, selected equipment was verified and approved by their HCP. The equipment was then delivered to the participant by the research coordinator and the research team's programmer who then sets up the devices and provides training to the participant. Training for usage of the CHR is provided by the research coordinator with the HCP in a one-to-one session. The participant completes their first interview upon discharge from the hospital prototype apartment. The participants complete a second interview at 6 months post-discharge.

The community phase is an expansion of the hospital prototype phase but participants are not crossed over, meaning that those who are discharged from the hospital prototype apartments do not enter the community phase. Upon enrollment into the study, participants for this phase of the project complete a baseline interview consisting of questionnaires pertaining to demographic data, health, housing, community integration and service utilization. Follow-up interviews are then conducted at 6 months and 12 months.

Focus groups are being provided to HCPs for both phases at the study's end allowing them to provide their observations and thoughts on the use of smart technology for the participants. A focus group at the study's end for participants will only be made available for participants in the community phase.

Instruments

In both phases of the study, the participants complete semi-structured interviews that include the following assessment tools: Community Integration Questionnaire - Revised (CIQ-R), Short-Form 36, EQ5D, the Housing History survey, the Health, Social and Justice Service Utilization (HSJSU) questionnaire, and the Perception of Smart Technology Questionnaire, a researcher-developed questionnaire that inquired about participants' attitudes and opinions of the equipment provided to them. Demographic data is also collected during these interviews.

Health data from the health monitoring devices include blood pressure, weight, blood glucose levels and heart rate. This data is backed up to the LIDB and made available to their HCPs for monitoring and tracking. Apps for these devices are preloaded onto the smartphones and tablets so that participants can also monitor their data. Participants could use the devices as and when they wished, or if directed by their HCP.

Data Analysis

Data is entered and stored on REDCap, a secure web-based database application by a research assistant. For quantitative analysis, the research team uses SPSS Statistics Software to generate descriptive statistics. It should be noted that data from the CHR's Qnaires have not, and will not, be analysed. The primary outcome of interest is the total score from the CIQ-R. Further quantitative analyses will investigate the housing history of the participant to assess housing stability, the health status of the participant, and experience with health, social and justice services to evaluate service usage.

Individual interviews are held with all participants enrolled in the study. Focus groups, as described by Krueger [16], are held with HCPs in both phases as well as participants in the community phase. Research assistants will conduct qualitative analyses by applying a thematic grouping of responses by identifying recurrent themes and opinions expressed by the participants and HCPs. Specifically, an ethnographic method of analysis will be used to observe the broader social and cultural contexts surrounding individual experiences as well as the impact on HCPs and how the intervention influenced their practice [17].

A standardised evaluation framework facilitated systematic effectiveness, economic, ethical and policy analysis of outcomes [18].

Effectiveness analyses will utilise the mixed-methods approach of this study by analysing the quantitative data from the instruments provided during the individual interviews to assess for any changes or improvements to the participants' health, service utilization and community integration. Common qualitative items from the focus groups will also assess the usage of the technologies and suggestions for improvement. By using a mixed methods approach, the research team is able to ascertain the participants' experiences with the technology as well as the effects on health, housing stability, and community integration.

The economic analyses will focus on the value for money aspect of the intervention as well as the costs and benefits. Specifically, the health costs of the intervention compared to usual care as well as the costs of hospitalizations, emergency room visits, outpatient visits and home care service.

Quantitative and qualitative findings related to views of fairness, benefits and social inclusion will be compared to ethical standards derived from welfare theory and accepted ethical principles of care providers (i.e. autonomy, beneficence and respect) as part of the ethical analyses.

Finally, policy analyses will address the implications that arise from the issues identified in the interviews such as access to and utilization of services, housing history, impact of severity of illness, and need for personal resources.

3 Results

Data collection and enrollment into the study is currently still ongoing. However, of all the participants approached so far, none have rejected to participate in the study and none have participated in the study without any equipment. All participants so far have met the study with great enthusiasm and eagerness. In terms of acceptability of the devices offered, the participants in the study so far have been positive about having the smart technologies in their home. When asked the question "How do you feel about having these smart technologies in your home/hospital?" on the Perception of Smart Technology questionnaire, preliminary analyses have revealed an average of 6.5 out of 7 demonstrating favorable attitudes towards having the technology.

Participants who have completed their interviews did not indicate any changes to their health after using the smart technologies they had selected. However, the ability to track health changes was seen as a benefit of the health monitoring devices. Number of steps measured by the activity tracker and weight was seen as useful. Furthermore, one participant highlighted that these devices aided them in making healthier choices by checking their weight two to three times per week and reaching their goals for walking. This could therefore reflect an uptake in healthier lifestyle choices as the devices provide an extra level of incentive and accountability. Although screen devices could not be used in the prototype apartment based in a forensic setting, one participant noted they would like to have a screen device in order to use apps for nutrition and fitness.

One of the concerns that arose from an interview with one participant was the issue of using small screens for those with visual impairments. Although the tablet used was 10.1 in. in size, the text on the screen was still too small to accommodate visual difficulties, even when the font size had been increased. The touch-screen monitor however was able to remedy this as the screen size was double that of the tablet and therefore the participant was able to clearly see their prompts and reminders. One suggestion was to use sounds instead of text thereby reducing the need to read prompts and reminders.

Future analyses will be able to provide more in-depth data and knowledge pertaining to changes in community integration, health and housing stability over the course of the study and after discharge from the hospital prototype apartments. We will also be able to perform more detailed analyses of the effects of the smart technology on the participants and to what degree they had an impact on their lives.

Part of this project was also to observe whether a smart technology system would be feasible and whether it could be used in a mental health care environment. This project has demonstrated that this system has been capable of funnelling various forms of data from a number of different sources. Key to mental health care treatment and recovery planning is the ability to tailor the intervention specifically to the participant. This was achieved as participants could pick and choose the devices specific to their care plans with no change or drop in performance from the system.

4 Discussion

Developing a reliable and secure system is a crucial step before community adoption of the intervention and must ensure the privacy of users and their data. This initial testing performed in the hospital prototype apartments allowed for further developments and refinements before going live in community-based environments. The intervention has undergone a number of enhancements from the time of its conception, mostly as a result of the fast-moving pace of technology but also the upgrades and additions to existing software and capabilities that meet the needs of the HCPs and participants.

To the researchers' knowledge, there are no other community-integrated, systems-level research studies underway that leverages novel state-of-the-art smart technology systems in community homes or in transitional hospital apartments. This project will advance the current knowledge of smart homes for individuals with severe mental illness by combining innovative health platforms (LIDB and CHR) and push smart technology to the forefront of mental health care within the home. With the infrastructure now in place, our team of researchers, health technology experts and software programmers are now equipped to support individuals with mental illness living in the community. Furthermore, this research project will have universal design potential across a range of mental illnesses for future research studies and/or interventions where optimal facilitation of healthy lifestyles may require smart technology support.

In terms of usage, the participants expressed they were generally satisfied with their usage of the devices provided to them. It was noted that the smartphone and tablet may be too small for individuals with visual impairments but the touch-screen monitor was able to provide suitable coverage. Training on using the devices was mostly straightforward as the activity tracker simply required the user to wear the device on their wrist and the weigh scale only required the user to stand on it. Similarly, the blood pressure monitor was easy to use, with the user strapping the cuff to their wrist then pushing one button located on the monitor attached to the cuff.

It has been reported so far that the health monitoring devices also helped to encourage weight and steps monitoring, which may be indicative of added motivation for the participants to maintain healthy lifestyles. The devices therefore may have acted as an accountability tool, providing the participants with their measurements and providing valuable feedback through enabling them to track their health. Previous studies have linked frequent observation to weight loss using personal digital assistants (PDAs) and daily feedback messages [19]. Research has also revealed that level of depression has been found to be a prognostic indicator for chronic illness such as coronary heart disease [20] and individuals with schizophrenia or depression have also demonstrated higher rates of diabetes and cardiac disease compared to the general population [3]. Therefore the use of health monitoring devices for individuals with mental illness cannot be understated.

A key benefit of this intervention would be the impacts on housing and economics. This project has allowed for the testing of commercial devices that can be easily purchased in the community or online and installed in community homes as opposed to expensive clinical equipment. This could inform housing policy decision-makers to consider the use of smart technologies for future housing development planning and for individuals with severe mental illnesses returning to the community. It is realistic to consider that future clinicians may prescribe smart devices and personalised health care technologies to support treatment or recovery. As the cost of mental care across Canada has been estimated to cost billions of dollars, this intervention may propose a more cost-effective alternative. At present, the cost of fitting an apartment with the devices plus CHR licensing and setup, and phone plan bills is less than $20,000 per year. St. Joseph's Hospital in London, ON, has estimated the mental health per diem cost as $454 per day ($165,710 per year) with a total of 10,699 patient days per year; which amounts to a net cost of $4,857,346 per year with the most prolonged stays being those with difficulty finding housing due to functional issues. Further costs can be saved by reducing travelling and improving efficiency in managing caseloads through greater monitoring and time-saving communication for HCPs [21].

Challenges

Many smart devices do not meet the security or privacy requirements of such a system or the compatibility requirements to connect with the other selected smart devices. For example, six different activity trackers were reviewed before one met the security and compatibility criteria. Finding a Cloud where it's Application Programming Interface (API) would grant the research team easy access to the data to be exported to the LIDB also proved to be challenging.

A challenge for this project was encouraging HCPs to adopt this technological approach. Although a number of HCPs embraced the technology and efficiency of the software available, others were skeptical. Due to the personal nature of the data being collected, some were concerned about the participants' privacy. However, concerns were allayed during the training sessions with HCPs as monthly meetings had been held between the hospital's IT and Privacy departments and the research team prior to the study's commencement. Some HCPs in the forensic setting felt more comfortable seeing the participant in person due to the close proximity between the prototype apartment and the HCP's office instead of viewing the CHR or the health data exported to the LIDB.

As one of the inpatient psychiatric facilities was a forensic mental health institution, a number of security protocols needed to be addressed. Internet usage specifically was prohibited due to the nature of the institution and the ease of access for harmful, dangerous or offensive materials on the internet. This therefore included the prohibition of screen devices that can connect to the internet. Further, devices with the ability to take photos or videos were also prohibited. The touch-screen monitor was acceptable as it could not be used for web-browsing and was programmed only to receive reminders as well as send acknowledgements back to the LIDB. However, this meant that the functions of a smartphone or tablet were not able to be replicated. The health monitoring devices were allowed as these did not allow for internet web-browsing.

5 Conclusions

Based on the preliminary findings of the current studies, the use of smart technology offers an alternative to traditional mental health care plans by allowing for enhanced connectivity and greater access to resources. The system described in this article is an efficient and reliable form of data management that can allow for tracking and monitoring of physical and mental health data. This intervention could enable mental health care strategies and inform policy decision-makers to adopt more smart technologies into care and treatment plans for individuals with severe mental illness. In addition, if implemented it can be cost-effective for individuals with mental illness living in the community and the lack of access to non-emergency health care services, the latter of which leads to an increase in emergency department usage and therefore funding. In providing a quality-assured smart technology system, individuals experiencing severe mental illness can gain access to mental health services that they may not have been able to access previously. Critical to this was the initial prototype apartment testing to ensure the intervention met the standards of those living in the community and their care teams. Full acceptability of smart technology within mental health care could support quality of care and improve integration for individuals living in the community. This can happen by combining mental health care legislation with public awareness to allay fears of personally identifiable data falling outside of the individual's circle of care, and assuring patients/tenants/HCPs that third parties will not have access to their information as the system is capable of managing electronic medical records.

Acknowledgments. We would like to acknowledge St. Joseph's Health Care, the Canadian Mental Health Association and London Middlesex Community Housing for facilitating the research environment. We would like to thank the participants and HCPs for their voluntary participation. Also, we appreciate the commitment of the research assistants for data collection and auditing to make sure the quality of research is assured. Finally, we would also like to acknowledge the two granting agencies - Canadian Mortgage & Housing Corporation, and Canadian Institutes for Health Research - for making the funding available.

Conflicts of Interest. The authors declare no conflict of interest.

References

1. Mental Health Commission of Canada: Making the Case for Investing in Mental Health in Canada. Mental Health Commission of Canada, Ottawa (2013)
2. Poirier, S., et al.: Schizophrenia patients with polydipsia and water intoxication are characterized by greater severity of psychotic illness and a more frequent history of alcohol abuse. Schizophr. Res. **118**, 285–291 (2010)
3. De Hert, M., et al.: Physical illness in patients with severe mental disorders. I. Prevalence, impact of medications and disparities in health care. World Psychiatry **10**, 52–77 (2011)
4. Dyck, K.G., Hardy, C.: Enhancing access to psychologically informed mental health services in rural and northern communities. Can. Psychol. **54**, 30–37 (2013)
5. Walker, E.R., McGee, R.E., Druss, B.G.: Mortality in mental disorders and global disease burden implications: a systematic review and meta-analysis. JAMA Psychiatry **72**, 334–341 (2015)
6. Ho, A., Quick, O.: Leaving patients to their own devices? Smart technology, safety, and therapeutic relationships. BMC Med. Ethics **19**, 18 (2018)
7. Forchuk, C., Csiernik, R., Jensen, E. (eds.): Homelessness, Housing and Mental Health. Canadian Scholars' Press, Toronto (2011)
8. Corring, D., Campbell, R., Rudnick, A.: A smart apartment for psychiatric inpatients. Psychiatr. Serv. **63**, 508 (2012)
9. Corring, D., Meier, A., Rudnick, A., Forchuk, C.: Using mobile technology to promote independence: an innovation in psychiatric rehabilitation – a feasibility study. Res. Insights **12**, 2–6 (2015)
10. Forchuk, C., et al.: TELEPROM-G: a study evaluating access and care delivery of telehealth services among community-based seniors. In: Future Technologies Conference: Proceedings of Future Technologies Conference, pp. 1346–1348. IEEE, San Francisco (2016)
11. Forchuk, C., et al.: Mental health engagement network (MHEN). Int. J. Adv. Life Sci. **5**, 1–10 (2013)
12. Forchuk, C., et al.: Mental health engagement network: an analysis of outcomes following a mobile and web-based intervention. J. Technol. Soc. **11**, 1–10 (2015)
13. Garafalo, J., Nathan-Roberts, D.: Assessment of the impacts from the addition of novel assistive technologies in mental health care. In: Proceedings of the Human Factors and Ergonomics Society 2016 Annual Meeting, vol. 60, pp. 1245–1248. Sage, Washington DC (2016)
14. Martin, S., Kelly, G., Kernohan, W.G., McCreight, B., Nugent, C.: Smart home technologies for health and social care support. Cochrane Database Syst. Rev. **4** (2008)
15. Goldman, H.H., Skodol, A.E., Lave, T.R.: Revising axis V for DSM-IV: a review of measures of social functioning. Am. J. Psychiatry **149**, 1148–1156 (1992)
16. Krueger, R.A.: Focus Groups: A Practical Guide for Applied Research. Sage Publications, Thousand Oak (1994)
17. Leininger, M.M.: Ethnography and Ethnonursing: models and modes of qualitative analysis. In: Leininger, M.M. (ed.) Qualitative Research Methods in Nursing, pp. 33–72. Grune & Stratton, Orlando (1985)
18. Forchuk, C., Rudnick, A., MacIntosh, J., Bukair, F., Hoch, J.S.: Evaluation framework for smart technology mental health interventions. In: Chang, C., Chiari, L., Cao, Y., Jin, H., Mokhtari, M., Aloulou, H. (eds.) ICOST 2016. LNCS, vol. 9677, pp. 203–210. Springer, Cham (2016). https://doi.org/10.1007/978-3-319-39601-9_18
19. Turk, M.W., et al.: Self-monitoring as a mediator of weight loss in the SMART randomized clinical trial. Int. J. Behav. Med. **20**, 556–561 (2013)

20. Nicholson, A., Kuper, H., Hemingway, H.: Depression as an aetiologic and prognostic factor in coronary heart disease: a meta-analysis of 6362 events among 146,358 participants in 54 observational studies. Eur. Heart J. **27**, 2763–2774 (2006)
21. Wurster, A.E., Archer, N.: Smart home technology and the needs of the aging population in Southern Ontario. Working Paper No. 59. McMaster eBusiness Research Centre (2016)

Transfer Learning for Urban Landscape Clustering and Correlation with Health Indexes

Riccardo Bellazzi[1(✉)], Alessandro Aldo Caldarone[1], Daniele Pala[1], Marica Franzini[2], Alberto Malovini[3], Cristiana Larizza[1], and Vittorio Casella[2]

[1] Department of Electrical, Computer and Biomedical Engineering, via Ferrata 5, 27100 Pavia, Italy
{riccardo.bellazzi, cristiana.larizza}@unipv.it, {alessandroaldo.caldarone01, daniele.pala02}@universitadipavia.it

[2] Department of Civil Engineering and Architecture, via Ferrata 3, 27100 Pavia, Italy
{marica.franzini, vittorio.casella}@unipv.it

[3] IRCCS ICS Maugeri, via S. Maugeri 2, 27100 Pavia, Italy
alberto.malovini@icsmaugeri.it

Abstract. Within the EU-funded Pulse project, we are implementing a data analytic platform designed to provide public health decision makers with advanced approaches to jointly analyze maps and geospatial information with health care data and air pollution measurements. In this paper we describe a component of such platform, designed to couple deep learning analysis of geospatial images of cities and some healthcare and behavioral indexes collected by the 500 cities US project, showing that, in New York City, urban landscape significantly correlates with the access to healthcare services.

Keywords: Transfer learning · Deep learning · Urban landscape · Health indexes

1 Introduction

Recent advances in machine learning and deep learning enable the design and implementation of novel data analysis pipelines that allow fusing heterogeneous data sources to extract novel insights and predictive patterns. These approaches seem particularly suitable to help increasing our insights in the relationships between the urban landscape of cities and the behavior of their residents, with particular focus on well-being and healthcare indexes. In this context, it can be of interest of health care planners and city decision-makers to have instruments able to find clusters of city areas that share similar urban structures and to analyze some behavioral indexes of their residents, in particular to see potential correlations and to plan similar interventions in the different clusters, even if such clusters contain areas that are geographically far. We have applied such approach in the context of the PULSE (Participatory Urban Living

J. Pagán et al. (Eds.): ICOST 2019, LNCS 11862, pp. 143–153, 2019.
https://doi.org/10.1007/978-3-030-32785-9_13

for Sustainable Environment) EU-project[1]. PULSE aims at developing a set of models and technologies to predict and manage public health problems in cities and promote health. It follows a participatory approach where citizen provide data through personal devices that are integrated with information from heterogeneous sources: open city data, health systems, urban sensors and satellites. The project deals with various issues concerning air quality, lifestyle and personal behavior and it aims to investigate the correlations between the exposure to atmospheric pollutants, the citizen habits and the health of the citizen themselves, focusing on asthma and type 2 diabetes. PULSE is being implemented in 5 major cities all over the world. Within PULSE, we are implementing a data analytic platform that will provide public health decision makers with advanced approaches to jointly analyze maps and geospatial information with health care data and air pollution measurements.

In this paper we will describe the results obtained with a prototypical component of such platform, designed to couple deep learning analysis of geospatial images of cities and some healthcare and behavioral indexes, showing that in New York City urban landscape significantly correlates with the access to healthcare services.

2 Deep Learning and Transfer Learning Models

Deep neural models provide flexible instruments to perform non-linear approximation of a variety of multivariate functions and to extract latent variables from a data set. In a nutshell, deep neural models are neural networks with many layers, able to map non-linear functions with a number of parameters that is typically lower than their equivalent models with one layer only. Such models are particularly attractive since they can be used to perform clustering, regression and classification starting from data sets made of images, texts, time series.

In dependence of the nature of the input data set, different architectures can be exploited, ranging from the combination of many Convolutional layers in the case of images to the use of Long-term/Short-term networks in the case of time series and speech/text data.

Recently, an increasing number of papers are using deep learning to examine the relationships between the urban landscape and some environmental or citizens' behavioral data [1–3].

One of the main limits of deep learning models is related to the need of very large data sets in order to be able to gain advantage of their capability of encoding even the finest details that can be important to map input data, without getting trapped into noise and poor parameters estimates.

Rather interestingly, in order to deal with this problem, it is possible to resort to an increasing set of pre-trained deep learning models that can be used for the task of transfer learning [4], i.e. models that are able to represent the input space into a set of latent variables on the basis of a mapping mechanism, usually a deep neural network, learned on a large (external) data set, so that the relationships between such latent

[1] "http://www.project-pulse.eu".

variables and the outcomes can be later learned on a specific and smaller data set. A well-known example is Inception-v3, a convolutional neural network trained on more than a million images from the ImageNet database (http://www.image-net.org). The network has 48 layers and can classify images into one thousand object categories, including trees and many animals. Another interesting example is represented by the Painters [5] networks, developed to automatically classify Paintings of famous artists. In principle, any of those methods can be used following the transfer learning paradigm to represent images coming from urban landscape of New York City.

3 Data and Methods

Our analysis is based on two data sources: NYC high resolution images and healthcare data coming from the 500 cities project [6]. NYC images have been collected by the "The National Agriculture Imagery Program" (NAIP) that acquires aerial imagery during the agricultural growing seasons in the continental United States. In particular, we have downloaded an image having an original resolution of 0.5 m and have downsampled it to 2 m which allows to have a fine-grained representation of the aerial urban landscape (see Fig. 1).

As it will be explained in the following, the reason for the downsampling is that the big image has been subdivided into tiles and the neural network adopted can accept images having maximum size of 299 pixel; we had to tune the ground resolution in order to have meaningful tiles, embracing a sufficiently-sized area.

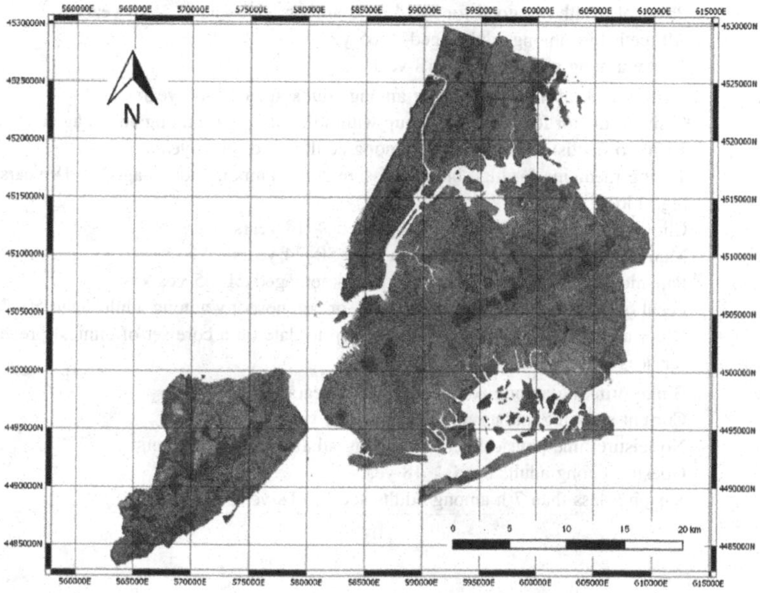

Fig. 1. NAIP image of NYC.

Health care data have been extracted from the repository made available by the 500 Cities project. “500 cities” is a collaboration between CDC, the Robert Wood Johnson Foundation, and the CDC Foundation[2]. The project provides city- and census tract-level small area estimates for chronic disease risk factors (unhealthy behaviors), health outcomes, and clinical preventive service use for the largest 500 cities in the United States. NYC is divided in 2166 census tracts and the latest data available concerns 2017. The 27 chronic diseases measures provided by the project are listed in Table 1.

The measures include major risk behaviors that lead to illness, suffering, and early death related to chronic diseases and conditions, as well as the conditions and diseases that are the most common, costly, and preventable of all health problems.

Table 1. 500 cities measures grouped by category. The 27 measures include 13 health outcomes, 9 prevention practices and 5 unhealthy behaviors.

Category	Measure
Health outcomes	Arthritis among adults aged ≥ 18 years
	Current asthma among adults aged ≥ 18 years
	High blood pressure among adults aged ≥ 18 years
	Cancer among adults aged ≥ 18 years
	High cholesterol among adults aged ≥ 18 years who have been screened in the past 5 years
	Chronic kidney disease among adults aged ≥ 18 years
	Chronic obstructive pulmonary disease among adults aged ≥ 18 years
	Coronary heart disease among adults aged ≥ 18 years
	Diagnosed diabetes among adults aged ≥ 18 years
	Mental health not good for ≥ 14 days among adults aged ≥ 18 years
	Physical health not good for ≥ 14 days among adults aged ≥ 18 years
	All teeth lost among adults aged ≥ 65 years
	Stroke among adults aged ≥ 18 years
Prevention	Current lack of health insurance among adults aged 18–64 years
	Visits to doctor for routine checkup within the past year among adults aged ≥ 18 years
	Visits to dentist or dental clinic among adults aged ≥ 18 years
	Taking medicine for high blood pressure control among adults aged ≥ 18 years with high blood pressure
	Cholesterol screening among adults aged ≥ 18 years
	Mammography use among women aged 50–74 years
	Papanicolaou smear use among adult women aged 21–65 years
	Fecal occult blood test, sigmoidoscopy, or colonoscopy among adults aged 50–75 years
	Older adults aged ≥ 65 years who are up to date on a core set of clinical preventive services by age and sex
Unhealthy behaviors	Binge drinking among adults aged ≥ 18 years
	Current smoking among adults aged ≥ 18 years
	No leisure-time physical activity among adults aged ≥ 18 years
	Obesity among adults aged ≥ 18 years
	Sleeping less than 7 h among adults aged ≥ 18 years

[2] https://www.cdc.gov/500cities/index.htm.

3.1 The Data Analysis Pipeline

The pipeline implemented in our work is described in Fig. 2. The NAIP NYC image has been subdivided into image square blocks having size of 256 × 256 pixels, corresponding to a 512 m edge. Therefore, it was possible to estimate the value of each of the 27 variables collected by "500 Cities" for each block. During this process, blocks out of the tracts or over the sea have been excluded, thus reducing the dataset. The images have been then processed by a pretrained deep model, thus extracting the final features for each image. Images are clustered by resorting to k-means clustering, and the clusters, confirmed with visual inspection, are associated to the healthcare indexes by statistical analysis.

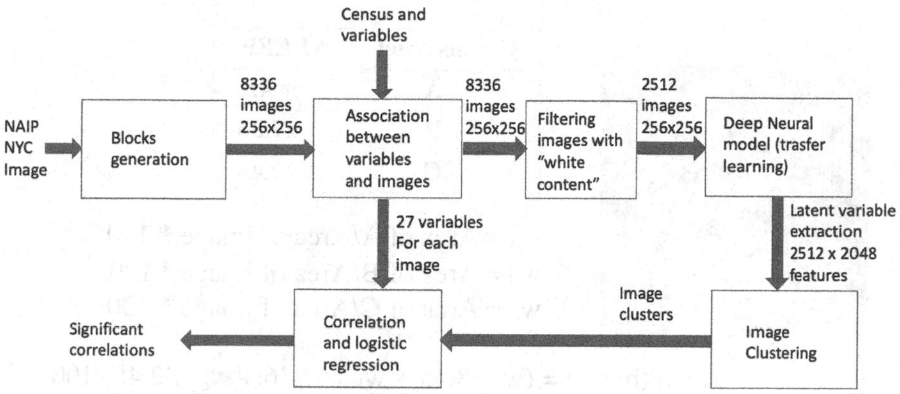

Fig. 2. The data analysis pipeline

3.2 Image Blocks

The NAIP NYC image has been subdivided into 8336 images of 256 × 256 pixels. Each image is a square with edge equal to 512 m. It must be underlined that the original image is georeferenced, meaning that each single pixel is precisely located in space. The small derived tiles are georeferenced as well and can be effectively overlapped to the health and well-being maps. The images have been processed resorting to the Matlab Image Processing and Mapping toolboxes, which are capable of properly managing georeferenced images. Figure 3 shows some examples of the resulting images.

It is possible to note that some of the squares have white areas, corresponding to unmapped zones, due to the irregular borders of the image and to the presence of sea, rivers. Due to the availability of the vector map of the borders of NYC, we have been able to quantify, for each tile, the amount of its surface lying inside the borders of the city; we then filtered the original tile set and maintained only those having a minimal overlapping of 90%.

3.3 Estimation of the Healthcare Indexes for Each Image Block

The healthcare indexes of the 500 Cities database are collected for census tracts and NYC has, as already reported, 2166 census tracts. In order to carry out our analysis, we had to determine the value of the considered variables for each image block. In fact, a given tile overlaps, in general, several tracts. Therefore, we had to implement a simple estimator of the healthcare index of the block, as:

$$hci(block) = \frac{\sum_j w_j hci(j)}{\sum_j w_j}$$

where $hci(j)$ is the value of the generic health care index for the j-*th* census tract and w_j is the percentage of the image block covered by the mentioned tract. An example is shown in Figs. 3 and 4.

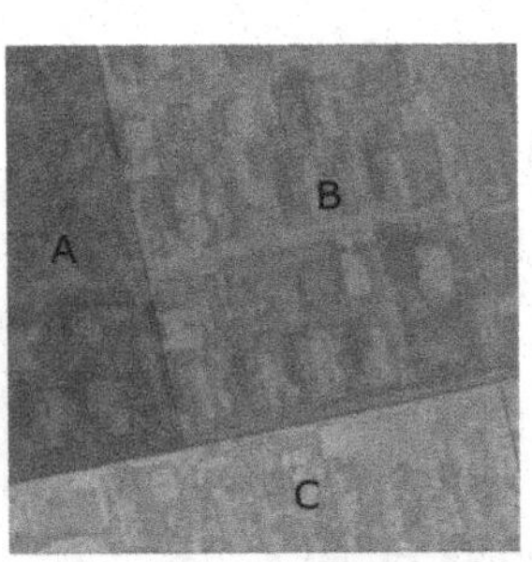

Census tract	SLEEP
A	8.45
B	47.36
C	32.48

w_A = Area of A/Area of image * 100
w_B = Area of B/Area of image * 100
w_C = Area of C/Area of image * 100

SLEEP(block) = (w_A * 8.45 + w_B * 47.36 + w_c * 32.48)/100

Fig. 3. The quantification of the healthcare index value (SLEEP) of a block.

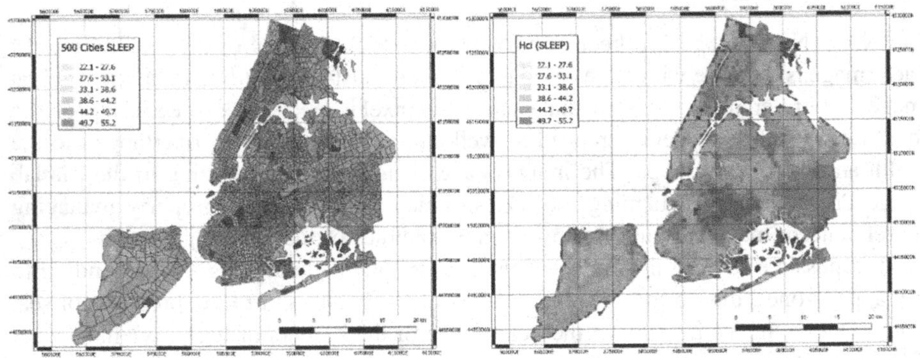

Fig. 4. Original census tracts with the 500 Cities SLEEP index (left hand side) and derived quantification of the healthcare index values for SLEEP variable (right hand side).

In order to properly quantify *hcis*, the blocks with a white area greater than 10% of the image have been removed. The final number of image blocks used for the following analysis has thus lowered to 2512 images. Each image has been then processed by resorting to a deep neural model to extract a set of latent features.

3.4 Deep Neural Networks Processing and Clustering

As a deep neural network model used for transfer learning, we have selected the network developed for the 2016 Painters by number competition [6]. In such competition the goal was to learn how to discriminate the authors of paintings between 1584 unique painters, starting from a training set of 79433 instances; the test set was composed of 23817 instances. In this case, a deep neural network model was learned, with 23 layers, mostly convolutional layers with some max pooling layer. The Painters network computes a layer of 2048 latent variables before the final discrimination layer implemented with a soft-max non-linear function. Those latent variables can be used as a way to embed generic images in the latent space. Therefore, using the software Orange (https://orange.biolab.si) and its Python pipeline, we have processed all image blocks with the Painters model, thus obtaining a final data matrix of 2512 examples with 2048 features.

Such features have been used to cluster the image blocks by resorting to the well-known K-means clustering algorithm. The value of K has been derived with a grid search between 2 and 6 and taking the value that maximize the Silhouette coefficient.

3.5 Correlation and Statistical Analysis

The final step of the data analysis pipeline is represented by the search of statistical correlations between the clusters and their *hci*s. Univariate multinomial logistic regression was applied to estimate the probability to belong to a specific cluster given single variables' values. Multivariate multinomial logistic regression was performed after removal of samples characterized by missing values. A backward stepwise selection procedure based on AIC was applied to identify the most informative set of variables jointly modulating the probability to belong to the clusters. Multinomial logistic regression and the stepwise selection procedure were implemented in the R packages "nnet" and "stats", respectively. Analyses were performed by the R software tool version 3.5.1 (http://www.r-project.org).

4 Results

4.1 Clustering

K-means was run on the 2512 instances with Euclidean distance and 10 reruns. 4 clusters were found to maximize Silhouette coefficient. The output of the clustering algorithm has been validated by analyzing the cluster distribution with the tSNE two-dimensional mapping, as reported in Fig. 5. It is easy to see that the four clusters are in general well separated in the two-dimensional space[3].

[3] It is worthwhile mentioning that this criterion was qualitatively used to assess also other deep neural networks model; Painters turned out to generate the clusters that had the best tSNE spatial distribution of clusters.

Thanks to visual inspection, it is possible to highlight that the four clusters well correspond to different urban landscapes. Cluster C1 corresponds to green areas, Cluster C2 to residential areas with small houses, Cluster C3 to industrial areas and larger buildings, Cluster C4 to residential with larger buildings. Four examples are shown in Fig. 6. Cluster analysis clearly show that the deep neural network model is able to map images in the latent space that share the intuitive notion of similarity that humans may use when they have to classify urban landscape. The method is thus able to automatically cluster similar areas where similar interventions can be planned.

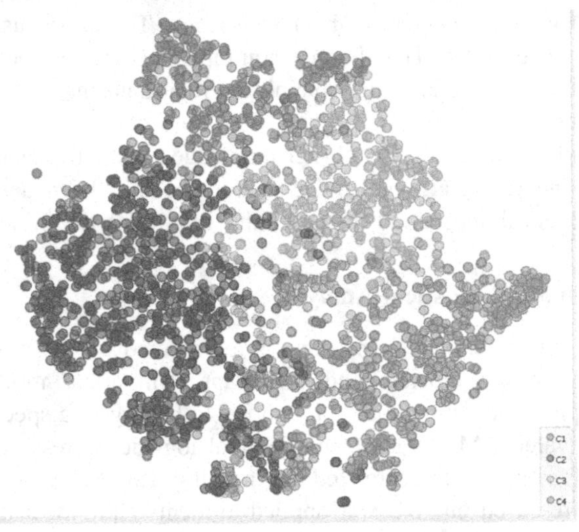

Fig. 5. The tSNE representation of the data with colors identifying the four clusters.

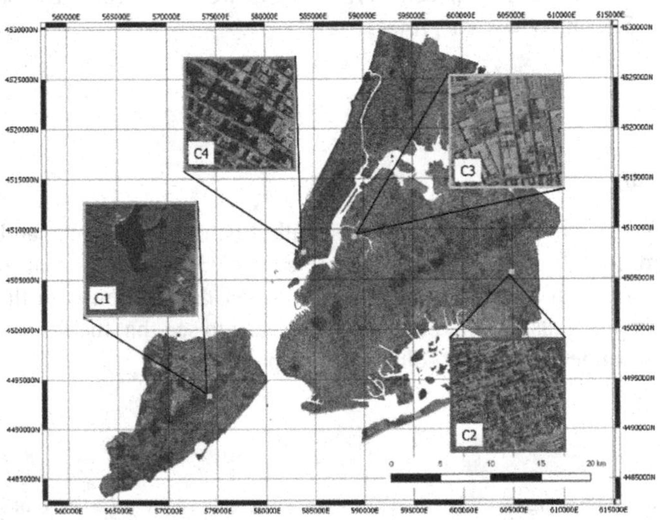

Fig. 6. Four images representing the clusters.

4.2 Correlation and Statistical Analysis

Univariate analysis shows that 22 over 27 variables were significantly correlated with the clusters. This is also confirmed with visual inspection showing the variables distributions after equal frequency discretization against the clusters, as shown in Fig. 7.

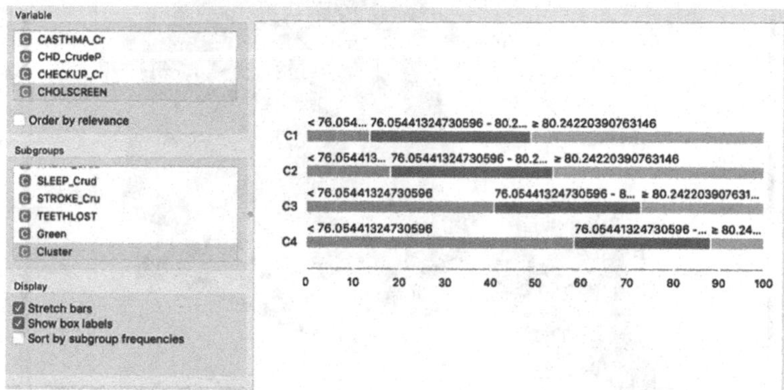

Fig. 7. The different distributions of Cholesterol screening among adults aged ≥ 18 years in the different clusters. Inhabitants of cluster C1 have much higher propensity towards screening than those who live in Cluster C4.

In general, cluster C1, which is the one that groups green areas, has consistently better prevention and health indicators, but worse sleeping indexes and leisure time. Overall, there is a gradient with all indexes moving from cluster C1, to C2, to C3 and finally to C4, which are the residential areas with large buildings.

A multivariate multinomial logistic regression has been performed to assess if significant correlations are present even in the multivariate setting. In this case, after a stepwise feature selection process, 20 variables have been selected. Of those, five variables have been found to be significant ($p \ll 0.01$) in all sub-regressions performed by the multinomial model: Colon screening (Fecal occult blood test, sigmoidoscopy, or colonoscopy among adults aged 50–75 years), Chronic obstructive pulmonary disease among adults aged ≥ 18 years, High cholesterol among adults aged ≥ 18 years who have been screened in the past 5 years, Chronic kidney disease among adults aged ≥ 18 years and finally Stroke among adults aged ≥ 18 years.

4.3 Mapping

The blocks and the clusters have been represented in the original map, confirming the qualitative evaluation of the clusters reported above (Fig. 8).

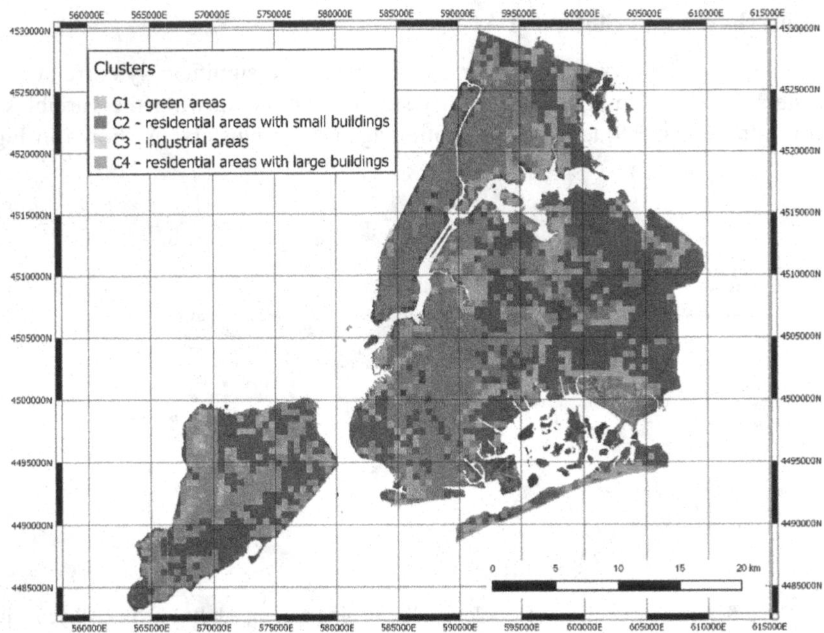

Fig. 8. The clusters remapped in NYC. (Color figure online)

We can find green areas (C1), residential areas with larger buildings (C2), industrial areas (C3) and finally residential areas (C4).

5 Discussion and Conclusions

The data analysis pipeline described in this paper shows that it is possible to automatically correlate urban landscape with healthcare indicators at the whole city level. In the NYC case, such correlation seems particularly strong, probably because of social factors, which, in the US society, makes health indicators related to the urban areas where people live.

Our work has a number of implications.

First of all, it shows that deep neural networks designed to encode image data can be successfully reused within transfer learning approaches. Their application to represent urban landscape seems very effective.

Second, in the context of the PULSE project, the capability of finding clusters of similar urban landscape may allow to profile city areas, in which health care decision makers may plan similar interventions.

Finally, the combination of urban landscape and healthcare indicators is not only useful to hypothesize the intertwining of these two dimensions, but also to further profile urban areas by finding similar areas with similar behaviors of their inhabitants, thus allowing also life style interventions and more "precise" health care policies.

Of course, the analysis has some limitations. First of all, the "quantification" of the health care indexes in the city blocks have been performed by a weighted averaging of the indexes of the census tracts included in the blocks. The weights are computed taking into account only the spatial overlap and not the actual number of inhabitants of the blocks. Second, the results obtained are probably "proxies" of the wealth of the people living in the different areas. For this reason, results may be representative of specific cities and not generalizable to other ones.

Acknowledgement. The work is part of the project PULSE, H2020 - 727816, funded by the European Union.

References

1. Helbich, M., Yao, Y., Liu, Y., Zhang, J., Liu, P., Wang, R.: Using deep learning to examine street view green and blue spaces and their associations with geriatric depression in Beijing. China. Environ Int. **126**, 107–117 (2019)
2. Hong, K.Y., Pinheiro, P.O., Minet, L., Hatzopoulou, M., Weichenthal, S.: Extending the spatial scale of land use regression models for ambient ultrafine particles using satellite images and deep convolutional neural networks. Environ. Res. **30**(176), 108513 (2019)
3. Zewdie, G.K., Lary, D.J., Levetin, E., Garuma, G.F.: Applying deep neural networks and ensemble machine learning methods to forecast airborne ambrosia pollen. Int. J. Environ. Res. Public Health **16**(11), 1992 (2019)
4. Sharma, S., Ball, J.E., Tang, B., Carruth, D.W., Doude, M., Islam, M.A.: Semantic segmentation with transfer learning for off-road autonomous driving. Sensors (Basel). **19**(11), 2577 (2019)
5. Painters by Numbers. http://blog.kaggle.com/2016/11/17/painter-by-numbers-competition-1st-place-winners-interview-nejc-ilenic/. Accessed 21 June 2019
6. Centers for disease control and prevention. National center for chronic disease prevention and health promotion. Division of population health. 500 cities project data (2019). https://www.cdc.gov/500cities. Accessed 21 June 2019

An IoT Architecture of Microservices for Ambient Assisted Living Environments to Promote Aging in Smart Cities

Hubert Kenfack Ngankam[1(✉)], Hélène Pigot[1], Maxime Parenteau[1], Maxime Lussier[2], Aline Aboujaoudé[2], Catherine Laliberté[1], Mélanie Couture[3], Nathalie Bier[2], and Sylvain Giroux[1]

[1] Laboratoire Domus, Université de Sherbrooke, 2500 boul. Université, Sherbrooke, QC J1K 2R1, Canada
{hubert.kenfack.ngankam,helene.pigot,maxime.parenteau, catherine.d.laliberte,sylvain.giroux}@usherbrooke.ca

[2] Centre de recherche de l'Institut de gériatrie de Montréal, 4565, rue Queen Mary, Montréal, QC H3W 1W5, Canada
maximelussier@gmail.com, aline.aboujaoude@mail.mcgill.ca, nathalie.bier@umontreal.ca

[3] Centre for Research and Expertise in Social Gerontology (CREGES), CIUSSS West-Central Montreal, 5800, Cavendish Boulevard, Côte Saint-Luc, QC H4W 2T5, Canada
melanie.couture.cvd@ssss.gouv.qc.ca

Abstract. Ambient Assisted Living (AAL) environments encompass technical systems and the Internet of Things (IoT) tools to support seniors in their daily routines. They aim to enable seniors to live independently and safely for as long as possible when faced declining physical or cognitive capacities. This work presents the design, development and deployment of an AAL system in the context of smart cities. The proposed architecture is based on microservices and software components. We examined the requirements and specifications of AAL systems in smart homes, in efforts to describe and evaluate how they would be transposable in the case of smart cities. The system has been tested and evaluated in the laboratory; it has been deployed in real life settings within city and is still in use by five elderly people.

Keywords: Ambient Assisted Living · Internet of Things · Architecture · Smart homes · Smart cities · Aging in place · Microservices

1 Introduction

As defined by Marsal-Llacuna et al. [1], Smart Cities aim to improve urban performance by using data, information and information technology (IT) to deliver

J. Pagán et al. (Eds.): ICOST 2019, LNCS 11862, pp. 154–167, 2019.
https://doi.org/10.1007/978-3-030-32785-9_14

more efficient services to citizens. IT must satisfy interconnected and smart characteristics. On one hand, city services may be interconnected through a distributed computing platform allowing integration, collection and dissemination of data; on the other hand, to become smart they must integrate information from various sources, analyze model, optimize and help visualization of these complex information to make better operational decisions.

The Centre of Regional Science at the Vienna University of Technology has identified six main components of a smart city: smart economy, smart mobility, smart environment, smart people, smart living, and smart governance [2]. The city of Côte Saint-Luc, Canada, faces an increased number of seniors that forces them to find solutions for promoting aging well at home, within the city. These circumstances leads the city to adopt a smart city approach mainly characterized by smart living for the aging population. Efficient and economical solutions may provide peace of mind, safety and support to limit isolation and promote social participation. Indeed, the administrative team of the city of Côte Saint-Luc believes that its intelligence relies on investments in human and social capital, as well as in technology infrastructure, sustainable growth and the quality of senior's life. These refer to the key components "smart living" of a smart city. The smart cities services must be able to interact with most of the aging population, offering non-complex interfaces that are well adapted to the abilities and preferences of each elder while maintaining functional efficiency in the delivery of services.

The needs of seniors and their state of health change over time as they age and loss of autonomy sets in [3,4]. Thus, as activities of daily living become more and more difficult to perform by the senior, increasing the number of situations of handicaps, institutionalization sometimes becomes the only solution [5]. Moreover, social interactions, community living and communication are factors that have an important influence on quality of life [6,7]. For seniors, interacting with citizens and participating in social activities and entertainment are essential for a good life [6,7]. Generally, seniors can communicate with family and friends by phone, email, and mail. However, seniors with cognitive or physical impairments have difficulty accessing social media and participating in social activities. This leads to social isolation and aggravation of the state of health [8].

To delay institutionalization and limit isolation, Ambient Assisted Living (AAL) systems build smart environment that provides assistance as well as healthcare and especially rehabilitation to seniors with physical or cognitive deficits. AAL systems include technology networks, heterogeneous information, smart devices, products and services. It is an ecosystem of connected objects, medical technologies, sensor networks and software applications for the monitoring and home support of frail people. To make everyday life easier, they propose to automate complex tasks and to monitor activities of daily living for facilitating independence. Above all, they offer continuous assessment of activities carried out, and a reduction in caregiver burden [3,6].

To design AAL system that fulfills the user requirements, the City needs action-oriented approach where research questions emerge through consultation and interaction among several disciplines and sectors to develop socially useful, feasible, practical, effective and sustainable solutions [9]. Stakeholders must work together in a transdisciplinary research approach and methodology. As defined by Harvard transdisciplinary research "Transdisciplinary Research is defined as research efforts conducted by investigators from different disciplines working jointly to create new conceptual, theoretical, methodological, and translational innovations that integrate and move beyond discipline-specific approaches to address a common problem". Indeed, transdisciplinary research provides an opportunity to bring out AAL relevant and appropriate solutions [9]. However, these solutions must be based on a reliable architecture to guarantee efficient services. As the domain of IoT is emerging, lack of standardization leads to a variety of products that provokes communication issues. It is then difficult to propose a coherent AAL system for the users. The goal of this work is twofold: (1) to identify the technical and technological requirements to be met to enable the city to promote aging in place for older residents; and (2) to design a software infrastructure that provides efficient and useful AAL applications that fulfill these requirements.

The rest of the document is structured as follows; Sect. 2 describes background and related works. Section 3 discusses the requirements and challenges an AAL system must satisfy in a smart city context. Section 4 describes the design and the implementation of the AAL architecture. Section 5 shows how the architecture was deployed in five participants home to fulfill their needs. A discussion of the deployment results follows. Finally, Sect. 6 concludes the paper and highlights the future work.

2 Background and Related Works

AAL is a multidisciplinary approach that leverages a wide range of technologies from different fields to deliver personalized services. Deployed AAL systems deal with many contextual information, based on a sensor/actuator information, user actions, user profiles, and ambient information [3]. The different AAL technologies that accompany aging in place are applied in various domains [3,5,6]:

- Facilitate communication between the senior and caregivers;
- Monitor the health parameters of the senior;
- Monitor the environment and the activities of the senior's daily life using sensors to ensure greater comfort and safety;
- Facilitate the mobility of people out of their homes.

To offer adequate services to the seniors, the scope of the AAL systems covers not only the measure, control and connection of the network of sensors and actuators, it also requires understanding the habits and the behavior of the inhabitants in order to react according to their needs, their state of mind and their desires [4]. A user-centered approach is therefore required, involving the elders themselves, as well as a transdisciplinary approach that includes the

City's administrators, computer engineers, geriatric specialists, caregivers and clinicians [9].

Most AAL systems are moving towards the IoT platform paradigm with programs to control devices, display monitoring recordings, adjust ambient settings, lock doors and windows, and so on [10]. The Internet of Things (IoT) is a technological paradigm derived from innovative concepts and developments in information and communication technologies associated with ubiquitous computing, and ambient intelligence [11,12]. Such an approach brings significant improvements to the interaction of users, but is often based on the presence of a monolithic architecture. Monolithic architecture is complex and costly in deployment time, with many limitations in terms of scalability and component reuse [13]. Yet, while connected to a wide range of independent devices and systems, the architecture of today's AAL systems tends to focus on service resiliency and software component integration.

The choice of a general structure has an impact on the reliability, performance, maintainability and therefore lifetime of the AAL systems. It needs a structure that is customizable, that could adapt to various features and react to dynamic changes to devices. Therefore, among the various infrastructure proposed, AAL middleware is mainly preferred to facilitate the homogenization of different technologies and to satisfy the prerequisite characteristics [14]. Also a microservices platform is favored because it makes possible to design an easy-to-scale IoT system that quickly integrates new technological components and allows each instance to be adapted to the profile of the user [13].

3 AAL Systems Requirements and Challenges

Designing AAL systems requires respecting several characteristics and norms. The general architecture of AAL systems must fulfill the following requirements: heterogeneity; interoperability; usability; security; accuracy; reliability; maintainability; efficiency and technological scalability [15]. In a smart city context, the vast number of users reached necessitates to assure effective services delivery. The scalability is then twofold. Its scope covers the increase of the number of users reached and the number of devices to integrate because of the personalization of the services offered to each senior.

The AAL system designed and presented in this paper is part of a transdisciplinary methodological approach, which ensures that the issues emerging from seniors and the city are satisfied. We will show in the following that designing AAL on a middleware architecture that integrates microservices will realize the pre-cited requirements and respond to transdisciplinary approach. These requirements are grouped into four categories:

- Modularity: heterogeneity – interoperability – maintainability;
- Availability of services: scalability of technology – reliability – efficiency;
- Services delivery: scalability for seniors – security;
- Adaptability: adaptation to the senior profile – usability – accuracy.

Indeed, scalability is required for the city to offer services to a large number of citizens. However, modularity is a key requirement for the city to offer multiples services that should evolve according to new services the city desires to offer and new devices the IoT improvements will make available. Citizens expect also that the city will comply with security, reliability and accuracy of the city services.

3.1 Modularity

Modularity is a concept that includes heterogeneity, interoperability and maintainability. Indeed, it expresses the fact that the technological components fit together despite their differences. Due to the rapid evolution of the IoT domain, no standard has yet emerged. Rather, a wide variety of IoT components appears on the market including network connectivity options, proprietary or standards-based protocols, and unknown communication methods. It is expected that for years, new devices, new services and new protocols force IoT systems to accommodate various components and let them interact despite the diversity. Users also ask to get access to IoT services irrespective to the medium used.

This heterogeneity requires interoperability without concession regarding maintainability. Interoperability refers to the ability for the AAL system to propose interfaces that are understood by all the IoT components and to allow access between them. Maintainability guarantees the ability of the AAL system to continue to be interoperable in the future despite the evolution of the technology, the update of each component and the apparition of new components.

To respect heterogeneity, ensure interoperability and maintain it over time, communication protocols as well as data format must be independent. Middleware and software components address this heterogeneity issue. Middleware is a feature that allows several devices to be managed by the platform. In general, middleware can be considered as a software construct mediating between two or more disparate software components [16]. The software components are part of a system or application. It is a web service, a software package, a web resource, or a module that encapsulates a set of functions or data. Components are a way to break down the complexity of the software into manageable parts [14]. Each component hides the complexity of its implementation behind an interface. This mechanism reduces the complexity of software development, maintenance, operations, and support, and allows to reuse the same code in many systems. To preserve this mechanism, the software components and the middleware for AAL must be kept simple and offer broad compatibility and interoperability with most of the IoT components. Excessive duplication of proprietary software must be prevented. Overall, it is better to opt for solutions and initiatives that are open source, easily to install, and quickly maintainable. Moreover, if the middleware is built on microservices, it guarantees flexibility and ease of work in large systems, reducing the amount of communication and coordination between entities [13].

3.2 Availability of Services

AAL systems are intended to change according to the needs of seniors and the configuration of the smart home that must integrate new IoT components. The user profile and his preferences are unique, necessitating the use of personalized sensors and actuators. Sometimes, it also requires to implement new services or modify existing ones. Despite the scalability of the technology induced by the changes, the AAL system must provide reliable and efficient services. This is all the more important given that the final users are not comfortable with technology. The software architecture must then be able to evolve with the senior needs and inspire confidence among the seniors and the city.

Each microservice can be: deployed independently; independently designed, developed and tested. As a result, this architecture style has a greatly increased responsiveness to change. It makes it possible to respond better to the objectives of responsiveness and adaptability of Agile approaches [13]. The individual components can be run across a variety of platforms. A layered and non-monolithic architectural organization makes it possible to promote the scaling up of components and technical requirements in a transparent manner. Indeed, each layer is responsible for the local management of a subset of information, while the overall management lies with all components. To ensure the availability of services, the system must be able to detect, to reason and act on the actions performed in the environment. The ability to communicate and interact with the surroundings is part of the AAL approach.

3.3 Services Delivery

The proposed architecture is intended for an entire city. It must then be able to be deployed to multiple participants. This scalability according to the number of seniors must not affect the quality of services offered. The AAL system must also guarantee security as it covers private issues.

The microservice architecture structures an application as a collection of services that are highly maintainable and testable, loosely coupled, independently deployable and organized around business capabilities. The microservice architecture enables the continuous delivery and deployment of large and complex applications. AAL system can be spread across multiple servers or even multiple databases. The architecture has better fault isolation; if one microservice fails, the others will continue to work. To evolve quickly, the system offers at least one local cache. This is necessary to ensure the resilience of the system. For example, if the microservice of the local user fails or is slow, other microservices will not be affected, they should be able to work independently. In the worst case, the remote information will be empty or classified with a default value. In this case, the microservices will also be faster, because they will not need to join data from a remote source to meet the demands of users.

3.4 Adaptability

To ensure that the smart home fulfills the senior needs, the design of AAL system must be participatory, transdisciplinary and user centered [9]. Interactions with the smart home remain simple and integrated into everyday life to facilitate its use by seniors. AAL systems should be able to anticipate the user's needs as much as possible and provide the necessary assistance in a non-intrusive and subtle manner. The profiles, the health status of seniors and the habitats are mostly different. The system must be organized to effectively manage these differences and offers equal, adapted and accurate services despite the underlying differences and the response of the users.

To ensure adaptability and ease of use, intuitive interfaces through voice control and tangible interfaces must be offered to provide for the seniors, easy ways to control the AAL system. At the reverse, the AAL system must put in place mechanisms to notify caregivers using IoT components that are dispatched into the home. Thus, the AAL architecture must share information between the IoT components to monitor the senior anywhere, at any time, regardless of the kind of action performed and assistance needed. Therefore, the information shared between the IoT components is described at a high level of abstraction in order for the IoT components to avoid specific implementation details and rather exchange semantic information.

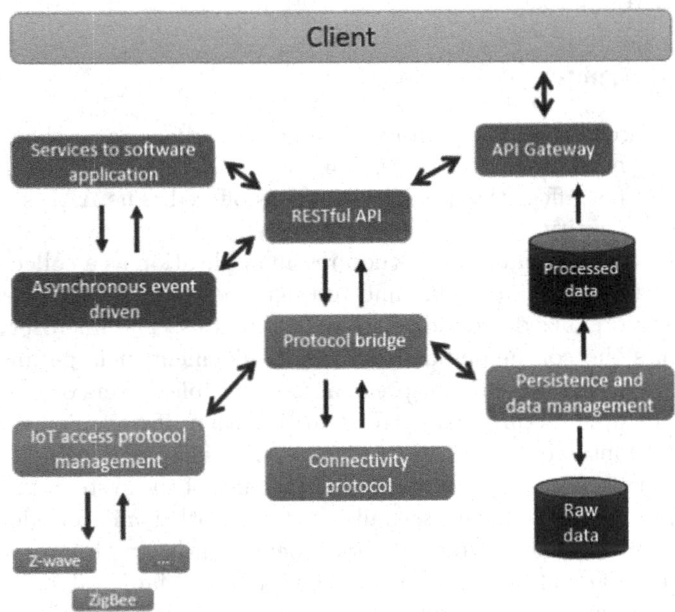

Fig. 1. AAL system logic architecture based on microservices.

4 AAL Systems Design and Implementation

Deriving from the previous requirements, the AAL architecture proposed in the City is based on a middleware that offers microservices described on a high level of abstraction. The microservice architecture ensures interoperability between distinct technologies over time. A microservice architecture is a specific software system design process that structures an application as a collection of loosely coupled services. The services work in cooperation to provide the features defined in the system. With microservices, each application runs independently from the others. Therefore, adding or changing features will affect only the service involved without affecting the others.

4.1 Architecture Design

Figure 1 illustrates the logical architecture of microservices that defines the distribution and relationship between AAL systems, subsystems, and components. This architecture, built as a set of independent microservice modular components, is easy to test, maintain and understand. It enables organizations to increase their agility while improving workflows and the time needed to enhance production.

The access protocol management module provides an interface for the handling of the different communication protocols based on the standard IEEE 802.15.x and 802.11. It usually acts as a driver for connected objects. Typically, this module provides wireless mesh technology designed to carry small amounts of data over short or medium distances.

The connectivity protocol module is designed as an extremely lightweight published/subscribed messaging transport. It is useful for connections to remote sites where a small code footprint is required or a reduced network bandwidth. It implements a channel subscription mechanism. Whenever an event occurs, it notifies all entities registered in the channel. Thus, when a new event occurs all registered components are notified, avoiding an active standby.

The microservice of persistence and data management deals with data backup in the appropriate databases. As part of this architecture, we deployed two database management systems. One deals with raw data and the other with processed data to increase efficiency in some monitoring operations.

The protocol bridge is a microservice that bundles devices and other technologies into a single solution. It provides a uniform user interface and a common approach to automating actions and rules across the system. It communicates electronically with smart and not-so-smart devices, performs user-defined actions, and provides high-level access to connected objects.

The asynchronous event driven is responsible for the web application server, for presenting information and notifications in a client's application. It communicates with the rest API by the PUT, GET, POST and DELETE commands. It spreads the data to the upper layers. The Gateway API manages access, certificates, and security protocols.

Physically, the proposed system is organized in six layers (Fig. 2). The lowest layer is composed of connected objects, including all the sensors, equipment and actuators that transform the habitat into a smart habitat.

Each data, each event, each action generating a stimulus is sent to the upper layer, the layer of controllers. This layer deals with the management of connected objects and the sensor network. It includes Sensors Controllers, Smart Lamp Controllers and Voice Command Controllers. This layer allows bidirectional communication between the connected objects and the middleware. The controller layer is implemented logically in our architecture by the access protocol management module.

Interoperability, subscription, notification, heterogeneity, and command execution are operations performed in the middleware layer. This layer offers mostly an abstraction to handle connected objects. It is just composed of few components: OpenHab and MQTT servers. It is deployed in a server running on a Raspberry Pi. Clients connect to an application server for data access. To ensure security, the Rest API is the only API able to connect to the Rapsberry Pi for data exploitation. All other layers consist of components that allow access and exploitation of data via Rest APIs or rich clients.

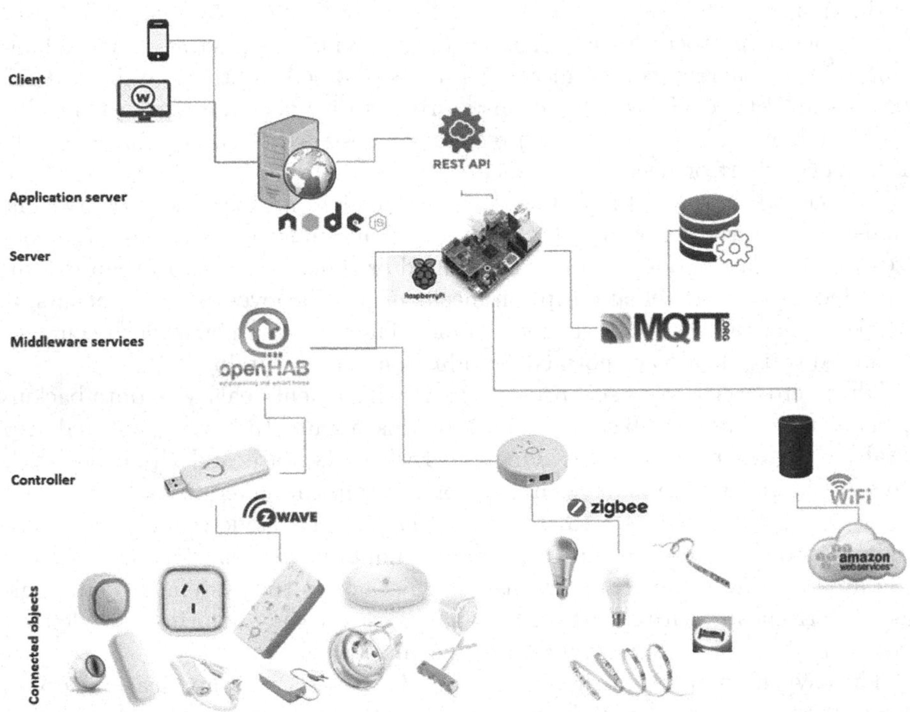

Fig. 2. Physical architecture of the IoT components for AAL system design.

5 Architecture Deployment

The experimental evaluation of the proposed system was performed in two phases. During the first phase, a functional test of the user's system assistance scenarios was run in the laboratory to establish the perceived usefulness of the system. During this phase, we emphasized the robustness and scalability of the system from a user and a technological point of view. During the second phase, we conducted a home experiment. We deployed the AAL architecture in five senior apartments in the city of Côte Saint-Luc, Canada.

The main objective of the proposed AAL system is to provide intelligent assistance and detect changes in the behavior of the occupant. The rest of the document focuses on the second phase experimentation that satisfies the requirements management on the heterogeneity, scalability and adaptation to the senior profile.

5.1 Materials and Method

The five participants involved in the experiment were living alone and showed quite diverse profiles (Table 1). They were between the age of 80 and 95. The proposed architecture of the system did not require any particular configuration for its deployment in different habitats. An installation at the participant's house required between one and two hours, depending on the layout of his apartment. To this must be added two hours of configuration of each kit, then about five minutes to adapt the services to the needs of a participant. The adaptation of the services is done by activation or deactivation of the docker corresponding to microservices.

Table 1. Profile of participants.

Participants	Sex	User profile
Participant 1	M	Rheumatism, uses a cane to get around
Participant 2	M	No physical and cognitive impairments
Participant 3	F	Overweight person, difficulty moving
Participant 4	F	Visual difficulties, poorly sighted
Participant 5	M	Walking with a walker

First in the laboratory, several user experiences and robustness tests were conducted to determine the behavior of software components in the face of profile changes, partial updating and technological scalability. Secondly, during the experience at home, a preliminary interview was conducted with each participant to explain technological tools. The participant was then invited during the usability testing phase to create real-life scenarios. Each situation was accompanied by a possible adjustment of the system, efforts were put to change as less as possible the participants' habitat. To meet the needs of the citizens, four assistance mechanisms were proposed:

- Automatic lighting controlled by voice;
- Automatic lighting when the person comes out of the bedroom and goes to the bathroom during night. A light path is installed between the bedroom and the bathroom;
- Spotlight lighting system to remind activity (It's time to take medication) or objects (Do not forget the keys when going outside);
- Automatic notification of community and social information organized by the town hall.

To illustrate the participation of seniors in the installation process, one of the participants preferred that the light path was installed along the stairs, instead of between the bedroom and the bathroom. He had expressed the need that the path from the garage to the ground floor be lit when needed. Another participant, presenting visual impairments, emphasized the advantage of ordering the turning on of lights by voice, as soon as she entered her home.

At the end of the installation, a summative evaluation of acceptability was requested from participants. Four of the five participants were satisfied with the test and would be curious to go further. They found the use of voice commands appropriate to their context.

The diversity of sensors and actuators used demonstrated the multiplicity of protocols and the technological scalability put in place. The 80 sensors used and distributed in about 20 devices per apartment materialize this part of the scalability. The local cache used for each installation makes it easier to partition the systems so that individual configurations and settings do not affect the entire system.

Figure 3 shows, for each AAL system requirement, the elements used to perform the evaluation.

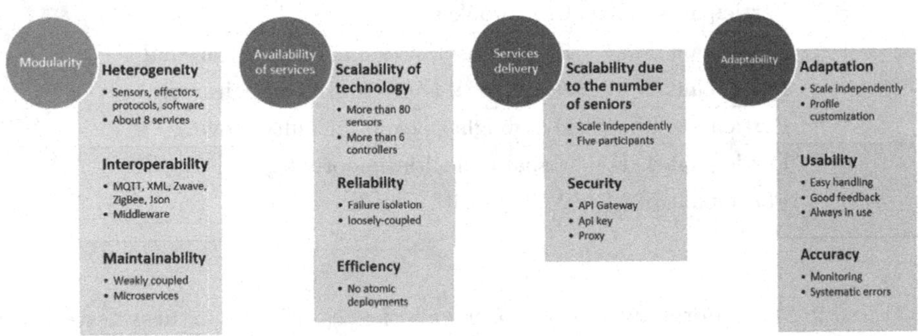

Fig. 3. Elements used by each requirement to make the assessment.

Many factors affect the performance of the AAL system, such as the performance of connected objects, the amount of available memory, the communication mode, the response time, the architecture and operating system of each component, the support of communication between the IoT, the algorithms used and the primary need of the system. In particular, heterogeneity induced by the disparity between IoT components may contribute to other factors, such as additional downtime while some components are waiting for others. It is therefore important to calibrate all relevant IoT components to provide information about events, such as communication time, system time, input output time and idle time. The six communication protocols and the eight services were interoperable to ensure the heterogeneity of the system.

The design of the modules in microservices brings a loosely coupling between component and a fault isolation these translate the reliability. Efficiency translates into the ability to perform non-atomic deployments and individually update components. For the moment, the number of five participants is too small to evaluate the capacity of our AAL infrastructure to support scalability. It is expected to deploy with more than 20 participants for better assessing this requirement.

6 Conclusion

This paper presents the design, development and deployment of an AAL environment which supports independent living in smart home for seniors. The system is based on a middleware that merges many different technologies to build the smart environment. The backbone of the system is its modular architecture based on microservices where different bundles (independent pieces of code) are in charge of providing the required functionalities. It allows adding easily new devices and new features, or replacing some devices without disrupting the system and minimizing the adaptation effort.

Another advantage of the proposed microservice architecture is its insulation quality and resilience. If one of the components fails, if the technology becomes obsolete or the code is out of date, the team can design another one without impacting the rest of the applications, which continue to operate independently.

The installation and evaluation of the AAL system in five seniors' home has shown that the system developed meet seniors needs. The seniors have expressed also how it is easy to use.

Ongoing research is currently conducted for analyzing the collected data and proposing new applications for satisfying new user requests. It has also shown that a middleware architecture based on microservices fulfills the requirements necessary for connecting citizens to smart city services. More technical investigations are planned to evaluate the scalability of the architecture and to deliver city services to the seniors thanks to the connected devices installed at home.

Acknowledgments. The authors want to thank all the partners and participants involved in the project. A special thanks to the Côte Saint-Luc city administrators.

References

1. Marsal-Llacuna, M.-L., Colomer-Llinàs, J., Meléndez-Frigola, J.: Lessons in urban monitoring taken from sustainable and livable cities to better address the Smart Cities initiative. Technol. Forecast. Soc. Change **90**, 611–622 (2015)
2. Giffinger, R., Gudrun, H.: Smart cities ranking: an effective instrument for the positioning of the cities? ACE Archit. Environ. **4**, 7–26 (2010)
3. Cook, D.J., Augusto, J.C., Jakkula, V.R.: Ambient intelligence: technologies, applications, and opportunities. Pervasive Mob. Comput. **5**, 277–298 (2009). https://doi.org/10.1016/j.pmcj.2009.04.001
4. Hwang, A.S., et al.: Co-designing ambient assisted living (AAL) environments: unravelling the situated context of informal dementia care. Biomed Res. Int. **2015**, 1–12 (2015). https://doi.org/10.1155/2015/720483
5. Blackman, S., et al.: Ambient assisted living technologies for aging well: a scoping review (2016). https://doi.org/10.1515/jisys-2014-0136
6. Rashidi, P., Mihailidis, A.: A survey on ambient assisted living tools for older adults. IEEE J. Biomed. Heal. Inf. **PP**, 1 (2013). https://doi.org/10.1109/JBHI.2012.2234129
7. Valkanova, N., Jorda, S., Vande Moere, A.: Public visualization displays of citizen data: design, impact and implications. Int. J. Hum Comput Stud. **81**, 4–16 (2015). https://doi.org/10.1016/j.ijhcs.2015.02.005
8. Li, R., Lu, B., McDonald-Maier, K.D.: Cognitive assisted living ambient system: a survey. Digit. Commun. Networks. **1**, 229–252 (2015). https://doi.org/10.1016/j.dcan.2015.10.003
9. Boger, J., et al.: Principles for fostering the transdisciplinary development of assistive technologies. Disabil. Rehabil. Assist. Technol. **12**, 480–490 (2017)
10. Yachir, A., Amirat, Y., Chibani, A., Badache, N.: Event-aware framework for dynamic services discovery and selection in the context of ambient intelligence and Internet of Things. IEEE Trans. Autom. Sci. Eng. **13**, 85–102 (2016)
11. Gubbi, J., Buyya, R., Marusic, S., Palaniswami, M.: Internet of Things (IoT): a vision, architectural elements, and future directions. Futur. Gener. Comput. Syst. **29** (2013). https://doi.org/10.1016/j.future.2013.01.010
12. Dohr, A., Modre-Osprian, R., Drobics, M., Hayn, D., Schreier, G.: The Internet of Things for ambient assisted living. In: ITNG2010 - 7th International Conference on Information Technology: New Generations, pp. 804–809 (2010). https://doi.org/10.1109/ITNG.2010.104
13. Alshuqayran, N., Ali, N., Evans, R.: A systematic mapping study in microservice architecture. In: Proceedings - 2016 IEEE 9th International Conference on Service-Oriented Computing and Applications, SOCA 2016, pp. 44–51. IEEE (2016). https://doi.org/10.1109/SOCA.2016.15
14. O'Grady, M.J., Muldoon, C., Dragone, M., Tynan, R., O'Hare, G.M.P.: Towards evolutionary ambient assisted living systems. J. Ambient Intell. Humaniz. Comput. **1**, 15–29 (2010). https://doi.org/10.1007/s12652-009-0003-5
15. Memon, M., Wagner, S.R., Pedersen, C.F., Aysha Beevi, F.H., Hansen, F.O.: Ambient assisted living healthcare frameworks, platforms, standards, and quality attributes (2014). https://doi.org/10.3390/s140304312
16. Albano, M.F., Ferreira, L.L., Pinho, L.M., Alkhawaja, A.R.: Middleware for smart grids. Comput. Stand. Interfaces **38**, 133–143 (2015)

Designing a Navigation System for Older Adults: A Case Study Under Real Road Condition

Perrine Ruer[1(✉)], Damien Brun[2], Charles Gouin-Vallerand[3], and Évelyne F. Vallières[4]

[1] HEC Montreal, Montreal, QC H3T2A7, Canada
perrine.ruer@hec.ca
[2] Université TÉLUQ, Montréal, QC H2S3L5, Canada
brund@acm.org
[3] École de Gestion, Université de Sherbrooke, Sherbrooke, QC J1K2R1, Canada
charles.gouin-vallerand@usherbrooke.ca
[4] Centre LICEF, Université TÉLUQ, Montréal, QC H2S3L5, Canada
evelyne.vallieres@teluq.ca

Abstract. Recent research allows envisioning what kind of sensory devices could be used for drivers' navigation in the future, particularly for older adults. Population all around the world is aging, older adults will be more on the road. In this paper, we present a contact-less navigation system dedicated to this category of people based on a mobile head-up display. The aim of this system is to preserve their mobility in order to promote their autonomy and daily social activities. To do so, we interviewed older drivers to design a driving assistance system and we assessed the system under real road conditions (N = 34) with measurement of older drivers' mental workload and the adequacy of users' expectations. We emphasize the need to combine both measures of mental workload. The contribution aims at providing a richer understanding of how older people experience navigation technologies and to discuss the design recommendations of digital devices for older people.

Keywords: Older people · Driving assistance system · Mental workload · Field studies

1 Introduction

Some research in Human-Computer Interaction (HCI) focuses on the kind of sensory devices that could be used for a driver's navigation in the future. That is convenient for the case of older drivers. This category of drivers will be more and more on the road in the next decades as shown from demographics prediction. Many physical and cognitive changes are associated with the aging process and could have negative impacts on driving activity. It is essential to preserve their mobility in order to continue to promote their autonomy and to have daily social activities.

In the last decade, little focus has been given to the driving assistance system focusing on older drivers' mobility that could help them to drive safely in the long

J. Pagán et al. (Eds.): ICOST 2019, LNCS 11862, pp. 168–179, 2019.
https://doi.org/10.1007/978-3-030-32785-9_15

term. To promote the autonomy of older drivers, one suggestion is to design navigation systems for and with the concerned users [1]. Several new cars are equipped with different driving assistance systems that have the potential to help older people to drive more safely as long as they are accepted and perceived as useful by these users with special needs and characteristics. Therefore, the aim of the present research was to propose a driving assistance system to promote driving for older drivers considering their aging impairments.

Usability is something to consider when dealing with older adults. Older people do not have the same familiarity with new technologies that young people [2]. If older drivers question the system, this may cause them to stop using the system. It is necessary to understand their expectations of technologies. In addition, if people are familiar with a system, they are likely to have a more favorable opinion of it [3].

After the definition of needs and expectations with older drivers, we designed a driving assistance system corresponding as closely as possible with these ones. The study involves the assessment of the newly designed driving assistance system from real-world experiments with 34 participants measures of objective and subjective mental workload. Our contributions are (1) to design a driving system assistance for older drivers based on Head-Up Display interactions (2) to assess the value of the system with the assessment of different measures of mental workload.

2 Related Works

The development of transportation technologies makes possible to maintain older drivers' mobility by allowing them to use a personal vehicle to reach their needs. In-vehicle systems support drivers. Their aims are to increase safety and save lives. These systems can help drivers in critical situations or in unfamiliar environments by giving driving information. For example: turn on your left at the next intersection [4]. However, these systems are developed most of the time for all drivers and few of them are assessed with older drivers [4]. Especially since older drivers have their own usability problem with computing systems [2]. They have particular needs and expectations which could differ from other categories of people (for instance, young people) [5].

A bad conception of a driving assistance system leads to the perception of the complexity of the driving task and a higher risk of accidents [6]. Furthermore, a bad conception induces more inconvenience for older drivers, whereas the system's role is to encourage mobility and security of the driver who uses it [6, 7]. User tests allow to assess a system and to verify its credibility [8]. A previous study was made with older drivers to assess a new driving system during user tests. Results indicated the system was positively perceived. Participants were able to better understand the benefits and limits of it [9].

Head-Up Display (HUD) is a recent interesting driving assistance system for older drivers. It is defined as a display mode which is used to present different information to the driver's field view (speed information, warnings or other indicators) [10]. The benefits of HUD are to allow quick reaction time; earlier detection of road hinders or to let more time to scan the traffic scene [10–12]. Most research focuses on the visual canal to provide information during the driving task. Older drivers are more sensitive to visual impairments with aging. Several authors agree that the main beneficiaries of HUD systems are aging people because of their narrower field of vision [11]. HUD is used to limit off-field sightings of the road scene by transmitting information directly into the driver's field of view and allowing a controlled driving task [12, 13]. A study indicated that the use of a head-up display system was assessed by participants as it was easy to use [10]. HUD has great potential to improve comfort for older drivers.

Interaction with driving assistance system can increase task complexity having consequences regarding safety (i.e. distraction or increased fatigue) [13]. Mental workload is a good indicator of distraction during the evaluation of a new driving assistance system [14]. A system should not increase distraction involving a higher mental workload with too much information to process [4, 13]. Mental workload allows assessing if a computing system supports or increases people's cognitive resources needed, particularly when a driving assistance system is added. The system could either assist the drivers or disturb them to drive more safely, especially older drivers [1, 4, 6]. Indeed, older drivers are more sensitive to distraction during dual tasks due to the aging process [15]. Mental workload is not directly observed. Two main measures are generally used to do so: an objective measure and a subjective measure. Objective measure is physiological cues such as heart rate, pupillary diameter, skin temperature, electrodermal activity [16, 17]. To detect these clues, biometric sensors are used to measure the body's reactions reflecting the driver's mental workload [17]. Subjective measures are questionnaires or scales to assess a specific event such as NASA Task Load Index (NASA-TLX). It is a multidimensional assessment tool with six different dimensions: mental demand, physical demand, temporal demand, effort, performance, and frustration [18]. It is strongly recommended to combine these different type of measurements in order to better assess mental workload when using a driving assistance system [14].

During the development of a driving assistance system, it is recommended to offer user tests, particularly for older drivers. The measurement of mental workload makes it possible to predict the influence (positive or negative) of a new driving assistance system during a driving task. The HUD seems to be an interesting system for older drivers, especially with the reduction of their field of view.

3 Methodology

The study consists of an implementation phase (3.1) and an exploratory study under real conditions (3.2).

3.1 Implementation Phase

Driving Assistance System Choice. Among driving assistance systems, HUD is interesting for older drivers. In our study, we used a commercialized system named HudwayGlass. This system consists of a phone holder and a tinted plastic blade covered with a mirror coating to reflect phone screen. This system can easily be purchased by any driver from the company's website[1]. The HudwayGlass HUD has three advantages: (1) the system is universal and can be used in all vehicles, (2) with any smartphone and (3) is customizable, letting the possibility to design any kind of mobile application adapted for this type of display (Fig. 1).

Fig. 1. HudwayGlass HUD

The HudwayGlass company offers specific mobile applications, but for our research, we developed our own mobile application for it to be well tailored for our intended older drivers.

Design of Mobile Applications. Regarding the design process, we assessed expectations of older drivers relative to mobile application interfaces with interviews. In these, we asked participants about pictogram and color for three types of interfaces. We implemented the most preferred interfaces in a mobile application (app.) named "AR-Driving Assistant". The mobile app has been divided into two sub-app. The first one presents information to the driver. This sub-app was built with the Unity software and was configured to run on an Android phone. It projects the information to the driver through the HUD interface. The objective was to provide driving notifications with pictograms and colors. These choices are important when designing technology interfaces [19]. Figure 2 presents the three selected interfaces according to expectations collected.

Fig. 2. Interfaces from the first sub-app. (in order of presentation: alert, information and advice)

1 http://hudwayglass.com.

The second sub-app allows control of notifications sent to the driver and collects data. The objective was to control the first sub-application by collecting data during driving for later analysis (i.e. speed, breaking, position, etc.). The application consists of a scrolling view containing several buttons including a dialog box to configure and start sensor monitoring (Fig. 3).

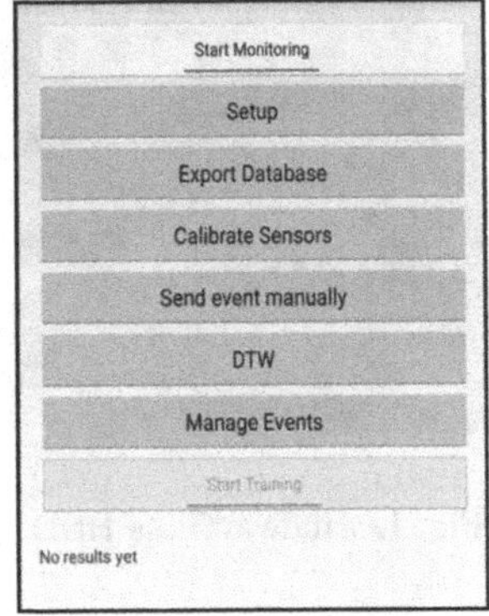

Fig. 3. Interface from the second sub-app.

This application was developed with the Android Studio software and the application code is available on GitHub (https://github.com/limvi-licef/AR-driving-assistant).

3.2 Assessment Under Real-World Conditions

The success or failure of a driving assistance system lies in a design for the targeted drivers.

Participants. Thirty-nine (39) participants were recruited, but only 34 took part in this study (41% of whom were women). Five participants withdrew a few days before their appointment for various reasons (loss of interest in the study, a problem with their personal vehicle or health problem). The sample was composed of older people between 60 and 85 years old (mean age: 68.8 years, standard deviation: 5.91). Participants lived in Montreal area (Quebec, Canada). We recruited participants with a local paper ad and with the university e-journal. Each participant was reached by phone to answer a pre-recruitment questionnaire to verify that they matched with the selection criteria. These criteria were to be 60 years old or more, to hold a valid driving license, to drive each week on a regular basis and to be in good health. To confirm the relevance of our system, we compared several measures by dividing our sample. Two groups were randomly composed: a control group and an experimental group. The experimental group (N = 17) drove with the prototype system, while the control group (N = 17) did not have the prototype system during driving. The control group was used as a reference group for the comparison of the collected measures. They were instructed to perform a routine driving task.

Procedure. Participants were invited to read and fill out a consent form. Once completed, they answered a questionnaire to collect sociodemographic variables, such as age, gender or driving experience. Participants were asked to drive on a highway in the greater Montreal area. The journey distance was a loop of 63 km and was completed in 40 min. All participants must respect traffic laws and driving speed limitations. The route drivers needed to drive was to follow the highway until exit 160. Then, they made a turn back to the outset. The journey was selected to a limited amount of traffic on the highway, with fewer stimuli than in urban road and to have a reproducibility of the scenario during experiments. Highway driving is known not to increase mental workload, unlike an urban road with the presence of less disruptive elements (e.g. pedestrians, parked vehicles, etc.) [14]. We also avoided as much as possible peak hours (8:00 am–9:00 am and 4:00 pm–5:00 pm) and intense traffic. We chose experiments in real-world conditions because they allow assessing variables with dynamic factors coming from the driving context [18]. Finally, they answered a questionnaire about their overall experience and received 30 Canadian dollars for their participation.

Collected Measures. We collected two objective measures: skin temperature and electrodermal activity. These two measures allow the assessment of the driver's mental workload [14, 17, 20]. During the driving task, all participants wore two biometric sensors from the Captiv' Solutions. These sensors are affixed with self-gripping tape and can be positioned at different locations on the body such as wrists or elbows. Each sensor weights 20 grams, measures 52 mm × 25 mm × 14 mm. Their sampling frequency is 32 Hz with a resolution of 16 bits and 0.05 °C. The amount of data collected is 1920 per minute for each sensor. These sensors are conveniently connected to a wireless box. Software is available to synchronize and display the data in real time, then record the data collected and perform subsequent analyses. Sensors were positioned on participants' left-hand fingers and a medical tape was added to hang the wires to the hand. They cause slight discomfort but do not prevent the steering wheel from being grasped or the execution of driving gestures with the right hand [21].

Regarding the subjective measure NASA-TLX, Participants answered it in the car straight after the driving task on the highway and before they got out. The first step of the NASA-TLX was to assess the six dimensions (mental demand, physical demand, time demand, effort, performance, and frustration) on scales ranging from low to high. We presented a definition for each dimension to ensure the participants' understanding. Then, participants carried out a comparison phase and chose from two dimensions that the experimenter said out loud. For example: "indicate the dimension required the most effort while driving between mental demand or performance".

All participants drove the University instrumented vehicle, named LiSA car. They all drove this vehicle to have better comparison and not have a vehicle change that would potentially influence the data collection. This vehicle is a Nissan Versa 2007 equipped with a data logger (AIM Evo4) and a computer embedded on board. An experimenter was placed in the back seat of the vehicle. The experimenter indicated to the participant that he or she could not speak during the whole driving task to not influence the driver. The experimenter could track the collected data in real time and complete the task with a paper-pencil statement with driving information (i.e. traffic, participant comments). The experimenter sent one of the three interfaces with the second sub-application to the first sub-application.

4 Results

As a reminder, our objective is to propose a driving assistance system to promote safe driving for older drivers. We did assessments under real-road conditions in order to confirm if this system meets the expectations of older drivers. First, we present results from the objective mental workload data (skin temperature and electrodermal activity) for control and experimental groups. Then we present the subjective mental workload's results for both groups. We study comparison between objective and subjective mental workload. Finally, we describe system usability assessment results completed by the experimental group.

4.1 Objective Mental Workload

Control group participants had a lower average skin temperature than experimental group participants (31.34 Celsius degree (°C) vs 31.81 °C). There is a small gap between the two groups for the skin temperature. For electrodermal activity, mean is lower for the control group than for the experimental group (2.20 micro-Siemens (μS) vs 3.51 μS). There is a higher variability into the experimental group. Table 1 shows descriptive results for each sensor by group.

Table 1. Descriptive results.

		Group	
		Control group	Experimental Group
Skin temperature	Mean	31.34 °C	31.81 °C
	Sd	2.3 °C	2.02 °C
Electrodermal activity	Mean	2.20 μS	3.51 μS
	Sd	1.59 μS	3.29 μS

A Mann-Whitney U test was used to compare the group's influence on skin temperature and electrodermal activity. There are no significative group's differences neither for skin temperature (U: 136.50; $p = .78$; $n = 34$) nor for electrodermal activity (U: 124; $p = .50$; $n = 34$).

Even if participants in the experimental group show higher skin temperature and electrodermal activity than participants in the control group, the differences are non-significant. Additional experiments should confirm whether there is a difference which can be inferred by the context or the stress induced by experimenting a new driving assistance system.

4.2 Subjective Mental Workload

For the control group, the most relevant dimension was mental demand (mean: 104.6), for the experimental group, it was performance (mean: 152.94). Figure 4 presents descriptive results.

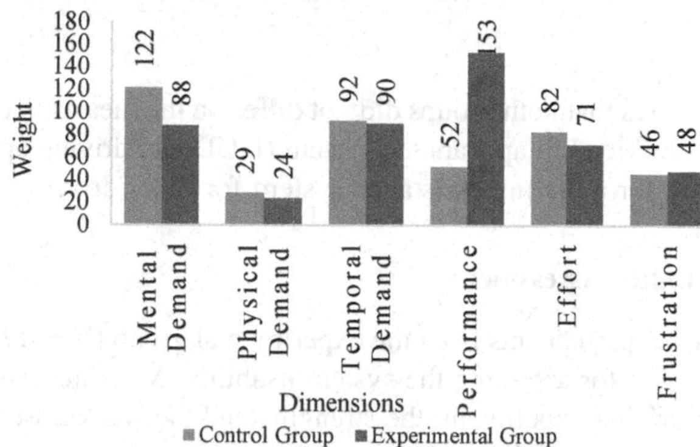

Fig. 4. NASA-TLX descriptive results.

A Mann-Whitney U test was used to compare groups' assessment of NASA-TLX dimensions. The hypothesis was that participants, regardless of group, would answer in the same way. This hypothesis was confirmed for five dimensions: mental demand (U: 121.5; $p = .43$; $n = 17$), physical demand (U: 124; $p = .49$; $n = 17$), temporal demand (U: 134.5; $p = .73$; $n = 17$), effort (U:143.5; $p = .97$; $n = 17$) and frustration (U:125; $p = .52$; $n = 17$). The hypothesis was rejected for performance. There is a significant difference for the performance dimension between control and experimental groups (U: 56; $p < .005$; $n = 17$). Subjective perception of participants mental workload is higher for performance. This result suggests that the system (HUD and driving mobile app.) had an impact on the performance dimension of driving, but not on the other dimensions of the NASA-TLX. It was more demanding for participants who drove with the system than those who drove without it.

4.3 Comparison of Objective and Subjective Mental Workload

Following the results presented above, a comparison was made on the three measures of mental workload (objective and subjective). We wanted to identify an effect between means of skin temperature; mean electrodermal activity; subjective conditions: mean total weight of NASA-TLX dimensions. The inter-subject factor was the group condition (control or experimental). Table 2 indicates no significant effect of objective and subjective mental workload conditions according to the group ($F [30] = .954$, $p < .50$).

Table 2. Multivariate ANOVA test.

Test name	Value	F	Hypoth. Df	Sig. of F	Sum of square	p
Pillais	.09	.95	3.00	.47	.09	.24
Wilks	.91	.95	3.00	.43	.09	.24
Hotelings	.09	.95	3.00	.43	.09	.24
Roys	.09	.95	3.00	.43	.09	.24

This result indicates that both groups did not differ on the measures of objective and subjective mental workload. It appears the system (HUD and driving application) is an interesting modality for a driving assistance system for older drivers.

4.4 System Usability Assessment

After the driving task, participants from the experimental group (N = 17) were asked to answer a questionnaire for assessing the system usability. Measures assessed were the satisfaction of the driving experiment, the strengths and the weaknesses of the system, and to judge the system usefulness. The overall driving experiment was rated satisfactory or very satisfactory for 94% of participants. Participants were surveyed about the strengths and weaknesses of the system (i.e. HUD and interfaces). They had to rate five strengths: reliable, high-quality, useful, singular and ergonomic. Classified in order from best to least strength, the first was its ergonomics, its usefulness, its singularity, its high-quality rate, and the last its reliability. The five weaknesses were: seems too expensive, impractical, ineffective, poor quality and unreliable. Amongst these, the first is its poor quality, its unreliability, its inefficiency, its impracticality, and it seems too expensive. These strengths and weaknesses allow us to determine what was considered interested and what has to be improved.

Most participants indicated that the system did not interfere during the driving task (70%). It means that the system in the participants' field of view is not perceived as a visual discomfort. About usefulness, 47% of participants considering the system useful or somewhat useful compared to 53% who considered it useless or rather useless. Subsequently, a question was asked about the benefit of the system to help driving safely. The system was rated as very beneficial or beneficial for 41% of participants. After testing the system, a quarter of participants would be interested in purchasing the system (24%). And the system did not seem like other computer systems with which participants were familiar (58%). The system was considered different from other known computing systems. These different aspects assessed allow us to know which ones need to be improved or preserved.

5 Discussion - Conclusion

Driving assistance systems are a solution to support the older drivers in their task. However, this type of assistance must be adapted and designed to meet the real needs of drivers. The assessment of the system influenced the subjective driving performance of older drivers, but not the objective mental workload where results did not indicate a significant difference between the two groups. Results of this work confirm the usefulness of measuring the mental workload of older drivers objectively and subjectively. Results of objective mental workload suggested there is no increased for the experimental group who assessed the system. Comparing both groups (control and experimental), mean skin temperature and mean electrodermal activity was slightly higher for drivers who had to assess the system. It means that the system tested would cause a slight increase in mental workload during driving activity, although there is no significant difference between groups. Objective mental workload measurements do not always correspond to the participants' feelings. It is the reason that we added to our objective measurements a subjective measure (NASA-TLX scale). This combination of mental workload measures should be encouraged in future research of older drivers. Our results indicated only one significant difference between the experimental and control groups: the performance dimension. The experimental group appears to have found it more difficult to drive than the control group. One explanation may be due to the novelty of the task, rather than the fact of driving with the system per se. Experimenting with a new system may have caused more anxiety. Combining mental workload measures is therefore recommended [14].

This study proposed to develop and assess new material based on expectations of older drivers in Quebec province (Canada). When a driving assistance system is designed with the intended users, it meets the expectations of users and will tend not to increase mental workload. The whole study provides new knowledge to think about improving driving for older drivers. A practical contribution is a development of HUD with adapted mobile applications which can be deployed quickly on the market and offered to older people by insurance companies.

In this study, the time to assess the system is a limitation. Participants discovered the system and drove with it for less than one hour. Since familiarity encourages opinion and system use [3], a longitudinal study is a proposal for future research in order to assess the system several times to encourage its usefulness.

As we wanted to validate the different interfaces with older drivers, it depended on the driving habits of each driver. Some would not have had as much information from the mobile app. while driving as they received during the experiments. It is necessary to propose a new study with the presentation of interfaces according to the context of the driving task through the analysis of data in real time. In the current mobile app., it is possible to collect contextual data (speed, brakes, acceleration, localization, etc.). It might be interesting to also include a data mining technique (e.g. decision tree) for real-time analysis of driving data. Future research could follow this direction and offer a personalized interface to the driver based on the driving context in real time.

Acknowledgments. This work was supported by MITACS. We thank all the participants from the user study and staff who wrote and provided helpful comments.

References

1. Reimer, B.: Driver assistance systems and the transition to automated vehicles: a path to increase older adult safety and mobility? Public Policy Aging Rep. **24**(1), 27–31 (2014)
2. Fisk, A.D., et al.: Designing for Older Adults: Principles and Creative Human Factors Approaches. CRC Press, Washington, DC (2009)
3. Duncan, M., et al.: Enhanced mobility for aging populations using automated vehicles (2015)
4. Eby, D.W., Molnar, L.J.: Has the time come for older driver vehicle? J. Ergon. (2014)
5. Williams, D., et al.: Considerations in designing human-computer interfaces for elderly people. In: 2013 13th International Conference on Quality Software. IEEE (2013)
6. Simões, A., Pereira, M.: Older drivers and new in-vehicle technologies: adaptation and long-term effects. In: Kurosu, M. (ed.) HCD 2009. LNCS, vol. 5619, pp. 552–561. Springer, Heidelberg (2009). https://doi.org/10.1007/978-3-642-02806-9_64
7. Davidse, R.J.: Older drivers and ADAS: which systems improve road safety? IATSS Res. **30** (1), 6–20 (2006)
8. Castillejo, E., Almeida, A., López-de-Ipiña, D.: User, context and device modeling for adaptive user interface systems. In: Urzaiz, G., Ochoa, Sergio F., Bravo, J., Chen, L.L., Oliveira, J. (eds.) UCAmI 2013. LNCS, vol. 8276, pp. 94–101. Springer, Cham (2013). https://doi.org/10.1007/978-3-319-03176-7_13
9. Reimer, B., Mehler, B., Coughlin, J.F.: An evaluation of driver reactions to new vehicle parking assist technologies developed to reduce driver stress. New England University Transportation Center, Massachusetts Institute of Technology, Cambridge (2010)
10. Tretten, P., et al.: An on-road study of head-up display: preferred location and acceptance levels. In: Proceedings of the Human Factors and Ergonomics Society Annual Meeting. Sage Publications, Los Angeles (2011)
11. Pauzie, A.: Head up display in automotive: a new reality for the driver. In: Marcus, A. (ed.) DUXU 2015. LNCS, vol. 9188, pp. 505–516. Springer, Cham (2015). https://doi.org/10.1007/978-3-319-20889-3_47
12. Tufano, D.R.: Automotive HUDs: the overlooked safety issues. Hum. Factors **39**(2), 303–311 (1997)
13. Kim, S., Dey, A.K.: Augmenting human senses to improve the user experience in cars: applying augmented reality and haptics approaches to reduce cognitive distances. Multimedia Tools Appl. **75**, 1–21 (2015)
14. Schneegass, S., et al.: A data set of real world driving to assess driver workload. In: Proceedings of the 5th International Conference on Automotive User Interfaces and Interactive Vehicular Applications. ACM (2013)
15. Lemercier, C., Cellier, J.-M.: Les défauts de l'attention en conduite automobile: inattention, distraction et interférence. Le travail humain **71**(3), 271–296 (2008)
16. Collet, C., Salvia, E., Petit-Boulanger, C.: Measuring workload with electrodermal activity during common braking actions. Ergonomics **57**(6), 886–896 (2015)
17. Solovey, E.T., et al.: Classifying driver workload using physiological and driving performance data: two field studies. In: Proceedings of the SIGCHI Conference on Human Factors in Computing Systems. ACM (2014)
18. Hart, S.G.: Theory and measurement of human workload. Hum. Prod. Enhanc. **1**, 396–456 (1986)
19. Leung, R., McGrenere, J., Graf, P.: Age-related differences in the initial usability of mobile device icons. Behav. Inf. Technol. **30**(5), 629–642 (2011)

20. Shi, Y., et al.: Galvanic Skin Response (GSR) as an index of cognitive workload. In: ACM CHI Conference Work-in-Progress (2007)
21. Clarion, A.: Electrodermal indices for mental workload analysis in car driving. Université Claude Bernard - Lyon I (2009)

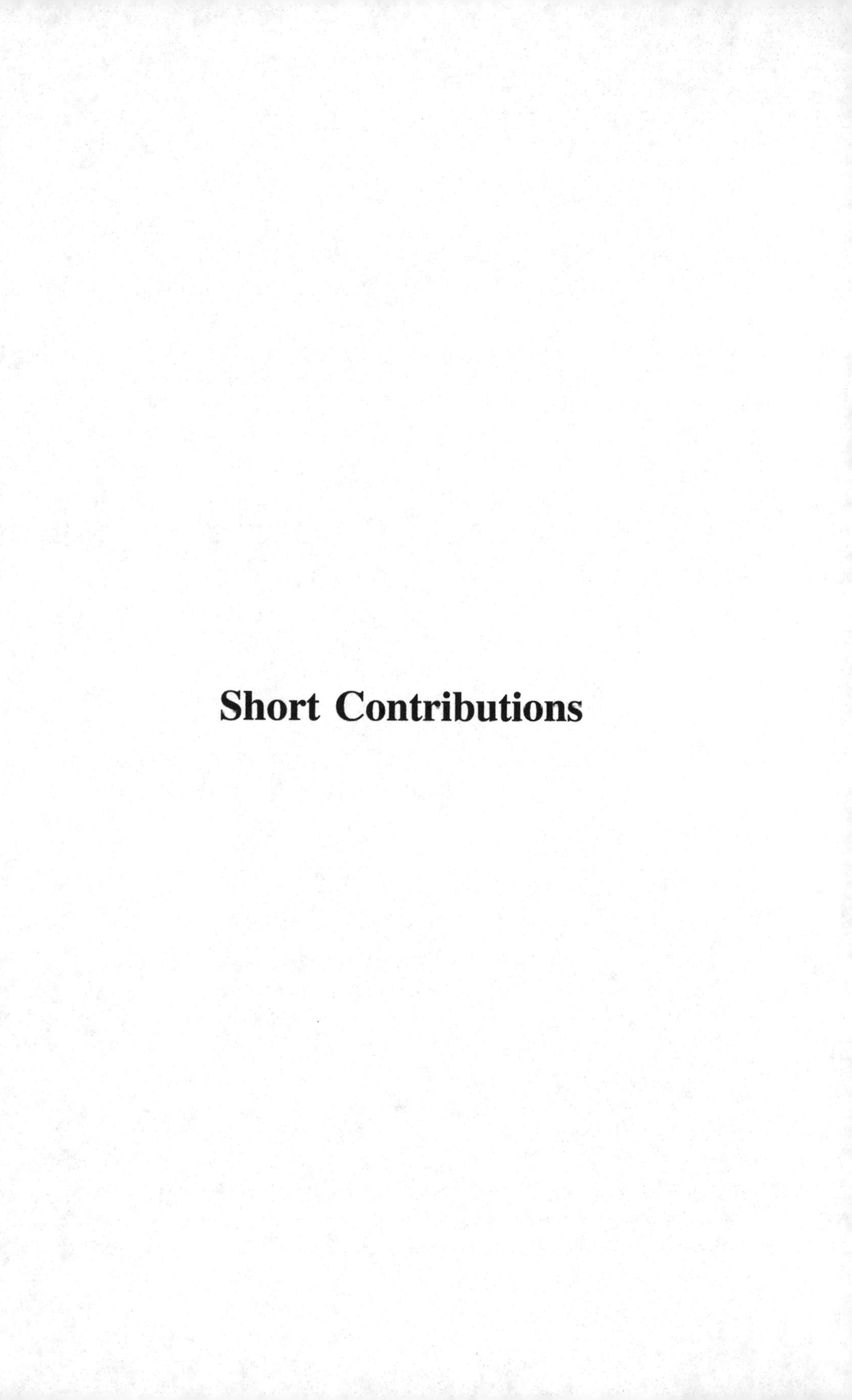

Short Contributions

User Embeddings Based on Mobile App Behavior Data

Kushal Singla[1(✉)], Satyen Abrol[1], and Sungdeuk Park[2]

[1] Samsung R&D Institute, Bangalore, India
{kushal.s,satyen.abrol}@samsung.com
[2] Samsung Electronics, Suwon, Korea
sdeuk.park@samsung.com

Abstract. We consider a smart phone scenario with a number of apps used by a user. The app usage data provides information about the user behavior, which can be used to identify the user demographics and interest and in turn is used to find similar users. In this paper, we propose a method to generate a latent space user embedding using the user app usage data, which is a dense low-dimensional representation of the user. This representation is used for low latency user similarity computation and acts as the user feature representation in user demographics prediction models.

Keywords: User2vec · AutoEncoder · User embedding

1 Introduction

User Modeling and User Profiling are well-studied areas of Computer Science finding applications in broad range of areas including recommendation systems and expert systems. Understanding the user preferences, interests and characteristics allows service providers to serve more personalized content to user resulting in improved user experience and increased success (engagement, purchases, etc.) for the business. In the domain of smartphones, a potential approach for building the user profiles is based on either developing a predictive model that map the user to a pre-defined taxonomy or creating user segments based on the app installation or app usage. In this paper, we present a novel approach to map a user to a latent space embedding which implicitly captures user behavior. In our work, we make several contributions in the field of user modelling based on app usage. First, we propose a user modelling method for creating a user embedding using Auto encoders. Second, we show the effectiveness of user embedding for different use cases such as demographics prediction. Thirdly, we show that this user representation can be used for user segmentation using vector operations.

2 Related Work

User modelling and Personalization has been studied extensively, especially since the advent of smartphones. Zolna et al. [1] present a method to build LSTMs to model user behavior on a website, with applications in e-commerce domain. The approach looks at

J. Pagán et al. (Eds.): ICOST 2019, LNCS 11862, pp. 183–189, 2019.
https://doi.org/10.1007/978-3-030-32785-9_16

user's browsing pattern and maps it into a fixed-size vector. Amir et al. [2] describe a method to create user embedding from text to capture latent user aspects. App2Vec [3] and AppDNA [4] are two such papers, which present methods to create embedding which captures semantic relationship between apps. The work done by us presents a novel unified method to compute user embedding based on the apps of the user instead of deducing user embedding from the app embedding. [5] Shows that usage of user embedding for the gender prediction task where the social context of the user is available but the social context is not readily available in all cases so in the absence of social context, the proposed approach doesn't require the user relations. Mannan [6] shows the use of artificial neural network for the user similarity computation but it is computationally expensive to compute the similarity between all the set of users and it cannot perform vector-based operations using this approach but the autoencoder fills this gap.

3 User Embeddings Model

User embedding can be used for finding similar user. The app space cardinality is very high but it is very sparse per user whereas dense user embeddings are usefull in this case. User embedding can be used as a feature for predictive analytics like classification of user into various categories extracted in an unsupervised manner. User embedding can be used to perform vector operations like addition, subtraction etc. This can be used to perform user analogy tasks. Our method is based on autoencoder. Autoencoder is a neural network model, which was developed for unsupervised learning and is used for feature extraction. [7] explains the usage of autoencoder for reducing the dimensions using a multi-layer neural network, which is proven to be better than the standard PCA approach. Amiri [8] presents a method to compute similarity between text pairs using autoencoder.

3.1 Method Explanation

In this subsection, we explain the architecture of the user-embedding model based on the autoencoder architecture. The layers of the encoder model are explained below (Fig. 1).

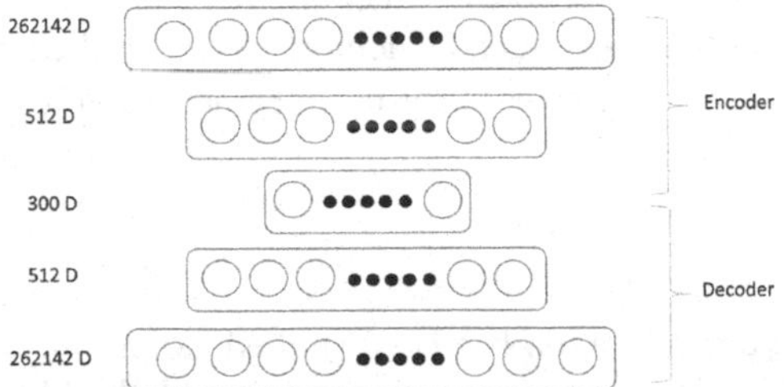

Fig. 1. Architecture for the autoencoder

(1) Input Layer – The input layer is 262,142 dimensional which is equal to the vocabulary of the app space.
(2) Hidden later – This layer is 512 dimensional which is followed by Relu, batch-norm, dropout respectively.
(3) Output later – This layer is 300 dimensional. Tanh computation is applied on the output layer

The layers of the decoder model are in the reverse order until the input layer. Sigmoid operation is applied to the output layer. Loss is optimized using the Adam optimizer and BCELoss. Number of epoch is equal to 6. Variable learning rate is employed per epoch- [0.1, 0.05, 0.025, 0.01, 0.005, 0.0001]. We ran the experiment on Amazon AWS p2.xlarge which has 12 GB of GPU memory which influences the autoencoder design (Table 1).

Table 1. Algorithm to compute the user embedding using the mobile app usage data

ALGORITHM: Algorithm to compute the user-embedding model using app usage
Input: User app usage vector for the app $A_1\,A_2\,A_{3\ldots\ldots}\,A_n$ ***Output***: User embedding vector for the user $U_1\,U_2\,U_{3\ldots\ldots}\,U_n$ 1. Pre-process the app usage vector and one-hot encode the vector 2. Train the auto encoder model using the user one-hot encoded vector. 3. Generate the user embedding from the output layer of the encoder section of the auto encoder. 4. *exit*: end procedure

4 Experiments

We evaluate the user-embedding model using a private dataset collected from a survey of the user app usage. We collected the app usage data of the users over a period of 2 months. The User set is composed of both the male and female users within the age group from 16 to 80. App usage data consists of the app ids (For example - com.whatsapp) of the apps used by the users within this period in the csv format. This dataset is used to evaluate the user embedding using various tasks. The app usage data is preprocessed using Spark to create the one hot encodings of the user app usage vector.

4.1 User Embedding Use Cases

4.1.1 Gender Clustering

In this sub section, we try to find the relation between the embedding and the user gender. In this case, we sampled 1000 user randomly from the two classes and generate the user embedding using the model training earlier and generate t-sne plots.

4.1.2 Age Clustering

In this sub section, we try to find the relation between the embedding and the user age. In the case of the age attribute based clustering of the user, we divider the user into two groups based on different point of age as the separation point and observe that the distinct clusters are formed at various age separation points. Figure 3 shows the user clusters based on different age threshold point. Equal numbers of users are sample from the two sets and t-sne plot are computed for the various threshold ages. This shows that distinct clusters are observed under various age thresholds (Fig. 2).

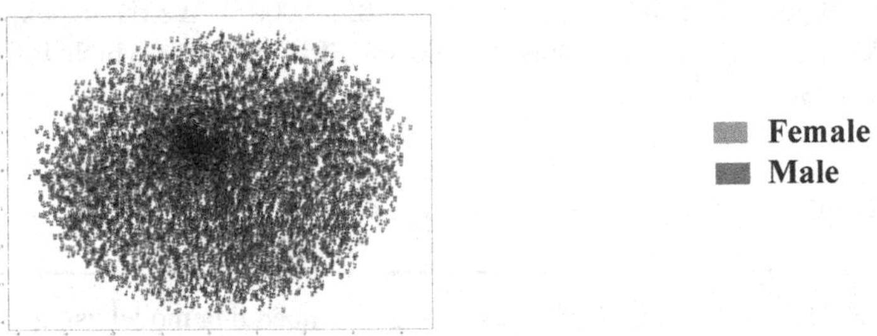

Fig. 2. T-SNE based gender plot of the users based on the autoencoder embedding

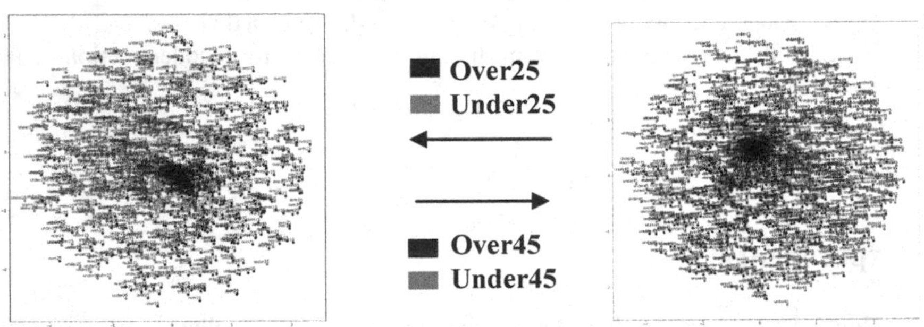

Fig. 3. T-SNE based age plots of the users based on the autoencoder embedding

4.1.3 Embedding for User Similarity Task

In this sub section, we evaluate the quality of finding users with similar attributes.

Figure 4a shows the quality of the user similarity task. In this experiment, we sampled a subset of users from the two age groups. This figure shows the probability of finding a user within the same age group by using the cosine distance between the user embedding lies within the range of 0.6 to 0.8. The app usage behavior of the people in the age group under 35 and over 35 is the least non-distinguishable in the experiment as it can be shown in lowest cosine distance of 0.6 whereas it's most distinguishable in the age-group under 75 and over 75 as shown by the cosine distance of 0.8. Figure 4b shows the quality of the user similarity task on dividing the user sample into two sets based on the age threshold.

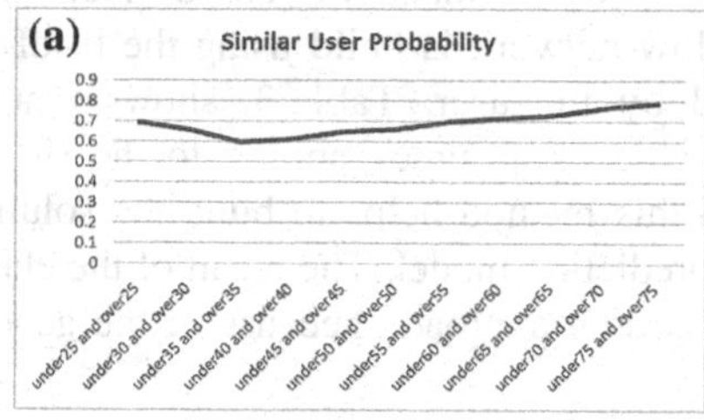

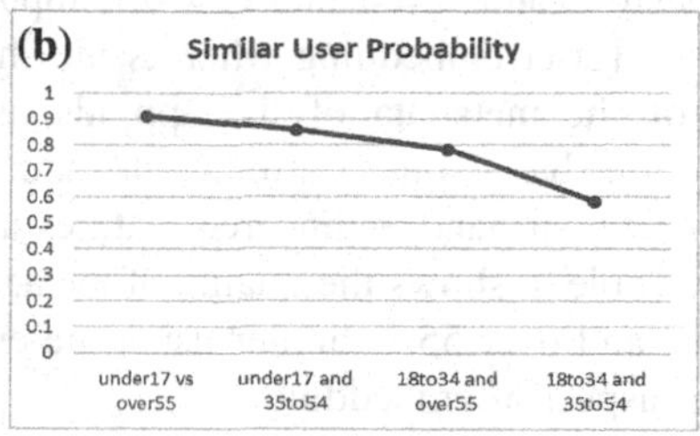

Fig. 4. (a) Probability of similar user in various age groups (b) Probability of similar user in various age groups

4.1.4 Validation Using Analogy Tasks

In this sub-section, we try to derive relationships based on multiple attributes. For e.g. the deduced semantic relation between an old woman user group and old man user group is similar to the semantic relation between young girl user group and young boy user group. These multi-attribute semantic relations can be evaluated by performing vector operation on the embedding. For example - To compute the semantic relation old_woman - old_man = young_girl - X, we sample 1000 users randomly from the each user group, compute the average of the vectors, perform this process for the old_woman, old_man, young_girl user groups and then search the vector space for the user_group vector closest to X using the cosine distance method and found that the closest vector is equal to the young_boy user group. We performed eight more experiments like this and the results are shown in the Table 2.

Table 2. Analysis of the classification quality for gender prediction using user embeddings and shallow network

Analogy	Actual test case
old_woman-old_man = young_girl-young_boy	60 to 65_F-60 to 65_M = 20 to 25_F-25 to 30_M
old_woman-young_girl = old_man-young_boy	70 to 75_F-20 to 25_F = 70 to 75_M-25 to 30_M
young_girl-young_boy = old_woman-old_man	20 to 25_F-20 to 25_M = 70 to 75_F-65 to 70_M
young_girl-old_woman = young_boy-old_man	20 to 25_F-70 to 75_F = 20 to 25_M-65 to 70_M
old_man-old_woman = young_man-young_girl	60 to 65_M-60 to 65_F = 20 to 25_M-25 to 30_F
old_man-young_boy = old_woman-young_girl	60 to 65_M-20 to 25_M = 60 to 65_F-25 to 30_F
young_boy-old_man = young_girl-old_woman	20 to 25_M-70 to 75_M = 20 to 25_F-65 to 70_F
young_boy-old_woman = young_girl-old_man	20 to 25_M-70 to 75_F = 20 to 25_F-60 to 65_M
young_boy-young_girl = old_man-old_woman	20 to 25_M-20 to 25_F = 70 to 75_M-65 to 70_F

4.1.5 User Embedding for Classification Task

In this sub-section, we use the embedding as feature for user attribute prediction and compare its performance with a shallow prediction model with manual feature engineering. The shallow prediction model is based on SVM [9] model with the following parameters: gamma = 1 and C = 0.1. Input data to the embedding based model is the app-based user embedding whereas the shallow network is build using the tf-idf features of the metadata of the app ids used by the user. Table 3. shows that the embedding based binary prediction model achieves accuracy similar to the shallow model without hand engineered features and this method helps to build the solutions faster. Table 4. shows the quality of the age prediction model. The recall of the classes 0 to 17 and over 55 is higher using the embedding approach because of the generalization aspect of embedding.

Table 3. Analysis of the classification quality for gender prediction using user embeddings and shallow network respectively

		precision	recall	f1-score	support
	F	0.8889	0.889	0.889	5083
	M	0.8853	0.8851	0.8852	4917
weighted	avg	0.8871	0.8871	0.8871	10000

	precision	recall	f1-score	support
F	0.8872	0.869	0.878	89299
M	0.8961	0.9109	0.9034	110701
avg/total	0.8921	0.8922	0.8921	200000

Table 4. Analysis of the classification quality for age prediction using embedding vector feature and shallow network

	precision	recall	f1-score	support
0to17	0.684211	0.537931	0.602317	145
18to34	0.767632	0.740511	0.753827	4189
35to54	0.693874	0.766928	0.728574	4711
over55	0.65047	0.434555	0.52103	955
avg	0.720486	0.7208	0.717502	10000

	precision	recall	f1-score	support
0to17	0.734463	0.463954	0.568679	1401
18to34	0.761585	0.759016	0.760298	41206
35to54	0.694594	0.774033	0.732165	46945
over55	0.695152	0.381508	0.492646	10448
avg / total	0.722815	0.722490	0.716442	100000

5 Conclusion and Future Work

In this paper, we have proposed a method to create user embedding for a smartphone user based on their app usage. Our experiments highlight the usefulness of such an embedding in capturing user behavior and for binary prediction tasks and vector operations. In future, we plan to evaluate the use of the user embedding for the recommendation task.

References

1. Zołna, K.: User modeling using LSTM networks (2017)
2. Amir, S., Coppersmith, G., Carvalho, P., Silva, M.J., Wallace, B.C.: Quantifying mental health from social media with neural user embeddings. arXiv preprint arXiv:1705.00335 (2017)

3. Ma, Q., Muthukrishnan, S., Simpson, W.: App2vec: vector modeling of mobile apps and applications. In: Proceedings of the 2016 IEEE/ACM International Conference on Advances in Social Networks Analysis and Mining, pp. 599–606. IEEE Press (2016)
4. Xue, S., Zhang, L., Li, A., Li, X.Y., Ruan, C., Huang, W.: Appdna: app behavior profiling via graph-based deep learning. In: IEEE INFOCOM 2018-IEEE Conference on Computer Communications, pp. 1475–1483. IEEE (2018)
5. Chen, L., Qian, T., Zhu, P., You, Z.: Learning user embedding representation for gender prediction. In: 2016 IEEE 28th International Conference on Tools with Artificial Intelligence (ICTAI), pp. 263–269. IEEE (2016)
6. Mannan, N.B., Sarwar, S.M., Elahi, N.: A new user similarity computation method for collaborative filtering using artificial neural network. In: Mladenov, V., Jayne, C., Iliadis, L. (eds.) EANN 2014. CCIS, vol. 459, pp. 145–154. Springer, Cham (2014). https://doi.org/10.1007/978-3-319-11071-4_14
7. Hinton, G.E., Salakhutdinov, R.R.: Reducing the dimensionality of data with neural networks. Science **313**(5786), 504–507 (2006)
8. Amiri, H., Resnik, P., Boyd-Graber, J., Daumé III, H.: Learning text pair similarity with context-sensitive autoencoders. In: Proceedings of the 54th Annual Meeting of the Association for Computational Linguistics, Long Papers, vol. 1, pp. 1882–1892 (2016)
9. Boser, B.E., Guyon, I.M., Vapnik, V.N.: A training algorithm for optimal margin classifiers. In: Proceedings of the Fifth Annual Workshop on Computational Learning Theory, pp. 144–152. ACM (1992)

Design, Development and Initial Validation of a Wearable Particulate Matter Monitoring Solution

José G. Teriús-Padrón(✉), Rebeca I. García-Betances, Nikolaos Liappas, María F. Cabrera-Umpiérrez, and María Teresa Arredondo Waldmeyer

Universidad Politécnica de Madrid, ETSI Ingenieros de Telecomunicación, 28002 Madrid, Spain
{jterius,rgarcia,nliappas,chiqui,mta}@lst.tfo.upm.es

Abstract. Air pollution in one of the main problems that big cities have nowadays. Traffic congestion, heaters, industrial activities, among others produce large quantities of Particulate Matter (PM) that have harmful effects on citizens' health. This paper presents the design, development and initial validation of a wearable device for the detection of PM concentration, with communication capacity via WiFi and Bluetooth Low Energy and an end user interface. The results are promising due to the high accuracy of measurements collected by the developed device. This solution is a step forward in empowering citizens to prevent being exposed to high levels of air pollution and is the beginning of what could be a macro-network of air quality sensors within a Smart City.

Keywords: Air pollution · Wearable sensor · Smart cities · Particulate matter

1 Introduction

Air pollution affects the quality of life (QoL) of people in large cities [1]. Vehicular traffic, heaters and lack of clean transport alternatives are some of the causes of this problem [2]. According to the World Health Organization, only 20% of cities worldwide comply with the required air quality standards [3].

Among the most dangerous pollutants, the Particulate Matter (PM) is one of the air pollutants that causes most damage to people's health due to its characteristics of size and composition [4]. PM_{10} or Coarse Particles have a diameter of less than 10 μg, $PM_{2.5}$ or Fine Particles less than 2.5 μg, and PM_1 less than 1 $\mu g/m^3$ [5].

Due to the long-term exposure to air pollutants, especially $PM_{2.5}$, the mortality of people with chronic diseases is increasing [6]. Cardiovascular, respiratory and neurodegenerative diseases are directly affected by the effects of these pollutants [7, 8]. One of the ways to reduce exposure to pollution is by providing awareness about the pollution levels within the cities. Smart Cities offer data that come from the air quality stations installed in the city from which different services and applications (e.g. PulsAir application [9]) could gather data to empower citizens with urban, environment and

J. Pagán et al. (Eds.): ICOST 2019, LNCS 11862, pp. 190–196, 2019.
https://doi.org/10.1007/978-3-030-32785-9_17

health recommendations. However, the data currently available come from fixed sensor stations, and do not necessary cover the entire city.

On the other hand, there are few wearable devices available in the market that seek to provide the user with the necessary information about the pollution levels in a precise location of the city. These solutions present certain weaknesses like the Sparrow [10] and ATMO sensors [11] only focus on $C0_2$ detection, and The Plume Flow [12] only uses Bluetooth as a communication protocol which limits the possibility to scale-up this solution to other services within a Smart City.

This manuscript presents the design, development and initial validation of a wearable real-time Air Quality (AQ) monitoring device based on PM concentration detection, with a user-friendly interface to show AQ levels, and to report warnings, alerts and recommendations based on the pollution levels detected. The device allows to send the gathered data to other devices or services through WiFi and Bluetooth Low Energy (BLE) and can be programmed to use different communication protocols. This solution is presented as the initial step for a result applicable to large Smart Cities in order to increase the granularity of air quality information that allows the public authorities to develop the appropriate policies to improve the QoL of the citizens.

The next sections are organized as follows: Sect. 2 presents the methodology and material used to develop the proposed solution; Sect. 3 includes the design, develop and evaluation of the system; and finally, Sect. 4 presents discussions, conclusion and future steps to extend this work.

2 Materials and Methods

The proposed solution includes the design development and initial validation of the wearable device for air quality measurement, with a user-friendly interface and multiple communication capabilities. The materials used throughout this work are the following:

- PMS7003 Air Quality Sensor (Plantower, Co.): this device can measure concentrations of PM_1, $PM_{2.5}$, and PM_{10}. It has a built-in flow system that allows air circulation through the device enabling to measure pollution levels.
- ESP32 microcontroller (Espressif Systems, Co.): it can establish communication via Serial, WiFi and BLE protocols, which gives great versatility when transmitting or receiving data to/from sensors, actuators and services.
- Sketch-Up software (Trimble, Inc.): is the software used to design the 3D case of the wearable device to be printed in the Ultimaker 3 extended (Ultimaker BV).
- Air Visual Pro Air Quality device (IQAir, Inc): a commercial fixed air quality device, capable to measure PM_1, $PM_{2.5}$, and PM_{10}. The device has a test configuration, that allows to run tests and extract the data collected.
- Arduino Integrated Development Environment (IDE): is an open-source development software to program multi-platform microcontrollers boards [13].

The following methodology has been established:

1. *First Phase, state of the art study of AQ sensors and protocols:*

In this phase, a research of the main air pollutants and their impact on the people health was carried out. Additionally, air quality protocols were studied in order to select the one to be applied in our system, based on current regulations and standards. Finally, a study of air quality sensors available in the market and comparisons were done in terms of size, accuracy communication and energy consumption. Findings of this phase were used to design the proposed device.

2. *Second Phase, design and development of the solution:*

Once the AQ sensor was selected the design and development of the electronics necessary for the operation of the device were conducted. As a final stage, the wearable case, where all the technology developed is built in, was designed with the 3D design sketch tool and produced in the 3D printer.

3. *Third Phase, initial validations:*

This phase consisted on analysing the operation of the device according to the established design, making the necessary adjustments and comparisons with a commercial device to study its accuracy.

Tests were carried out following two stages to analyse the measured quality of the solution developed compared with the Air Visual Pro air quality monitor. In the first stage, the PM sensor was placed without any encapsulation. In the second stage, the same test was conducted with the final design (including the case) in order to verify that the design of the 3D encapsulation did not affect the sensor accuracy. The devices were placed in a home kitchen and synchronized to measure $PM_{2.5}$, PM_1 and PM_{10}, every five minutes. These tests were carryout for a total of six days, three continuous days in each test.

3 Results

This section presents the results obtained from the design, development and initial validations according to the methodology described in Sect. 2.

3.1 Main Components and Design

The designed solution has been conceived with the purpose of being wearable, easy to use and with multiple communication capacity. There are 5 main components: (1) a microcontroller, that mange the sensor, actuators and interface, makes the necessary calculations, and establishes the communications via BLE or WiFi to other devices. It has a lithium battery port and an embedded charger module, which guarantees the portability of the solution; (2) a sensor, that detects the $PM_{2.5}$, PM_1 and PM_{10} concentration and sends it to the microcontroller via serial communication; (3) a screen to show the levels of air quality detected by the sensor; (4) a button which has the functionality to activate the screen. In this way, battery consumption is decreased by not activating the screen unless the user decides to do so; and (5) a sound emitter, which is activated in case of any health risk due to high pollution levels.

3.2 Development

For the development of the firmware, the Arduino IDE has been used taking advantage of the compatibility with the ESP32 microcontroller.

The Air Quality Index (AQI) has been calculated with the data received through the sensor, based on the Environmental Protection Agency standard [14], where 6 levels of pollution are established according to the concentration level of PM. The system will respond in different ways, depending on the AQI value, as presented in Fig. 1.

Three functionalities have been established: to sense the pollution levels, to show the data collected, and to present the information through a user-friendly interface. The measurements are later sent to other devices or services. The functionalities established are the following:

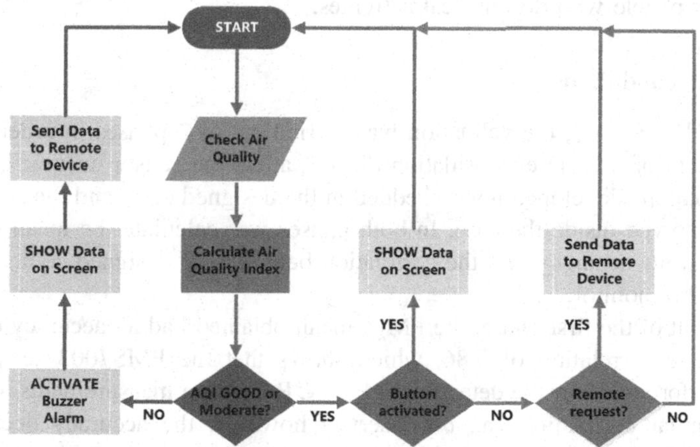

Fig. 1. Flow diagram of the solution.

1. *Activation by button:* when the button is pressed the device calculates the AQI and shows on the screen the AQI levels, taking into consideration the colour scale described by the AQI standard.
2. *Remote communication:* the device measurements and the calculated PM concentration are sent, via BLE, to another device (e.g. smartphone) or service. This functionality allows to present the historical data in a mobile application or to be used by other services.
3. *Pollution levels*: the device reacts autonomously depending on the AQI calculated. When the levels are in a safe range for health ($PM_{2.5}$ concentration between 0 and

12 μg/m^3), the device remains in passive mode. However, when the detected levels are harmful ($PM_{2.5}$ concentration above 35.5 μg/m^3), the system proceeds to alert the user by emitting an alarm sound and showing on the screen the appropriate icon. Furthermore, if a device or service are connected, the information is sent in order to have a historical record of the event.

Each of the functionalities described above were developed individually, and later assembled and incorporated into the case.

4 3D Case Design

Taking into account that the users of this device can have different needs, the case has one top cover, were all the components developed are embedded, and then includes three exchangeable lower caps, describes as follows: (1) lower cap with a clip to attach the device on the side of the pants or belt; (2) lower cap with a hole in one side to hang it on bags or purses; (3) lower cap with two holes to be used with an arm band, designed for people who do physical activities.

4.1 Initial Validations

As described in Sect. 2, the validation was carried out in 2 phases in order to ensure that the design of the 3D encapsulation did not affect the sensor accuracy. The first, with the prototype developed not embedded in the designed case, and the second, with the final prototype inside the case. In both phases was calculate the mean of the PM concentration the accuracy and the correlation between the designed solution and the Air Visual Pro monitor.

As a result of the first phase, the $PM_{2.5}$ mean obtained had an accuracy of 91.42% and a positive correlation of 0.86, which shows that the PMS7003 sensor has an excellent performance for the detection of $PM_{2.5}$. Regarding measurements of PM_1 and PM_{10}, a similar correlation can be observed however, the accuracy decreases but remains over 75%.

On the second tests, the measurement of $PM_{2.5}$ concentration has an accuracy of 92.69% and a correlation of 0.87. In the case of PM_1 and PM_{10} measurements, the data collected show a high accuracy, over 70%, and a positive correlation.

5 Discussions and Conclusion

The system developed represents a novel monitoring device that will help improving the quality of life of people within a smart city environment. Thanks to its small design and wearability, users can have air quality information when moving around city areas where the monitoring stations do not cover. Big cities have insufficient air quality monitoring stations, hence there is no granularity in the provided air pollution data, so that the impact that public policies have on pollution levels cannot be measured with total accuracy.

The proposed solution can be useful to implement a macro network of distributed air quality sensors, monitoring the pollution levels in every corner of the city and thus implement more efficient and effective public policies that will impact positively in the quality of life of the citizens. Taking advantage of the portability and communication capabilities of both BLE and WiFi technologies, the developed sensor can be easily scalable and adaptable to other communication systems and protocols such as Web of Things [15]. The initial validation demonstrates that there are no differences in the measures made by the proposed solution and the commercial device Air Visual Pro monitor.

Future research lines include: (1) the conduction of usability tests in order to improve the design of the final product; (2) largest validations of the device with respect AQ monitoring stations in major cities; and (3) the incorporation of this technology as part of an innovative distributed sensor network for large Smart Cities.

Acknowledgment. This work has been funded by the European Union Horizon 2020 research and innovation program under the Marie Skłodowska- Curie grant agreement ACROSSING No 676157.

References

1. Kelly, F., Fussell, J.: Air pollution and public health: emerging hazards and improved understanding of risk. Environ. Geochem. Health **37**, 631–649 (2015)
2. Ambient air pollution: Pollutants. www.who.int/airpollution/ambient/pollutants/en
3. Health, environment and sustainable development: Air Pollution. https://www.who.int/sustainable-development/cities/health-risks/air-pollution/en/
4. Kim, K., Kabir, E., Kabir, S.: A review on the human health impact of airborne particulate matter. Environ. Int. **74**, 136–143 (2015)
5. Zhang, L., Ninomiya, Y., Yamashita, T.: Formation of submicron particulate matter (PM1) during coal combustion and influence of reaction temperature. Fuel **85**, 1446–1457 (2006)
6. Cohen, A., Brauer, M., Burnett, R., Anderson, H., Frostad, J., et al.: Estimates and 25-year trends of the global burden of disease attributable to ambient air pollution: an analysis of data from the global burden of diseases study 2015. Lancet **389**, 1907–1918 (2017)
7. Zaheer, J., Jeon, J., Lee, S., Kim, J.: Effect of particulate matter on human health, prevention, and imaging using PET or SPECT. Prog. Med. Phys. **29**, 81 (2018)
8. Underwood, E.: The polluted brain. Science **355**, 342–345 (2017)
9. Ottaviano, M., Beltrán-Jaunsarás, M., Teriús-Padrón, J., et al.: Empowering citizens through perceptual sensing of urban environmental and health data following a participative citizen science approach. Sensors **19**(13), 2940 (2019)
10. Sparrow Sense. https://www.sparrowsense.com/
11. AMTO. https://atmotube.com/?view=es
12. Plume Labs. https://plumelabs.com/en/flow/
13. Boxall, J.: Arduino Workshop: A Hands-on Introduction with 65 Projects. No Starch Press (2013)

14. US Environmental Protection Agency, US Environmental Protection Agency, Office of Air Quality Planning and Standards, Outreach and Information Division. Air Quality Index: A guide to air quality and your health. EPA-456/F-14-002 (2014)
15. Teriús-Padrón, J., et al.: Autonomous air quality management system based on Web of Things standard architecture. In: The 5th IEEE Smart World Congress (In press)

Cooperative System and Scheduling Algorithm for Sustainable Energy-Efficient Communities

Esther Palomar(✉), Carlos Cruz, Ignacio Bravo, and Alfredo Gardel

Department Electronics, University of Alcala, Madrid, Spain
{esther.palomar,carlos.cruzt,ignacio.bravo,alfredo.gardel}@uah.es

Abstract. The High connectivity among devices within the Internet-of-Things facilitates two-way flow of information throughout the infrastructure reaching homes and the consumers targeting broader energy goals. Our proposal encompasses consumers cooperating in response to utility supply conditions, i.e., electricity available from renewable sources. Such a smart and green community of consumers autonomously adapts its energy consumption by enabling a local aggregator to (1) integrate their demand into a common view and, (2) re-schedule the community demand given the renewable energy supply and the consumers' demand time preferences. In this paper, we evaluate the developed scheduling algorithm using benchmark data to validate our proposal implementation over existent technology.

Keywords: Cooperative demand response · Scheduling algorithm · Consumer time preferences · Renewable supply

1 Introduction

Information and communication technologies (ICT) are essential tools for enabling energy efficiency as well as establishing new energy services and solutions [4]. In particular, the Internet of Things (IoT) [2] and the Smart Grid [3] together can provide the foundational infrastructure and use of advanced information, control and communication technologies to save energy, reduce cost and increase reliability and transparency. Connected devices (e.g, household items, machines, or gadgets) can automatically influence each other so increasing the overall potential for energy savings and the range of management systems' involvement. ICT can also play an important role in shaping consumer behaviour [5]. Furthermore, the real exploitation of renewable sources for energy supply presents multiple challenges not only for utilities, grid and system operators, but also for the consumers who do not see this type of information on their utility bills [6].

Supported by Comunidad de Madrid (Spain) under the grant Talent Attraction with reference 2017-T1/TIC- 5184.

J. Pagán et al. (Eds.): ICOST 2019, LNCS 11862, pp. 197–203, 2019.
https://doi.org/10.1007/978-3-030-32785-9_18

Demand response (DR) programmes appear to bolster not only energy efficiency but also renewable energy resource management initiatives as to handle their sophisticated planning and operation scheduling requirements [1,7]. In this short paper, we present a cooperative DR system model which is designed to promote behavioural changes in small or large communities of electricity consumers. The community will target common interests (i.e., to be green) that create the need for involved entities to reach binding agreements and coordinated behaviour. We implement and analyse the resource (i.e., the renewable supply) allocation process, initially conceived in a centralised way by means of a data collector called the *Aggregator*. This entity provides the community with the scheduling of the total demand taking into account both the renewable supply available from the local utility providers and the costumers' consumption time preferences. Experimentation with estimated values and benchmarks throws feasible performance cost that validates the viability of the system implementation over existent technology (i.e., Z-Wave or IEEE 802.11i standards).

2 System Model

Figure 1 illustrates the main roles and processes within the adopted cooperative demand response framework. In our proposal, Consumers adapt their energy consumption cooperatively on a centralised way; that is, they share their demand schedule with a data collector called **Aggregator**. The **Aggregator** facilitates the integration of the energy consumption information and implements an optimised resource allocation algorithm in response to the Utility's supply conditions, in particular, targeting renewable sources.

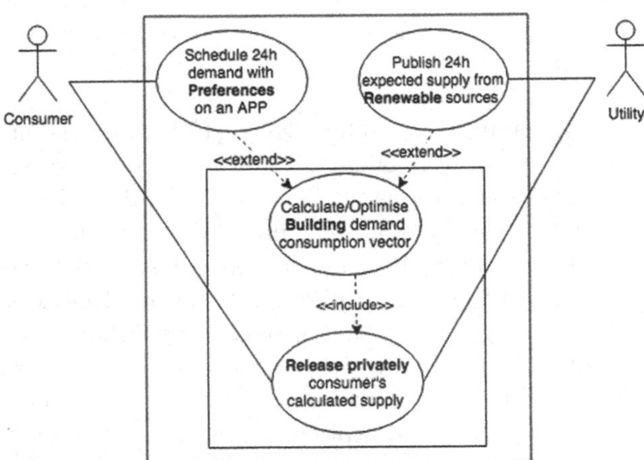

Fig. 1. A user (or household) equipped with an energy consumption scheduler or home energy manager on a portable device (i.e., an app on a smartphone or tablet) that is connected to a communication network. A community consists of a set of Consumers sharing electricity supplier or substation.

2.1 Consumer System Design

Let $\mathcal{N}$ denote an ordered set of Consumers that are willing to cooperate in the pursuit of global community targets (i.e., become greener), sending their data to the *Aggregator*. Each Consumer $i \in \mathcal{N}$ has a set of household appliances $\mathcal{A}_i = \{$washer, dryer, coffee makers, cooker, fridge, TV, alarm, light controller, water heating, AC system,...$\}$. Each consumer then pre-allocates[1] a certain amount of fixed demand[2] as well as variable consumption resulting from their utilisation planned for the upcoming 24 h. The daily fixed demand for consumer $i \in \mathcal{N}$ is denoted by $f\mathcal{D}_i = \sum_{t=0}^{23} \sum_{a_{ij} \in \mathcal{A}_i} fx_{i,a_{ij}}^t$ as the aggregated load of non-shiftable local consumption of the appliances and frequent behaviours. Variable energy demand is considered *flexible* since consumer preference for an appliance to start within a particular time interval is also taken into account. For each appliance, there is a execution window (i.e., a closed interval) denoting a minimal starting time and a maximal ending time. In other words, Consumer i will keep/set the following data for his/her appliance $a_{ij} \in \mathcal{A}_i$ as in Table 1.

Table 1. Appliance configuration

Consumption (KW/h)	Fixed consumption (KW/h)	Duration (hours)	Time ON	Time OFF

2.2 Aggregator System Design

A centralised system with aggregation tasks communicates with the Utility as well as with the Consumers as shown in Fig. 1. An algorithm is originally built to optimise the allocation of the expected electricity supply from renewables amongst the community's Consumers and according to the their expressed preferences. We denote by $\mathcal{RW}^t$ the energy supply generated from a set of renewable sources at a time slot $t \in \{0, \ldots, 23\}$. The *Aggregator* can easily compute the daily fixed demand for the whole community of consumers at a time t as $f\mathcal{D}^t = \sum_i^N f\mathcal{D}_i^t$, which should not reach the worst case such that $\sum_i^N \sum_{t=0}^{23} f\mathcal{D}_i^t \gg \sum_{t=0}^{23} \mathcal{RW}^t$. By contrast, aggregation of the variable consumption is an optimisation problem given the consumers' time preferences.

[1] We consider a discrete time slot system, which granularity is one hour of the day. We have developed an energy consumption scheduling app (or home energy manager) that connects via a home area network (HAN) and/or lower power wireless such as ZigBee, with all the appliances at home and the Aggregator. The app provides the Consumer with an interface to control, monitor, visualise and program the functioning of appliances.

[2] Formulae and benchmarks can be used to estimate appliance and home electronic energy use in kilowatt hours (kWh) as well as household local records.

Algorithm 1. Demand Calculation Function ($\mathcal{DCF}$)

1: **for** iappliance 1 to size of appliances configuration ($\mathcal{A}_i$) **do**
2: $\mathcal{RW}^t = \mathcal{RW}^t - \mathcal{A}_i(f\mathcal{D}_i^t)$
3: **end for**
4: $\mathcal{A}_i(v\mathcal{D}_i^t) = \mathcal{A}_i(v\mathcal{D}_i^t) - \mathcal{A}_i(f\mathcal{D}_i^t)$
5: $\mathcal{A}_i(\mathcal{D}_i^t(\mathcal{D}_i^t < 0)) = 0$
6: $\mathcal{A}_i(f\mathcal{D}_i^t) = \mathcal{A}_i(f\mathcal{D}_i^t) - \mathcal{A}_i(f\mathcal{D}_i^t)$
Objective Function $\mathcal{F}(\mathcal{A}_i, \mathcal{RW}^t, t_{osi})$
Require: $\mathcal{A}_i$ configuration: $v\mathcal{D}_i^t, f\mathcal{D}_i^t, \mathcal{L}_i^t, st_i, et_i$
Ensure: $st_i < et_i$
7: $\mathcal{HC}$ initialisation (consume Hourly Energy)
8: **for** iappliance 1 to size of appliance configuration **do**
9: Set t_{sti}
10: Set t_{eti} based on $\mathcal{L}_i$ and t_{sti}
11: **for** ihour time to the total number of hours **do**
12: **if** ihour belongs to interval $[st_i, et_i]$ **then**
13: $\mathcal{HC}(ihour) \leftarrow \mathcal{HC}(ihour) + \mathcal{A}_i(v\mathcal{D}_i^t)$
14: **else**
15: $\mathcal{HC}(ihour) \leftarrow \mathcal{HC}(ihour) + \mathcal{A}_i(f\mathcal{D}_i^t)$
16: **end if**
17: **end for**
18: **end for**
19: $\mathcal{RW}^t s = \mathcal{RW}^t - \mathcal{HC}^t$
20: $\mathcal{RW}^t s(\mathcal{RW}^t s < 0) = 0$
21: $Demanded\_\mathcal{RW}^t \leftarrow min(\mathcal{RW}^t, \mathcal{HC}^t)$
22: $\mathcal{R}1 = sum(\mathcal{RW}^t s)$; $\mathcal{R}2 = max(\mathcal{HC})$
23: $Result = sum(\mathcal{R}1 + \mathcal{R}2)$
24: **return** $Result, Demanded\_\mathcal{RW}^t, \mathcal{HC}^t(t_{osi}, t_{oei})$

The *Aggregator* will execute a scheduling of the community's requested variable demand per hour $v\mathcal{D}_i^t$ when the aforementioned worst case does not apply, and aiming at $\forall t \in \{0, \ldots, 23\}, \sum_i^N (f\mathcal{D}_i^t + v\mathcal{D}_i^t) \leq \mathcal{RW}^t$. We face here a global centralised optimisation problem to which there exists a unique *Nash bargaining solution* such that: $\forall i \in \{1 \ldots \mathcal{N}\}, \mu_i^t = f\mathcal{D}_i^t + min\{\mathcal{F}(v\mathcal{D}_i^t)\} \leq \mathcal{RW}^t$, where $\mathcal{F}(\cdot)$[3] is in charge of shifting the variable demand given Consumers' appliance preferred activation time. Algorithm 1 displays a round-robin strategy over the matrix of all appliances' operation preferences and the remnant of the *RW* supply vector after deducting the total fixed demand (Algorithm 1 – lines 1–3). Upon reaching the optimisation objective, the *Aggregator* will notify the community that an agreement has been reached and privately release the reallocated demand vector $\overrightarrow{\mu}_i, \forall i \in \mathcal{N}$.

[3] The *Aggregator* can apply different strategies to the aggregated load vector $v\mathcal{D}$ by shifting appliance's demand within their preferred activation time frame as well as by selecting one or another appliance to serve first.

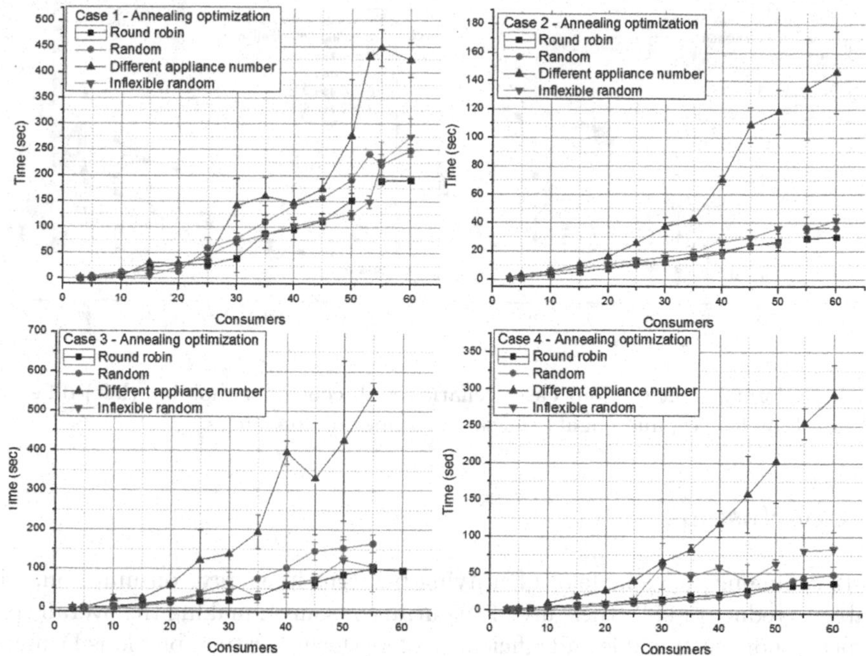

Fig. 2. Computational cost in Cases 1–4 using SA and strategies RR, randomness and consumers with heterogeneous/homogeneous number of appliances.

3 Algorithm Validation

We evaluate the performance of Algorithm 1 with simulated[4] data of consumers' fixed and variable consumption demands at different case scenarios for appliances' fixed and variable consumption, i.e., Case 1 for high consumptions, Case 2 for high fixed expends, Case 3 when variable is high and, Case 4 for low consumption communities.

Figure 2 illustrates the reallocation processing cost of communities with up to 60 consumers with up to 4 appliances, which is taking 3 min in the worst case. In fact, worst case occurs when appliances demand high variable consumption (Cases 1 and 3) and the algorithm performs a random strategy. On the other hand, we found that the factor incurring the highest performance cost on our algorithm is consumers holding a different number of appliances to schedule; 6 min in the worst case (triangle-up line in Fig. 2) and applying a sequence with the first player being the same every time. Figure 3 throws best outcomes over communities with low variable demand and the same number of appliances per consumer.

[4] Simulation run on a computer with the following specifications: CPU: 2.3 GHz Intel Core i5; Memory: 8 GB 2133 MHz LPDDR3 and MATLAB R2018b. Data is estimated by applying manufactures' benchmarks.

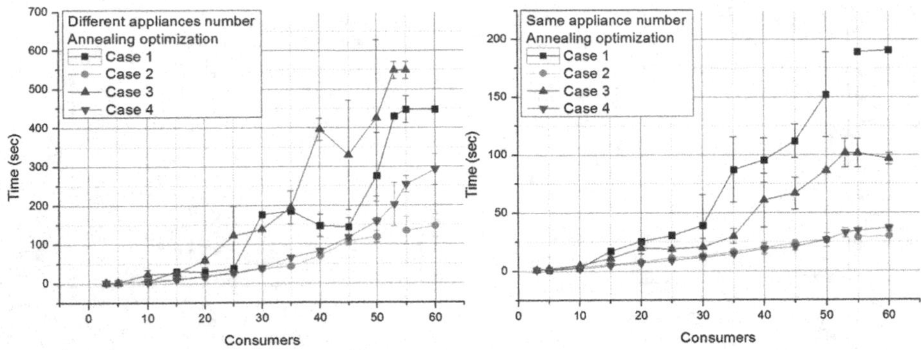

Fig. 3. Performance at the four case scenarios with consumers holding (left) different number of appliances, and (right) the same number of appliances.

4 Conclusions

Smart communities, capable of identifying patterns in energy consumption, will be able to reduce or shift their use of the utility resource, making the overall consumption more sustainable and efficient. Unlike the majority of previous Demand Response strategies that focus on pricing and aim at reducing the energy cost and the peak-to-average ratio, our solution tends to promote a transformation of the whole energy value chain by making consumer communities cooperate targeting the available renewable energy supply. In this paper, we have shown the performance cost of a centralised scheduling algorithm (less than 1 min cost) for different size of communities and consumption patterns. Immediate future work relates to the algorithm testing with real traces from the Birmingham Living Lab and the real implementation of both algorithm and home controllers on a pilot testbed, paying special attention to the system and network security.

References

1. Aghaei, J., Alizadeh, M.I.: Demand response in smart electricity grids equipped with renewable energy sources: a review. Renew. Sustain. Energy Rev. **18**, 64–72 (2013)
2. Gubbi, J., Buyya, R., Marusic, S., Palaniswami, M.: Internet of Things (IoT): a vision, architectural elements, and future directions. Future Gener. Comput. Syst. **29**(7), 1645–1660 (2013)
3. Ipakchi, A., Albuyeh, F.: Grid of the future. IEEE Power Energ. Mag. **7**(2), 52–62 (2009)
4. Lui, T.J., Stirling, W., Marcy, H.O.: Get smart. IEEE Power Energ. Mag. **8**(3), 66–78 (2010)
5. Mattern, F., Staake, T., Weiss, M.: ICT for green: how computers can help us to conserve energy. In: Proceedings of the 1st International Conference on Energy-Efficient Computing and Networking, e-Energy, pp. 1–10. ACM (2010)

6. Palensky, P., Dietrich, D.: Demand side management: demand response, intelligent energy systems, and smart loads. IEEE Trans. Ind. Inform. **7**(3), 381–388 (2011)
7. Qayyum, F., Naeem, M., Khwaja, A.S., Anpalagan, A., Guan, L., Venkatesh, B.: Appliance scheduling optimization in smart home networks. IEEE Access **3**, 2176–2190 (2015)

ForeSight - Platform Approach for Enabling AI-based Services for Smart Living

Jochen Bauer[1(✉)], Hilko Hoffmann[2], Thomas Feld[3], Mathias Runge[4], Oliver Hinz[5], Andreas Mayr[1], Kristina Förster[1], Franz Teske[1], Franziska Schäfer[1], Christoph Konrad[1], and Jörg Franke[1]

[1] Institute for Factory Automation and Production Systems, Friedrich-Alexander-University Erlangen-Nürnberg, Egerlandstraße 7-9, 91058 Erlangen, Germany
jochen.bauer@faps.fau.de
[2] Deutsches Forschungszentrum für Künstliche Intelligenz GmbH, Stuhlsatzenhausweg 3, 66123 Saarbrücken, Germany
[3] Strategion GmbH, Albert-Einstein-Straße 1, 49076 Osnabrück, Germany
[4] IoT connctd GmbH, Hardenbergstraße 32, 10623 Berlin, Germany
[5] Faculty of Economics and Business Administration, Goethe University Frankfurt, Theodor-W.-Adorno-Platz 4, 60323 Frankfurt am Main, Germany

Abstract. In future, smart home and smart living applications will enrich daily life. These applications are aware of their context, use artificial intelligence (AI) and are therefore able to recognize common use cases reliably and adapt these use cases individually with the current user in mind. This paper describes a concept for such an AI-based platform. The presented platform approach considers different stakeholders, e.g. the housing industry, service providers and tenants.

Keywords: Artificial intelligence · Ecosystem · Platform · Smart home · Smart living

1 Motivation

The term "Smart Living" comprises several areas that are separated today: energy management, health and home automation [1]. Furthermore, smart home is a core element in a connected world. There is need for intelligent applications, which fulfil cross-domain use cases. Smart buildings, which include smart homes and commercial buildings, will take an important role to enable smart grid [2] and smart city related approaches. Such approaches can only be realised with intelligent, situation-adaptive control opportunities and building related services [3]. This leads to more comfort, better assistance and increased safety and security as well as improved resource efficiency and reduced overall costs. The reason

Supported by German Federal Ministry for Economic Affairs and Energy.

J. Pagán et al. (Eds.): ICOST 2019, LNCS 11862, pp. 204–211, 2019.
https://doi.org/10.1007/978-3-030-32785-9_19

for such advanced opportunities is the intense usage of AI. This paper describes a concept for a platform approach to enable such an intense AI usage in smart living.

The economic relevance of connected homes or buildings is proven by several key figures [4,5]. In Germany there are currently approximately 19 million residential buildings and around 42 million households. The residential buildings have a share of approximately 98% of the total building stock. 57% of all Germans and 72% of single households lived for rent in 2015. [6] The 23 million rental housing units are managed by about 68,000 companies. Due to the situation described above, it is demanded at government level that the topic of digitisation and connectivity for the housing industry will be addressed. For other European countries, the situation seems not exactly the same, but similar.

2 State of the Art

There are currently various stand-alone smart home systems on the market. Some of these are based on wired or wireless technologies, e.g. KNX [7], Homematic [8, S. 231], Z-Wave [8, S. 216], free@home or digitalSTROM [9]. Moreover, most of the systems offer cloud-based remote access possibilities as an additional option for controlling the building from abroad. Of course, the biggest value proposition for the tenant is if he is able to add various devices from different vendors and consume third party services in his system. There are various middleware systems, which follow this idea like the openHAB system [10] or ioBroker.

Middleware systems usually provide an abstraction layer for devices. Thus, these systems are able to ensure data transfer between such systems and therefore achieve interoperability. In smart homes and for assistance systems in general, privacy and security issues [11] play an important role in Europe. This means that each data record should be extended with the information, who is allowed to do what actions at what time with it.

According to the paragraph before, it becomes obvious that available semantic information is useful to include domain knowledge in suitable data structures. For this purpose the concept of ontologies exists. Ontologies are semantic orders of domain related terms and their relationships [12]. Due to ontologies it is possible to start semantic search operations, combine two knowledge bases or test data for inconsistencies [13]. In the domain of smart living the SAREF ontology [14], BRICK [15] and Web of Things [16] are ontologies or approaches which should be investigated. The world of ontologies and knowledge representations lost some importance in recent years because solutions for numerous challenges were delivered by another part of AI, so-called machine learning (ML). In ML, algorithms and statistical methods are used to find solutions for optimization problems, e.g. more and more pre-trained neural networks offer robust high-quality answers to related questions [21]. In the context of smart living, speech recognition [22], object identification or energy management are relevant examples, where ML is used successfully.

3 Challenges

Requirements are rapidly increasing in the smart building context, i.e. for achieving the energy transition flexible control and monitoring mechanisms need to be offered. Another challenge for German society is to assist elderly people and enable them to live in their preferred environment as long as possible. To achieve this, AI-based smart living technologies can help to extend this period of time. Thus, it is necessary to increase the amount of connected devices and enable energy consumption measurement and localisation technologies to create individual adaptable use cases. Currently, systems lack this functionality and do not offer such individually profile-based approaches. Future smart home systems need to have the specific user in mind, detect users' behaviour and make the correct conclusions. Smart speaker can help here to locate and identify persons. Moreover voice user interfaces (VUI) can bring smart home technology to people who are not used to smartphones. The first numbers of sold smart speakers show that VUIs are a game changer. Anyway, there are lots of people who are still reluctant, because they do not know what happens to their data. Summing up, promising smart home platforms should offer a VUI and address privacy issues as well.

Existing middleware systems are slowly beginning to ensure interoperability [18,19]. In addition to automating tasks, smart home systems begin to offer authentication options based on OAuth. This is pretty common for social media websites, i.e. signing in with your Google or Facebook account to another website [20]. On the one hand, this is quite comfortable for the user but on the other hand it will be even more advanced to sign in with your preferred service and avoid sharing data to lots of different servers abroad. Current platforms and eco systems lack organizational interoperability. This interoperability level should be persuaded, because only then it will be possible to create a flexible eco system with different partners, who are able to include their specific services and corresponding business models. The ideal place to store semantic information is in an ontology, e.g. the SAREF ontology. Ontologies can be extended [17], hence this should be considered by almost any platform project in the smart living domain.

Furthermore, concepts are needed which enable the transition from hard-coded if-else-statements towards context aware, dynamic and situation adaptive, self-learning approaches, which consider future trends as well. These new approaches need to add to current best practice approaches, e.g. plug-and-play mechanisms like the OSGI-based openHAB system. Changing the perspective from system to device, it is possible to speak from "Thinking Objects".

4 Approach

The following ForeSight platform approach was initiated from members of the German Smart Living Business Initiative, a network of smart home and smart building experts. The goal of the ForeSight platform is to create a significant contribution to the further development of smart buildings and homes by providing cross-domain AI-based solutions in combination with established building automation technologies.

In the past, there have been various platform approaches, most of these were not able to conquer the market. There are technical, legal and economic challenges to deal with. In a first step core partners were allowed to found ForeSight. In this six months lasting project a useful platform concept needs to be created and relevant partners have to be identified, so that the value added chain is completed. In addition to that, established research institutes and organisations are added to the consortium to develop the concept further and further.

Due to literature research and experience, possible partners were detected. Afterwards, the team decided to start the working phase by founding a matrix based organisation, composed of several working groups (WG) (see Fig. 1). The figure shows WGs with domain specific focus and groups with cross-sectoral topics. The WG coordinators need to collect relevant data of their WG and interconnect with other WGs.

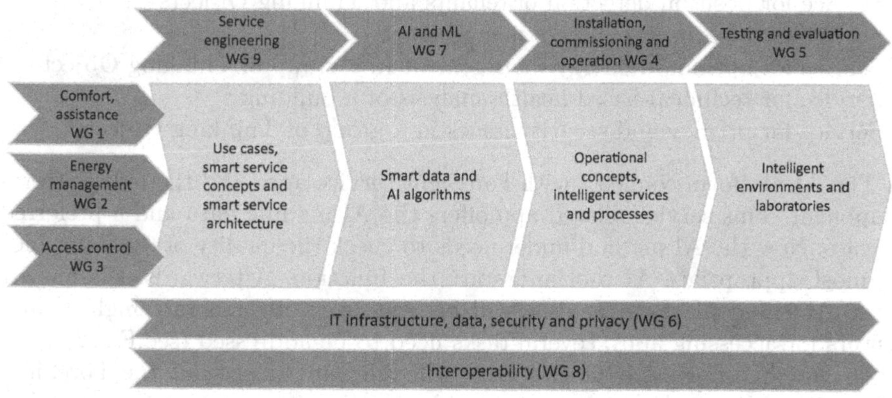

Fig. 1. The consortium created working groups to start an efficient process to push the ForeSight concept creation.

The created ForeSight platform concept should be evaluated and verified in laboratories and real world environments. Therefore, possible user stories and use cases need to be identified and implemented. There are several user story catalogues but usually there is no direct combination with AI, which is one of the core elements of this platform approach. Therefore, a new template for user stories was created and given to the members of the different WGs. This template considers relations to AI services, which are necessary for the specific use case.

With reference to the challenges section, ForeSight wants to reach a high level of interoperability, i.e. that service providers with different business models can replace their services without much effort. The resident focuses on one use case and the platform takes care of necessary processes in the background. To identify users is one of ForeSight's basic features and the key to enable user specific use case adaptions. Horizontal interoperability ensures that the manufacturers and cross-domain interchangeability of devices works. Vertical interoperability considers that interoperability between two services is available, i.e. energy management use cases are interchangeable, although tenants are clients from different energy providers. Following the thinking objects approach it is necessary to offer the most appropriate AI method in relation to a client's use case. It makes sense to offer three subsystems: first, the AI method platform module; second, an IoT platform module to make sure that all commands can be transported to several vendor-independent devices and third, service-related apps which can be built and ran on the IoT platform module and are allowed to connect to the AI module. Several AI base services are necessary and will be made available in ForeSight:

- Service for activity recognition of tenants
- Service for object identification
- Service for predictive maintenance related to Thinking Objects
- Service for self-configuration of Thinking Objects
- Service for position detection of tenants and Thinking Objects
- Service for identity and access management
- Service for optimized energy management in a group of Thinking Objects
- Service for technical-based health analysis of a building
- Service for privacy and security issues in a group of Thinking Objects

The AI platform connects with ForeSight service apps and the IoT platform component. This service-related app offers the AI module data and a preferred use case. Now the AI method finder needs to check the quality of the data, pick the most appropriate AI tool and start the function. Afterwards, the answer of the AI based platform module will be sent back. To generate high quality answers for accessing apps, several tasks need to be addressed (see Fig. 2).

To get an impression of the time schedule, an excerpt of the ForeSight roadmap is shown below.

- 2019, 2020: creation of the ForeSight platform concept and identification of all project partners
- 2020, 2021: implementation of reference architecture and AI-based context sensitive services
- 2021, 2022: realization of service layer to achieve interoperability on business model layer
- 2023, ... : ForeSight entering the market for third party service providers

In addition to the time schedule we defined some milestones and evaluation steps:

- 2019: Partners are able to contribute to all steps of the value added chain.
- 2020: Partners are willing and able to run the platform from 2020 to 2030.

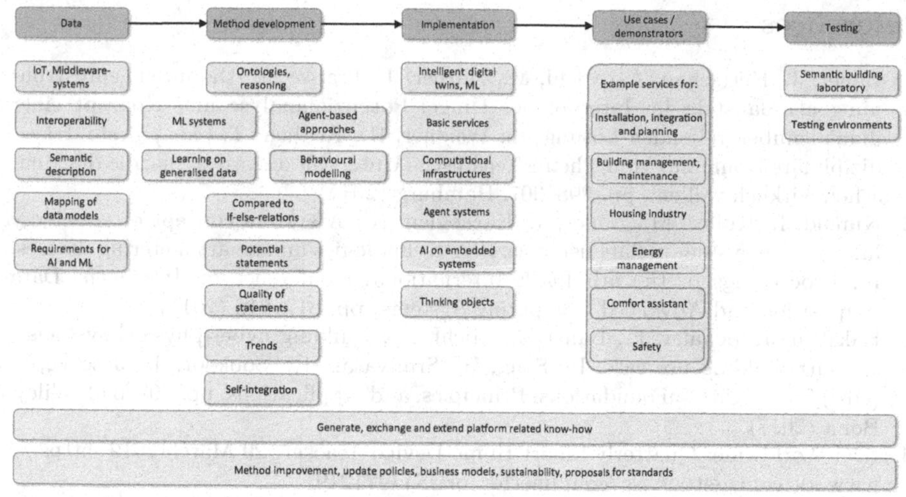

Fig. 2. The AI method platform offers different components to fulfil the needs of accessing service apps.

- 2021: Tests in labs and real world scenarios achieve satisfactory results and robustness.
- 2022: 10 third-party companies connect to the ForeSight platform with their own services.
- 2023: More than 80% of existing smart living systems are using a ForeSight platform service.

5 Discussion

When designing a platform, one of the first questions which arises is who wants to operate such a platform. The ForeSight consortium consists of several companies, which are experienced in running platforms. A flexible service-based approach for running the platform seems to outperform a monolithic approach, as first interviews showed.

Numerous use cases from the ML area require high quality data in order to train the ML models, e.g. neural networks. Such data is often not available and must be generated, which usually takes an enormous amount of time. It will be hard to consider such soft facts in the AI method finder function to answer the service-based apps.

In the past, several critical factors for smart home platforms were identified, i.e. IT security, privacy and economic beneficial business models for all stakeholders. The appropriate treatment of these topics needs to be considered from the very beginning to avoid major concept changes later, which results in high costs.

References

1. Bauer, J., Kettschau, A., Michl, M., Bürner, J., Franke, J.: Die intelligente Wohnung als Baustein im Internet der Dinge: Potenzialanalyse und Konzept einer domänenübergreifenden Lösung. In: Weidner, R., Redlich, T. (eds.) Erste Transdiziplinäre Konferenz zum Thema Technische Unterstützungssysteme, die die Menschen wirklich wollen., pp. 298–307. Hamburg (2014)
2. Kunold, I., Kuller, M., Bauer, J., Karaoglan, N.: A system concept of an energy information system in flats using wireless technologies and smart metering devices. In: Proceedings of the 6th IEEE International Conference on Intelligent Data Acquisition and Advanced Computing Systems, pp. 812–816 (2011)
3. Bakakeu, J., Schäfer, F., Bauer, J., Michl, M.: Building cyber-physical systems - a smart building use case. In: Song, H., Srinivasan, R., Sookoor, T., Jeschke, S. (eds.) Smart Cities: Foundations, Principles, and Applications, pp. 605–640. Wiley, Bonn (2017)
4. IDC Worldwide: Quarterly Smart Home Device Tracker, 29 March 2019. https://www.idc.com/getdoc.jsp?containerId=prUS44971219
5. MarketsandMarkets: Smart Home Market by Product (Lighting Control, Security & Access Control, HVAC, Entertainment, Smart Speaker, Home Healthcare, Smart Kitchen, Home Appliances, and Smart Furniture), Software & Services, and Region - Global Forecast to 2024. https://www.marketsandmarkets.com/Market-Reports/smart-homes-and-assisted-living-advanced-technologie-and-global-market-121.html
6. Statista: Übersicht Wohnen. https://de.statista.com/themen/51/wohnen/. Accessed 16 June 2019
7. Kriesel, W., Sokollik, F., Helm, P.: KNX/EIB für die Gebäudesystemtechnik in Wohn- und Zweckbau. Hüthig Verlag, Heidelberg (2014)
8. Heinle, S.: Heimautomation mit KNX, DALI, 1-Wire und Co. Rehinwerk Computing, Bonn (2016)
9. Dickmann, G.: DigitalSTROM®: a centralized PLC topology for home automation and energy management (2011)
10. Spiller, M.: Smart Home mit openHAB 2. Rheinwerk Computing, Bonn (2018)
11. Zibuschka, J., Nofer, M., Zimmermann, C., Hinz, O.: Users' preferences concerning privacy properties of assistant systems on the internet of things. In: American Conference on Information Systems (AMCIS 2019) (2019, forthcoming)
12. Gruber, T.R.: A translation approach to portable ontology specification. Knowl. Acquis. **5**, 199–220 (1993)
13. Sabou, M.: An introduction to semantic web technologies. Semantic Web Technologies for Intelligent Engineering Applications, pp. 53–81. Springer, Cham (2016). https://doi.org/10.1007/978-3-319-41490-4_3
14. Daniele, L., den Hartog, F., Roes, J.: Created in close interaction with the industry: the Smart Appliances REFerence (SAREF) ontology. In: Cuel, R., Young, R. (eds.) FOMI 2015. LNBIP, vol. 225, pp. 100–112. Springer, Cham (2015). https://doi.org/10.1007/978-3-319-21545-7_9
15. Balaji, B., et al.: Brick: towards a unified metadata schema for buildings. In: ACM Proceedings of the 3rd ACM International Conference on Systems for Energy-Efficient Built Environments, New York, pp. 41–50 (2016)
16. Guinard, D., Trifa, V.: Towards the web of things: web mashups for embedded devices. In: Workshop on Mashups, Enterprise Mashups and Lightweight Composition on the Web (MEM 2009), In Proceedings of WWW (International World Wide Web Conferences) Madrid (2009)

17. Daniele, L., Solanki, M., den Hartog, F., Roes, J.: Interoperability for smart appliances in the IoT world. In: Groth, P., et al. (eds.) ISWC 2016. LNCS, vol. 9982, pp. 21–29. Springer, Cham (2016). https://doi.org/10.1007/978-3-319-46547-0_3
18. Kreuzer, K.: Semantic modelling of smart buildings with the open source software openHAB smart public building website. http://www.hft-stuttgart.de/Forschung/i_city/Handlungsfelder/Explorative-Projekte-i-city/Exploratives-Projekt-SPUB/de/. Accessed 16 June 2019
19. Broering, A., et al.: Enabling IoT ecosystems through platform interoperability. IEEE Softw. **34**(1), 54–61 (2017)
20. Rossnagel, H., Zibuschka, J., Muntermann, J., Hinz, O.: Users' willingness-to-pay for web identity managment. Eur. J. Inf. Syst. (EJIS) **23**, 36–50 (2014)
21. Bauer, J., et al.: Camera-based fall detection system with the service robot sanbot ELF. In: Uckelmann, D., (ed.) Smart Public Building 2018 Conference Proceedings, Stuttgart, DE, pp. 15–28 (2018)
22. Pan, Y., Shen, P., Shen, L.: Speech emotion recognition using support vector machine. Int. J. Smart Home **6**(2), 101–108 (2012)

Mobility Application with Semantic Reasoning

Martin Kodyš[1,2(✉)], Antoine de Marassé[1,3], and Mounir Mokhtari[1,3]

[1] Image and Pervasive Access Laboratory (IPAL), CNRS UMI 2955, Singapore, Singapore
martin.kodys@univ-grenoble-alpes.fr
[2] Université Grenoble Alpes, Grenoble, France
[3] Institut Mines-Télécom, Paris, France

Abstract. Active mobility is a way of keeping oneself in a good health, although it may cause some discomfort. Globally, and specifically in Singapore context, several elements can influence our decisions. The choice of the right time for active mobility depends not only on available vehicles but also on the weather and the air quality. Popular fitness trackers motivate users by a daily step count goal. At the same time, open data, bus arrival times or shared bicycles availability help optimise the planning of the active mobility. Given these elements, a personalised mobile application was designed in order to facilitate the mobility choice. The paper describes how this application was constructed. It focuses on the use of semantic web reasoning for the integration of all factors and the recommendation inference. The outcome of the ongoing deployment with 36 participants is presented.

1 Introduction

It is well known that physical exercise enhances blood circulation, which in turn has additional health benefits [5]. Even in advanced age, it is not too late to start even a simple exercise, such as a walk, to notice improvements [1]. Walking, a light physical activity, has been recommended to cope with type 2 diabetes [2].

We consider *active mobility* to be one or a combination of the following activities: walking, jogging, cycling and, to a certain extent, using a scooter or even taking public transportation as there is an additional physical effort compared to use of a private car or a motorcycle.

Getting physical exercise through active mobility is convenient. It has the potential to decrease the cost of commute if it can replace some parts of one's journey. It can save time as well – time that would be needed to get to an activity-specific environment like a gym. Although active mobility is essentially an outstanding way of improving one's health, the outdoor environment is an important risk factor. For instance, air pollution, noise, and risk of accidents [3]. Air pollution becomes dangerous due to increased respiration rate during a physical activity. For that reason, the authorities usually discourage people from performing them if the concentration of particles reaches defined thresholds.

J. Pagán et al. (Eds.): ICOST 2019, LNCS 11862, pp. 212–221, 2019.
https://doi.org/10.1007/978-3-030-32785-9_20

At the same time, other research evidence suggests that the benefits of physical activity due to walking and cycling outweigh the detrimental effects of air pollution exposure and the risk of traffic incidents [4].

Our aim is to promote active mobility by making it more accessible and preferable to other kinds of transportation, such as personal vehicles, taxis and or other similar services. The focus is thus on maintaining and enhancing the health of our users. This has to be done with respect to their profiles and the potential environmental impact of the chosen mobility solutions. Other useful indicators include current daily progress, e.g. using step count, as well as other real-time and near real-time data.

We approached it by providing a unified interface for services that have been already made available by local companies or government agencies. In the back-end, we used semantic technology to facilitate the evolution of the application in order to integrate new features. We also made it modular and allow administrators to create new content that are directly visible to our participants.

Context in Singapore. As in other cities, in Singapore, public transportation faces the problem of the first and the last mile; the distance between the starting point of the commuter's journey and the most convenient transportation node (bus stop, interchange or Mass Rapid Transit (MRT) station) and similarly, the exit point of the network and their real destination.

The city-state allows bicycles-riding on both walkways and roads (unlike, for example, France where riding a bike on a walkway is tolerated but not officially allowed). In 2016, shared bicycles became very popular and the trend is now decreasing. Meanwhile, the use of personal mobility devices (PMDs), mainly electric scooters is rising. In the latest legislation in effect since February 2019, the maximum riding speed on walkways is 10 km/h for all devices. Shared paths (bicycles, rollers, walking) and park connector network allow 25 km/h.

2 Research Problem

This paper presents an approach to tackle the issue of sedentary life-style in a non-intrusive way, that is suitable to everyone regardless of age or health conditions.

The main interest of ours is to motivate the user while ensuring maximum convenience given the space we have. This means we need to push our message without too much pressure in order to retain the user's attention and interest. From the layout point of view, all necessary information should be provided without overwhelming the user.

In the back-end side of the application, which is our main focus in this paper, we ought to provide the aforementioned services in a dynamic way, transparent to the user, having a lot of flexibility as the parameters might need to evolve over time. New sources can be added and discontinued sources must not affect the functionality of the technological solution. Therefore, the proposed solution is expected to be modular.

Semantic web technologies provide interesting tools to create knowledge-based systems. They provide modularity and flexibility when removing or inserting the information. However, the main difficulty is that the logical inference may produce unexpected results and therefore, verification mechanisms have to be implemented (Fig. 2).

From the point of view of semantic technologies in mobile applications surveyed in [7], we position our software as a client-server architecture where the reasoning is performed in a remote server. In this setting, the client only formats and displays the information. The application would belong to several categories: health, recommendation, map-based.

To the best of our knowledge, no holistic application focused on mobility solution was available. We believe that a way of merging the heterogeneous data is a valuable contribution to possible uses of the semantic web technologies.

For instance, Google Maps application, offers different mobility solutions (public transport, walk, taxi). It even offers a travel time estimation. However, the mobility offer is not adapted to the user's profile nor to the current weather. On the other hand, "fitness" applications (Fitbit, Google Fit, Apple Health) are oriented more on achieving better values, being competitive. Therefore, we believe this fusion of multiple functionalities has an added value for the user.

3 Application Design

The resulting Android application data flow is depicted in Fig. 1. Upon opening, our application sends a geo-located request to our server. The server interacts with necessary APIs to obtain the data: the current *physical activity* progress rate from the fitness tracker, e.g. 90 %; the weather 2 h *forecast*, e.g. rain,and current *temperature*, e.g. 26 °C; and the current *air quality* index (AQI), e.g. 140. From the **profile** stored in the database, information about one's personal condition is retrieved: *asthma*, e.g no; *disability*, e.g. yes. All the information is injected into a semantic graph structure using an ontology model in which the parameters fit: the knowledge base. The reasoning process applies our set of rules on this knowledge base. The rules keep producing new knowledge until a "desirability" of modelled mobility solutions is obtained. This information is returned to the client and along with environmental factors (forecast, temperature, AQI). The mobile application then presents this information to the user using colour codes for each mobility solution.

3.1 User Interface

This part of the design process was performed by our industrial partner, having a user-centred approach in mind. The design of the system started with an overview of applications currently offered for major operating systems in sections concerning mobility, well-being and physical activity. Opinions of potential users and other stakeholders were collected in a workshop setting, using questionnaires and brainstorming techniques.

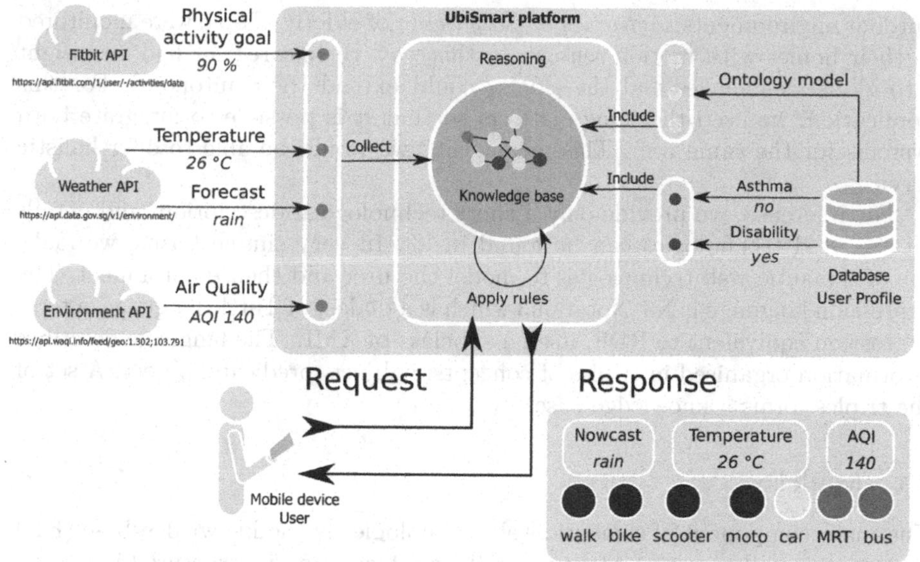

Fig. 1. On a request from the application, platform UbiSmart (designed according to [6]) injects available information from multiple sources into the semantic structure of the knowledge base, applies rules and serves a comprehensive decision and its context.

The outcome showed that a most adapted application would have a very simple interface so that it could be used without a lot of interaction, with few indicators. Then, incrementally complex view was defined for each indicator and service integrated onto the application (Fitbit integration, API for bus arrivals, points of interest, bike-sharing integration).

We defined the simple interface as a three-level indicator according to a colour level: green, yellow and red with the intuitive meaning of the traffic lights or gauges indicating a measure of danger.

Around this basic indicator, we developed an algorithm that aggregates available dimensions and projects them in a one dimensional variable "desirability", having value between 0 and 1, for each of the selected mobility solutions. It represents to what extent we recommend the given mobility solution provided the available information. The interval was divided into three segments, one for each colour.

[0, 1/3]: red – mobility solution is discouraged given the circumstances;
(1/3, 2/3]: yellow – not recommended;
(2/3, 1]: green – recommended.

4 Reasoning

The core of the application was the engine for decision process about each mobility solution. Our reasoning processes has already been deployed in indoor and outdoor environments. *Activities of daily living* of elderly people were monitored in their homes with motion sensors. In this way, their caregiver had an insight into global tendencies and the elderly could extend their autonomy. For this application, we used the same platform so that it is possible to integrate both systems for the same user. This means that we would be able to offer holistic services.

For reference, we provide only a short technological description, and details on the used technologies can be found in [6]. In very simple terms, we make use of semantic web technologies to model the user and their environment. The expression language is N3, Notation3 which is a dialect of Turtle language, a terse expression equivalent to RDF, itself a subclass of XML. The language describes information organised in triples of concepts: subject, predicate, object. A set of the triples forms a knowledge base.

4.1 Model

The main component of semantic web technologies is the knowledge base (KB) that contains all pieces of information. This information is structured in triples. A triple has a form of a three-term sentence, e.g. "hom:aqi qol:hasValue 105". Each term is either a concept or a literal. Each concept is identified by a unique identifier – URI that points to its definition. A literal is a value of one of usual data types: string of characters, numerical value, boolean value, ... The dictionary of the terms and a "grammar" are defined in an *ontology*. An ontology describes what can exist in the world described by our knowledge base. In simple words, it defines the hierarchy of concepts. For instance, "cycling" is a "mobility solution", which translates to concept of "cycling" being a subclass of the concept of "mobility solution".

4.2 Rules

Rules define the mechanics of our world and are also expressed as a special kind of triples - subject is a formula, i.e. zero or more triples, enclosed in curly braces, predicate is the string "=>", object is another formula written in curly braces. Formulas can contain special terms beginning with a question mark, e.g. "?weather". They are similar to variables in imperative programming languages. Their scope is limited to the rule.

A set of rules applied on the current knowledge generates new information. Depending on the evaluation of the output, appearance of some specific triples may trigger actions on the outside world (notification), removal of the information from the KB. Rules can be used to perform arithmetic operations, aggregation or simple inference "if ..., then ...".

The following is an excerpt of the rule set used in our application to determine the coefficient of air pollution from the measure of AQI obtained from a public source.

Soundness of the manually generated rules must be verified and along with the rules a table of all combinations was generated and is presented in Fig. 2.

```
# 100 < AQI < 150
# For all users that do not have asthma, if (100 < AQI < 150) then aqiFactor equals 0.8
{hom:aqi qol:hasValue ?v. ?v math:lessThan 150. ?v math:notLessThan 100.
  []e:findall((){hom:johndoe qol:hasMedicalCondition qol:asthma}()).
  (hom:walk hom:bike hom:scooter hom:moto hom:mrt hom:bus hom:car)  list:member ?mode}
=> {?mode hom:aqiFactor 0.8}.

{hom:aqi qol:hasValue ?v. ?v math:lessThan 150. ?v math:notLessThan 100.
 hom:johndoe qol:hasMedicalCondition qol:asthma.
 (hom:scooter hom:moto) list:member ?mode}
=> {?mode hom:aqiFactor 0.6}.
```

4.3 Reasoner

Once the description of our universe (knowledge base) and its laws (rules) is ready, we apply a reasoner. A reasoner is an application that takes our triplets in input, along with the rules to be applied and a query that defines a selection of the knowledge base that is of interest for us. The reasoner we use is called "eye" shorthand for "Euler yet another proof Engine". The choice of this tool is discussed in [6]. Eye is accessed via a Javascript interface inside our NodeJS application. Components of our application can add, remove and update the knowledge base.

4.4 Implementation of a Decision Table

For this application, we defined basic statements and implemented the rules. However, the most useful was the enumeration of all possible states in a table. It is automatically generated from a list of conditions for each dimension and their combinations. It was very helpful during verification process.

For the proof of our concept, the we integrated 6 dimensions with the segmentation as follows. The full table contain 5 weather conditions $\times$ 2 temperature cases $\times$ 4 AQI intervals $\times$ 1 scalar goal measure $\times$ 2 disability $\times$ 2 asthma $=$ 160 cells (each having a value for every mobility solution).

The visualisation of this space is presented in Fig. 2. This matrix of 16×10 cells represents the different cases taken into account. Each cell contains a combination of digits that denote conditions in order weather (1–5: unknown, rain, fair, danger, wind), AQI (1–4: from better to worse), asthma (0 no or 1 yes), disability (0 no or 1 yes), temperature (0: under 36 °C or 1: over 36 °C).

There are 8 coloured segments, each of them represents a specific configuration of the aforementioned binary parameters. They are coded in RGB 3-dimensional colour space with following attributions: temperature $=$ red, asthma $=$ green, disability $=$ blue. Their combinations give a colour combination: e.g. *black* (gray background) is at all values are 0, *cyan* has blue and green components so it depicts disability and asthma.

Within the coloured cluster, horizontal position indicates 4 cases of air quality indicator AQI with healthiest lowest values on the left and in this order: under 50, up to 100, up to 150, over 150. Vertical position within each coloured block are 5 cases of weather condition in this order: unknown, rain, good weather (fair, overcast, cloudy), dangerous (heavy rain, thunderstorm), and windy.

Inside each cell, 7 mobility solutions are indicated in order: walk, bicycle, scooter, motorbike, car, MRT, bus. Their vertical position within the cell is a measure of recommendation which also defines the colour according to their appearance in the application: red, yellow or green. The lower the mobility is placed, the lower is the score.

The indicated values are the *maximum score* the mobility can obtain in the configuration, and passive mobilities are weighted with current progress in goals. This means that "car" will be *red* if there was no physical activity progress in the day, even if it appears *green* in the cell.

In the case of non-use of the fitness tracker, we decided to show the results as if the daily goal was achieved (we show the colour as in this table).

The current progress is adapted to the time of the day – 100% score is obtained if at 50 % of the day, the user completed 50 % of their goal.

The importance of explicitly drawing this table is for validation of the approaches to make sure that all cases are covered with values that make sense. We made use of it during the verification process and it helped to discover issues with the model.

Product of all values is the measure of desirability of given mobility solution for the currently known situation.

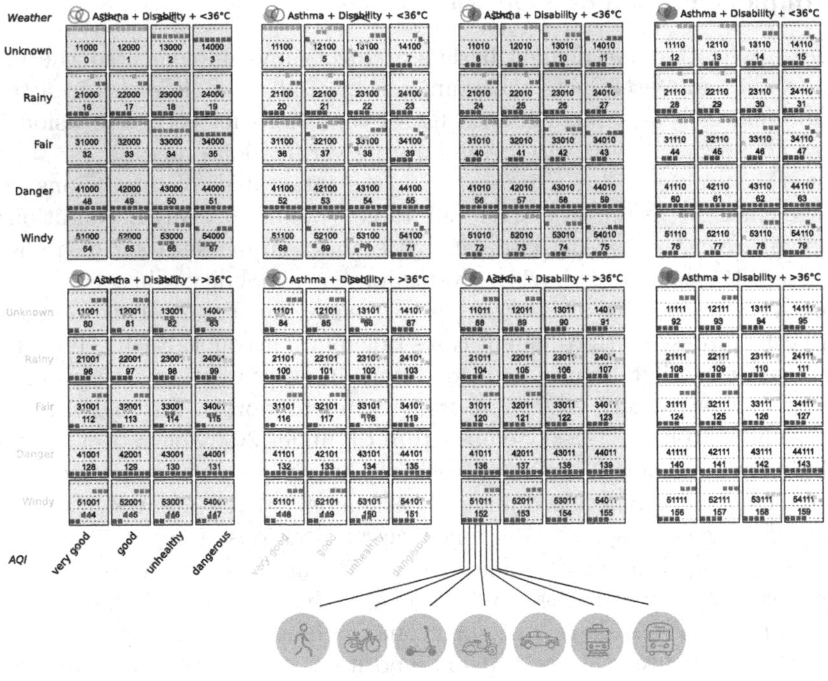

Fig. 2. Six dimensions for each mobility solution as implemented in our application

4.5 Deployment

The application was distributed to participants along with an optional Fitbit device. We were interested in the usage rate of the application and in gathering feedback from the users. Users own a smartphone and know at least basic interactions. In order to encourage users' feedback, the participants were invited to a lucky draw where two participants would win an upgrade of their Fitbit device to a newer model.

5 Results

The application was deployed to 36 very heterogeneous group of users. In the latest phase, of 4 months, we monitored application start, reasoning cycle trigger, and Fitbit synchronisation time-dates.

Very few participants used the application extensively. We recognise that the installation was cumbersome due to the necessity to connect user's Fitbit account to our application and several runtime errors in the application linked to the use of the GPS that need to be addressed in future versions. However the idea of a mobility application with these features seems appreciated. The deployment shows that 15 out of 36 users downloaded the application but needed a guided help to set it up with Fitbit or make the reasoning work (e.g. not activated geolocation services and hence, the application couldn't operate).

According to 17 valid profiles, the age of participants ranged from 22 to 59 years, with an average of 31.5 years and median of 30.

The feedback from our active users include following categorised statements:

Data Empowerment. "The great power of data is when you can communicate it to people at an individual level that makes sense for them, for example: at a neighbourhood level . . . this is what air pollution looks like around you; what it means for you; and what the advice is."

Near Geolocated Data. "Using the mobile App together with the wearable device is motivating, this is my one-stop-app for my personal data activity crossed with impactful Urban data. Those data are geo-located and enhance the use of the public space for citizens."

About the Concept of Service. "Encouraging the people to be physically active and crossing this data with urban data makes sense to empower individuals in their daily lifestyle."

Behaviour Change. "The mobile app enables to track your physical activity, it is very motivating. For instance, I will more likely try to walk or run more, also simple changes have an important impact on our daily lives, for example I take the stairs instead of the escalators to exit the subway. The sport side of the project, improving my physical activity is my main motivation."

We also asked participants about the application's ease of use and their feedback was used to solve technical issues. The need of providing a walk-through of the application was noted but scheduled for a further release.

6 Conclusion

We presented a functional concept application for mobility solutions based on symbolic reasoning. It combines the data from an activity tracker (Fitbit), publicly available environmental data (weather forecast, local temperature and air quality), and private profile data (asthma, disability). We described the functioning and the design, and in particular, the implementation of a 6-dimensional table used for validation of the rules.

Our solution was implemented and as an Android application deployed to 36 users. We are continuing the data collection in order to understand their use of the application. A positive user feedback shows that the application is able to fulfill new needs and it is encouraging us to enhance the interface and performances.

Acknowledgements. The work presented in this paper was supported by the PSA Group.

References

1. DeSouza, C., et al.: Regular aerobic exercise prevents and restores age-related declines in endothelium-dependent vasodilation in healthy men. Circulation **102**, 1351–1357 (2000)
2. Duclos, M., et al.: Physical activity and type 2 diabetes recommandations of the SFD (francophone diabetes society) diabetes andphysical activity working group. Diab. Metab. **39**(3), 205–216 (2013). https://doi.org/10.1016%2Fj.diabet.2013.03.005
3. Johansson, C., et al.: Impacts on air pollution and health by changing commuting from car to bicycle. Sci. Total Environ. **584–585**, 55–63 (2017)
4. Mueller, N., et al.: Health impact assessment of active transportation: a systematic review. Prev. Med. **76**, 103–114 (2015). http://www.sciencedirect.com/science/article/pii/S0091743515001164
5. Nystoriak, M.A., Bhatnagar, A.: Cardiovascular effects and benefits of exercise. Front. Cardiovasc. Med. **5**, 135 (2018). https://doi.org/10.3389/fcvm.2018.00135
6. Tiberghien, T.: Strategies for context reasoning in assistive livings for the elderly. Ph.D. thesis, Institut National des Télécommunications (2013)
7. Yus, R., Pappachan, P.: Are apps going semantic? a systematic review of semantic mobile applications. In: MoDeST@ISWC (2015)

BY

Author Index

Printed in the United States
By Bookmasters